COUNSELLING SKILLS FOR

WORKING WITH SHAME

also in the Essential Skills for Counselling Series

**Counselling Skills for Becoming
a Wiser Practitioner**
Tools, Techniques and Reflections for
Building Practice Wisdom
Tony Evans
ISBN 978 1 84905 607 6
eISBN 978 1 78450 143 3

Counselling Skills for Working with Trauma
Healing From Child Sexual Abuse,
Sexual Violence and Domestic Abuse
Christiane Sanderson
ISBN 978 1 84905 326 6
eISBN 978 0 85700 743 8

by the same author

**Introduction to Counselling Survivors
of Interpersonal Trauma**
Christiane Sanderson
ISBN 978 1 84310 962 4
eISBN 978 0 85700 213 6

Counselling Survivors of Domestic Abuse
Christiane Sanderson
ISBN 978 1 84310 606 7
eISBN 978 1 84642 811 1

Counselling Adult Survivors of Child Sexual Abuse
Third Edition
Christiane Sanderson
ISBN 978 1 84310 335 6
eISBN 978 1 84642 532 5

The Seduction of Children
Empowering Parents and Teachers to Protect
Children from Child Sexual Abuse
Christiane Sanderson
ISBN 978 1 84310 248 9
eISBN 978 1 84642 060 3

COUNSELLING SKILLS FOR
WORKING
WITH
SHAME

CHRISTIANE SANDERSON

Jessica Kingsley *Publishers*
London and Philadelphia

First published in 2015
by Jessica Kingsley Publishers
73 Collier Street
London N1 9BE, UK
and
400 Market Street, Suite 400
Philadelphia, PA 19106, USA

www.jkp.com

Library of Congress Cataloging in Publication Data
Sanderson, Christiane.
Counselling skills for working with shame / Christiane Sanderson.
pages cm. -- (Essential skills for counseling)
Includes bibliographical references and index.
ISBN 978-1-84905-562-8 (alk. paper)
1. Shame. 2. Counseling psychology. 3. Counseling. I. Title.
BF575.S45S26 2015
152.4'4--dc23

2015005465

British Library Cataloguing in Publication Data
A CIP catalogue record for this book is available from the British Library

ISBN 978 1 84905 562 8
eISBN 978 1 78450 001 6

Printed and bound in the United States

To my mother and my children, James and Max

ACKNOWLEDGEMENTS

I would like to thank all my clients who have helped me to develop deeper understanding of the crippling effects of shame. They have been an inspiration and taught me about resilience and what it means to be human. I would also like to thank the many students, trainee counsellors, therapists and colleagues who through numerous discussions enabled me to develop the ideas and exercises in this book. In particular I would like to thank Linda Dominguez and all the staff at One in Four UK, Tony Evans, Jo Cruywagen, Nicole Proia, Matthew Trustman, Henrietta Seebohm, Diane Bray, Jean O'Callaghan, Mick Cooper, Marcia Worrall, Elwyn Taylor and Michael, for their unwavering support. Special thanks for their creative input go to Sigal Shalev for designing the Shame Tree and Nine Rogers at Circle Services for designing the shame images in the book, in particular the Circle of Shame and Pride. My appreciation and thanks as always go to Jessica Kingsley, Stephen Jones and the production team at Jessica Kingsley Publishers whose continuing support brought the book to fruition. Finally to James and Max for their love and support.

CONTENTS

SERIES PREFACE

The landscape of therapeutic practice is a constantly changing terrain that reflects current mental health concerns and increasingly diverse client populations. This, along with keeping up to date with the latest research in the field of mental health and good practice, poses considerable challenges for practitioners as they try to balance the demands of their practice with continuous professional development. The Essential Skills for Counselling Series is designed to provide clinicians, therapists, counsellors, health professionals, social care practitioners and trainees with a range of tried and tested skills to enable them to enhance their practice. The emphasis is on exploring current changes in knowledge and practice which can be incorporated into their existing practice and theoretical model or orientation. The books in the series will focus on skills and techniques that are particularly useful when working either with particular client groups, such as survivors of childhood sexual abuse, or specific presenting symptoms, such as complex trauma or shame.

Many practitioners are not always able to keep abreast of the latest research or be familiar with developments in practice and the range of therapeutic techniques across different modalities. The handbooks in this series aim to provide current knowledge in working with particular client groups or specific mental health issues that practitioners may not have encountered in their original training. To enhance awareness and understanding, the books in this series will encourage practitioners to challenge their own perceptions and practice through self-reflection and a series of tried-and-tested exercises that they are invited to engage with and which can be used with clients.

The books in the series will be user friendly in using clear, accessible and easy-to-understand language with icons to signpost important information and good practice points. There will be boxes for experiential exercises and skills and exercises to use with clients. The series will encourage practitioners to dip in and out as they need to enable them to access relevant information and skills without having to read extensively. To enliven the text, case examples will be included to show how the skills can be employed. The focus throughout is on clear and succinct descriptions of skills, how they can best be employed and making the practitioner more aware of their own process in their work, enabling them to become more sentient practitioners.

Christiane Sanderson 2015

INTRODUCTION

Shame is a soul eating emotion. (C.G. Jung)

Shame is a social emotion which is elicited when in the presence of others to regulate social interaction and social bonding. It can be a powerful way to facilitate affiliation and prosocial behaviour but can also be used as a means of social control and oppression. If shame is used in a healthy way to guide social behaviour and aid social cohesion it can lead to empathy and compassion for others. If, however, shame is used to humiliate and degrade others, it can become toxic and elicit rage and humiliated fury, which results in destructive attacks on self or others. To manage overwhelming or unbearable shame it needs to be hidden from self and others through denial and disavowal. It can metastasise into narcissism, grandiosity, self-harm, addictions and shameless acts of rage as seen in seemingly senseless acts of violence, domestic abuse, rape and sexual violence. To ensure empathy and compassion for self and others it is necessary to have a healthy amount of shame and accept that it is part of what makes us human. When we are able to do this we are able to give voice to shame and break the silence and secrecy that maintains and perpetuates it. However, when we are afraid to show our vulnerabilities or flaws, and become fearful of being exposed, the need to hide or mask shame is amplified and thereby intensified.

As social animals humans are dependent on others for care and support to develop a sense of self and relational worth. This need is most pronounced in early childhood interactions with significant others in which a positive sense of self ensues from the loving gaze of the primary caregiver. When the sparkling-eyed gaze of the primary caregiver reflects back a sense of joy and pleasure the child's sense of self becomes one of being valued and affirmed (Schore 1998). If the reflection is one of disappointment and disgust, shame ensues. This leads to what is the central paradox in shame, wherein the need to be visible increases the risk of exposure to shame. This delicate balance between the wish to be seen and express the self, and the need to suppress the self (Mollon 2002), can be precarious and lead to either healthy shame or chronic shame.

For many this balance has to be negotiated on a daily basis through social interactions and the use of social media. While social media like Facebook, Instagram and Twitter are primarily a way to connect to others and share aspects of ourselves, they can also be a source of intense scrutiny and potential exposure to shame. In many ways the use of Facebook, Instagram or Twitter has become a powerful substitute for the reflection and mirroring of the primary caregiver as a way to validate our way of being and to seek approval from others. In this we are able to share aspects of ourselves that we value and allow us to have a sense of belonging. However, in exposing so many aspects of our lives, there is an increased risk of exposure which renders social media a potent instrument for social comparison, and thus a source of shame. The pressure to reveal or compare appearances, lifestyles, holidays and opinions can lead to intense scrutiny as photos are uploaded, Twitter feeds are analysed and profiles compared. Such scrutiny can lead to exposure to shame especially for those who do not fit into social norms with regard to appearance, status or lifestyle.

The fear of being found to be 'less than' or lacking in some way has led to a need to control what we reveal about us so that any sources of shame can be hidden. Common examples of this are tweaking or editing profiles, airbrushing or photoshopping photographs or only ever revealing what is deemed to be socially acceptable. The fear of being shamed for not fitting in or not being perfect enough can have severe consequences in terms of extreme cosmetic surgery or body modification in order to look a certain way. In addition, those who are deemed 'less than' are in danger of being shamed and humiliated, which can reinforce social isolation and loneliness, and increase the risk of suicide.

Social media and its capacity as an instrument of shame, along with the need to live up to the expectations of others, has prompted a resurgence of interest and research in shame, especially as more and more people enter therapy with shame-based problems such as social anxiety, a sense of isolation and exclusion, and depression and loneliness. This is reflected in the work of Brené Brown and her hugely popular books and podcasts about shame and letting go of the need to be perfect.

As more clients enter counselling suffering from shame-based anxieties such as failing to live up to others' expectations, it is critical that counsellors develop an understanding of the language of shame. This is particularly so as shame is ubiquitous in therapy where clients often feel under the scrutiny of the therapist's gaze. In encouraging clients to reveal all of themselves we need to be mindful that this can make them vulnerable to re-experiencing shame. Despite this, shame as a crucial component of the therapeutic process is rarely explored in counselling or psychotherapeutic training, which makes it hard for counsellors to know how to address shame, either their own or the client's. As a result shame is typically 'the elephant in the room' with clients avoiding talking about shame and practitioners being anxious about bringing it into the room. This is exacerbated when counsellors have little or no awareness of their own shame, and yet it invades the therapeutic process. To prevent shame becoming the elephant in the room, it is helpful to understand the language of shame, how it manifests and the range of strategies used to mask shame. With such awareness and understanding practitioners will be better equipped to express empathy and compassion for clients suffering from chronic shame and minimise the risk of re-shaming the client.

Shame is often associated with discomfort and overwhelming emotions, which makes it difficult to talk about. To manage this, clients typically tend to use less threatening or synonymous words such as guilt, embarrassment or self-blame when really they feel ashamed. This is compounded by the fact that much of shame is implicit and therefore right brain dominant and thus lacks language and words. In not being able to give voice to shame individuals are forced to suffer in silence, which intensifies shame and the need to mask it. As a result they become drenched in shame, which can infect the soul and lead to negative self-evaluations and self-beliefs. The need to hide shame and fear of exposure means that there is little or no opportunity to explore or release it, which intensifies the shame and traps the individual in a never-ending cycle of shame.

This book aims to provide a general introduction to the universal nature of shame and examine how this manifests in both client and counsellor. It will look at the myriad sources of shame and how these impact on individuals and relationships. It will explore the range of defences to ward off shame, such as withdrawal, in which the client renders themselves invisible so they are no longer a source of shame;

attacking the self through self-criticism and self-harming behaviours; avoidance through dissociation; numbing through alcohol, food, drugs or sex; or attacking others, whereby shame is expunged by projecting it into others through humiliation and shameless acts of violence. In addition it will link these to a range of clinical problems such as addictions, abuse, domestic violence, sexual difficulties, sex addictions, eroticised rage and sexual violence.

To facilitate working with shame the book will focus on providing skills and exercises for counsellors to use with clients to identify shame, what elicits, evokes or triggers it and how they manage feelings of shame. The objective is to release shame and to build shame resilience and reduce the inhibiting effects of shame. Alongside this, consideration will be given to how being in the presence of shame and listening to accounts of shameful acts can elicit practitioners' own experience of shame. In gaining greater awareness and being able to voice shame counsellors will be able to be more sensitive to the felt sense of shame and minimise the risk of further shame. It is only when clients are given a voice with which to break the silence and secrecy surrounding shame that they can be released from its crippling effects. This, together with compassion and empathy, is the most powerful antidote to shame, allowing it to be expressed rather than suppressed so that the client can be seen rather than rendered invisible.

The handbook is designed in such a way that you can dip in and out of it as you need to. You do not have to read all the chapters, or in any particular order. It is a flexible resource to be used in the way it most suits you. It is designed to help you to create a safe, secure base in which you can introduce skills and exercises that facilitate the exploration and management of your own as well your clients' shame and how this impacts on their sense of self and their relationships. The range of exercises and reflection points have a dual purpose in being directed at practitioners to increase self-awareness of their own shame experiences and how these have impacted and can also be used with clients to enhance their awareness. Moreover, the exercises and techniques can be adopted and adapted in whatever way suits the practitioner and their particular therapeutic mode. Each chapter can be read as a stand-alone topic and will include a range of top tips, warnings and exercises.

USE OF LANGUAGE

While the author acknowledges the differences and similarities between counsellor and therapist, these terms will be used synonymously, alongside the terms clinician and practitioner.

STRUCTURE OF THE BOOK

Chapter 1 explores the language of shame to make it easier to give clients a voice to their shame. It will look at the universal nature of shame and its role in bonding and prosocial behaviour, and highlight both the positive aspects of shame in regulating social interaction and the negative aspects which can infect and erode the self. The focus will be on how external shame is internalised and how it drenches the soul. In mastering the language of shame you will be able to work more effectively in releasing clients from the prison of shame, to develop empathy and self-compassion, and learn to live more authentically.

In Chapter 2 the focus is on the nature of shame and how it develops in early attachment relationships with significant others and how these impact on the regulation of shame experiences. It will also examine how shame manifests in shame-based families and the intergenerational transmission of shame and how these shape later responses and reactions to shame throughout the life span. Typical triggers and the cycle of shame will be explored to help you identify these when working with clients who are not able to verbalise feelings of shame.

Chapter 3 will examine shame anxiety and how this elicits shame-proneness, leading to shame loops which intensify shame. The emphasis will be on the impact shame has on the self and how it results in negative self-evaluations, low self-esteem, self-blame, social comparison, negative thoughts and negative self-talk. It will also look at how shame underpins defences such as perfectionism and the need for control and how this can lead to grandiosity, narcissism, anger and violence.

To better understand shame, Chapter 4 will explore the many sources of shame including the body, mind, achievement and status; sexual, relational and cultural shame; and shame associated with ageing. In identifying common sources of shame you will be able to facilitate clients in identifying their own shame and how this impacts in the present.

Chapter 5 looks at shame reactions as a survival strategy that elicits a range of protective mechanisms. It will identify the four predominant defence strategies used to cover up shame. In looking at the defence of withdrawal, attacking the self, avoidance or attacking others it will highlight the function and purposes of these defences and how they commonly manifest in everyday encounters and the therapeutic process.

Sex and sexuality are common sources of shame, and Chapter 6 will explore how the relationship between sex and shame is forged from early childhood. It will look at the development of sexual shame in early childhood development and adolescence and how this shapes later adult sexual behaviour. Particular attention will be focused on the different sources of shame in males and females in terms of arousal, performance and relational dynamics, as well as cultural and religious sanctions that can intensify shame. In addition, it will examine defensive reactions to sexual shame and how these link to a range of sexual difficulties, sexual compulsions, sex addictions and variant sexual behaviour. The emphasis throughout is to enhance awareness of sexual shame and how this impacts on sexual behaviour and the range of sexual difficulties that present in clinical practice.

Chapter 7 looks at how defences against shame can lead to addictions and compulsions as a form of escape and distraction from overwhelming thoughts and feelings. It will also highlight how addictions become a substitute for relationships and a way to avoid intimacy and closeness to mask lack of relational worth. Emphasis will also be placed on enhancing awareness of the role of shame in the addiction cycle and how this intensifies and perpetuates shame. The role of shame in compulsions and obsessive compulsive disorders such as Pure O will also be examined to have a better understanding of how shame drives addictions and compulsions.

The relationship between shame and rage and how this is enacted is explored in Chapter 8. The focus is on how shame is converted into anger and rage and then directed at others through shameless acts of rage and violence. Attention will be on how shame can be disavowed by shaming and humiliating others and how this manifests in abusive relationships such as domestic violence. It will also explore how shame-related rage can become eroticised, leading to the sexual abuse and sexual exploitation of children, sexual violence, rape and sexually motivated murder.

Chapter 9 will look at how shame manifests in the therapeutic process in both client and counsellor. It will examine how client and counsellor responses can evoke shame in clients, and how these become entwined in the therapeutic process. Emphasis will be placed on taking responsibility for the co-creation and maintenance of shame in therapy and how to regulate exposure to shaming experiences to minimise therapeutic ruptures. In addition, it is crucial to balance exploring a client's shame with apposite reminders of their sources of healthy pride.

To facilitate this, Chapter 10 will look at how to work with shame in the counselling process by exploring the main aims of working with it, and the role of psycho-education in enhancing awareness of the origins of shame and its impact. It will provide a range of skills and exercises to help identify layers of shame, interrupt shame loops and circumvent cycles of shame. Emphasis will be placed on helping clients to break the silence and secrecy of shame by giving it a voice without fear of judgement or being re-shamed. A range of skills will be presented to help clients regulate and manage their shame.

In Chapter 11 the focus is placed on the counsellor's shame and how this manifests in the therapeutic process. It will look at the counsellor's own experience's of shame and how this might be reactivated in the therapeutic relationship by the client's shame and how these intermingle and are enacted in the therapeutic process. Emphasis is placed on ensuring that you can identify your own shame and ensure that this does not become entwined with your client's shame. Particular consideration will also be given to the impact of shaming experiences whilst in training, especially in supervision, training programmes and clinical placements.

The final chapter will look at how clients can consolidate the skills they have learnt in understanding shame and how these can be honed through daily practice to build resilience to shame. The emphasis will be on encouraging mindfulness, reaching out to others and developing self-acceptance through empathy and self-compassion. This will allow both clients and counsellors to embrace who they are rather than who they are supposed to be. In having the courage to accept the self and develop authentic pride both you and your clients will be able to cultivate self-acceptance in which imperfections and flaws are embraced and seen as marks of wisdom that increase our value rather than needing to be hidden or disguised.

ICONS

The following icons are used to signpost the book's main features:

Exercise

Reflection

Remember

Top tip

Warning

1

THE LANGUAGE OF SHAME

Shame is a primary emotion that facilitates social bonds, allowing us to connect to others and experience a sense of belonging. This is necessary for survival, prosocial behaviour, empathy and compassion. As social animals that live in groups it is crucial that we are accepted by others to avoid the humiliation and shame of rejection or exclusion. In building social bonds, shame acts as a regulator of behaviour in acknowledging to others that a social norm has been violated or an individual has acted in an unacceptable way. In this, a fleeting expression of shame signals to others that you recognise that you have broken a social code and feel embarrassed or ashamed. In expressing an appropriate amount of shame, not too much or too little, others are more likely to make allowances and remain connected, rather than reject or condemn. Thus the healthy expression of shame is a powerful adaptive strategy that ensures survival and promotes affiliation.

However, when shame is too harshly imposed, it can become toxic and imprison the individual in an abyss of self-hate and self-blame and becomes what Jung describes as 'a soul eating emotion.' (Jung 1957, p.23). To avoid further shame they withdraw into an iron fortress to keep themselves safe and others at bay. This is especially so when individuals are exposed to repeated humiliation and shame experiences in which no attempts at reconnection are made no matter how much shame might be expressed (see Chapter 2). Such shaming experiences produce a deep sense of alienation from self and others in which the sense of self becomes inextricably linked to shame. This is often seen in physical, sexual and emotional abuse, domestic abuse, sexual violence and in the persecution of marginalised groups. Individuals or groups who are perceived as a threat to the dominant group, be that due to their gender, sexual orientation, religious beliefs or ethnicity, are shamed and excluded in order to silence them and render them invisible.

To be repeatedly humiliated and shamed can engender a chronic and crippling sense of shame. The overwhelming emotional pain is often so unbearable that individuals have to push the feelings out of conscious awareness and thereby decouple it from the original shame experiences. When such individuals enter therapy they are often unable to link their distress or presenting symptoms to shame. Equally, practitioners may also be out of contact with their own shame experiences, making it hard to explore this most private and hidden emotion. As a result shame becomes an omnipresent elephant in the room.

As many shame experiences are encountered in early childhood and stored implicitly in the right brain they are often not available to left brain cognitive processing or language. This chapter endeavours to provide you with a lexicon, or language, for shame so as to make it easier to give a voice to shame. It will explore the language of shame by looking at shame as a primary emotion that is universal and necessary to regulate social interaction and cohesion. In this it will explore the two faces of shame by highlighting both the positive aspects which promote bonding and prosocial behaviour and the negative aspects which can erode the self. Alongside this the chapter will look at the definition of shame and a range of synonymous feelings and words that are typically used to hide the sting of shame. It will also look at conscious and unconscious shame and how external shame can become internalised and infect the sense of self. Shame will be contextualised within a number of other emotions associated with shame such as embarrassment, humiliation, guilt and pride. In uncovering shame you will become aware of both the positive value of shame and its destructive nature. This will enable you to develop a more nuanced language and understanding of shame in the therapeutic process. In mastering the language of shame you will be able to work more effectively in releasing clients from the prison of shame, develop empathy and self-compassion, and learn to live more authentically.

DEFINITION OF SHAME

The word shame originates from the Teutonic root word '*skem*', which means 'to cover oneself', which is a typical expression of shame, as is the Old Norse word '*kinnrooi*', which means 'red-cheeked', as in the blushing associated with shame. The ancient Greeks further distinguished between positive shame, as in modesty, and negative shame, as in disgrace or dishonour. The *Oxford English Dictionary* definition of shame is 'A painful feeling of humiliation or distress caused by consciousness of wrong or foolish behaviour, a loss of respect, esteem or honour'. This suggests that shame is an intense reaction to the pain of humiliation which is mediated by an awareness of doing something dishonourable, improper or ridiculous. As this can be judged not just by the self but also by others, it usually necessitates a degree of deception to keep it concealed rather than risk further exposure to shame.

Definitions of shame in the therapeutic literature go beyond this definition by elaborating on the corrosive effect chronic shame can have on the sense of self. Thus, Tomkins (1963, p.118) defines shame as a 'sickness of the soul, an inner torment', while Lewis (1992, p.81) describes it as 'a global attack on the self-system'. Gilligan (2001, p.48) expands on this in arguing that when we are humiliated, ridiculed or rejected 'the self collapses and the soul dies'. More recently Brené Brown has defined shame as 'the intensely painful feeling or experience of believing we are flawed and therefore unworthy of love and belonging' (Brown 2007b, p.5). The focus in these definitions is that shame is essentially an intense and enduring reaction to a threat to the sense of self, sense of belonging and self-acceptance.

Clinical definitions imply that shame is primarily a negative or soul-destroying emotion in which the self is compromised. More recent research, however, has challenged this in proposing that shame is also a positive interpersonal emotion that is adaptive in the development of prosocial behaviour (Barrett 1995; de Hooge 2014; Fessler 2007; Gilbert 1997). Wurmser (1995) argues that shame has a number of positive values in promoting humanity, humility, autonomy, competence and humour, all of which contribute to the development of empathy and compassion. Given the adaptive nature of shame it is critical that you are aware of the two faces of shame to avoid pathologising all shame experiences and to acknowledge the positive interpersonal benefits of shame as well as the negative.

In addition, you need to be sensitive to cultural variations in the experience of shame and how this might manifest in the therapeutic process. Research has shown that the primary focus of shame experiences in Western culture is on the violation of social norms and failure, compared to other cultures where the focus is on social status and the need for appropriate expressions of shame in the presence of someone of a higher rank (Haidt 2003). This may manifest in the therapeutic process where some clients may experience and express shame simply by being in your presence since you are perceived as a higher-ranking authority figure.

THE TWO FACES OF SHAME

Shame is a universal emotion that is highly adaptive in regulating appropriate behaviour in social groups. It is part of a family of emotions that curb our primitive instincts and regulates these to be more compatible with the demands of belonging to a social group. However, it needs to be attenuated to avoid eliciting a more destructive, maladaptive version which can become inhibiting. The two faces of shame consist of healthy shame, which promotes affiliation with and connection to others and prosocial behaviour such as cooperation, compassion and empathy, and chronic or toxic shame, which paradoxically severs connections, destroys social bonds and can lead to antisocial behaviour, hostility, rage and violence. These two faces of shame represent the extreme ends of a shame spectrum – with healthy, adaptive or constructive shame at one end and chronic, maladaptive or destructive shame at the other end.

Top tip

To avoid pathologising all shame experiences you need to distinguish between the positive and adaptive aspects of shame and the more negative and destructive aspects.

THE SPECTRUM OF SHAME

Given the positive and negative elements associated with shame you need to be aware of the spectrum of shame to avoid pathologising all shame experiences (see Figure 1.1). Clients will enter therapy with a variety of shame experiences; some will have had relatively mild experiences of feeling slighted, embarrassed or awkward with positive outcomes, while others will have been treated with contempt and disdain, and exposed to more annihilating experiences such as humiliation, denigration, dehumanisation and mortification in which the core-self ceased to exist. You will need to explore individual shame experiences with an open mind in order to assess to what extent these have had a positive impact on the client and when these have become corrosive. Alongside this you need to be mindful of cultural variations in the experience and expression of shame. Clients will differ in how they perceive and recollect their shame experiences depending on the cultural context in which they occurred. You need to be sensitive to these nuances rather than impose your own interpretation of shame.

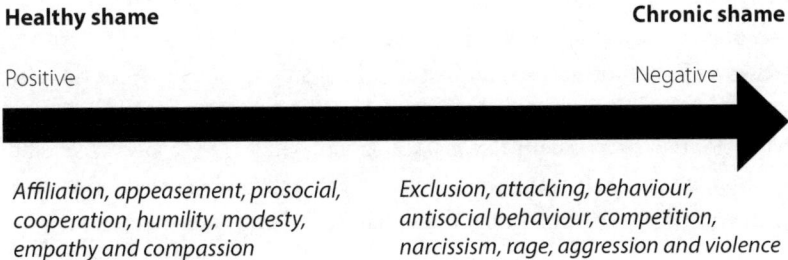

Healthy shame   **Chronic shame**

Positive   Negative

Affiliation, appeasement, prosocial,   *Exclusion, attacking, behaviour,*
cooperation, humility, modesty,   *antisocial behaviour, competition,*
empathy and compassion   *narcissism, rage, aggression and violence*

Figure 1.1 Spectrum of healthy and chronic shame

Healthy shame

Healthy, or adaptive, shame is experienced by all humans to varying degrees on a daily basis and as such it is a normal response to faux pas, errors in social etiquette or failure to live up to expectations. Such experiences are positive in reminding us that we are human and make mistakes, and that we need to be valued, respected and accepted despite this. These basic needs are mediated through shame in regulating relationships to maintain close bonds, attunement and proof of relational worth through prosocial behaviours such as cooperation, empathy, compassion and acceptance. In this sense healthy shame is constructive (Nathanson 1992) as it provides the necessary moral guidance to facilitate self-awareness of behaviour in relation to others and encourages a deeper appreciation of relationships. In addition it teaches individuals vital human qualities such as modesty, humility, gratitude and respect for others (Potter-Efron 2011). Most importantly, healthy shame can be a powerful motivator for personal change, especially in building interpersonal bridges (Kaufman 1992), to create more harmonious relationships and to feel valued and accepted by others.

Reflection

To identify healthy shame take a moment to reflect on any shame-based experience that helped guide your behaviour in a positive way, or helped you to realise that you are no better or worse than any other person.

The appropriate expression of shame signals to others that a social code has been broken and that the individual recognises this. In acknowledging a transgression or failure the individual shows contrition, which reduces the risk of rejection and exclusion while increasing connection and acceptance. As a result, the experience of shame is fleeting and transitory. However, when others do not respond to the contrition and continue to shame or humiliate the individual, healthy shame can become chronic with no relief or reconnection (see Chapter 2). These pervasive and continued acts of shaming ultimately lead to unbearable levels of chronic shame in which the individual feels abandoned and utterly rejected.

Chronic shame

Over time the pervasive nature of chronic or toxic shame and the accompanying intense and overwhelming feelings lead to the belief that the core-self is defective, inadequate and unacceptable to others. For some people, these negative self-beliefs can become so corrosive that they infect the very being of the person with the sense that they are irredeemably flawed and therefore unworthy of love or being alive. This renders the individual extremely vulnerable, fearful and psychologically fragile. To manage these painful feelings and internal states, psychological defences such as dissociation are activated to protect the individual from the experience of shame by placing it outside of conscious awareness. In doing so a range of defensive strategies may emerge which are decoupled from the original shame experience. Typically these manifest in a multitude of emotional reactions such as anger, rage, blame and despair. This in turn can prompt a range of behaviours such as hostility, aggression, violence and desire for revenge. Not surprisingly, such antisocial behaviours decrease opportunities for connection and increase the likelihood of rejection and social exclusion. You may like to take a moment to reflect on how shame has impacted on you in terms of inhibiting or blocking you in making choices. You can also use this exercise with your clients.

Reflection

Take a moment to reflect on your experiences of shame. Reflect on how these impacted on you at the time and how they have influenced you, and to what extent they still persist.

In contrast to the fleeting nature of shame which is more easily discharged, chronic shame is more likely to be internalised and turned against the self through rumination, self-harm, compulsions, risky behaviour and addictions (Tangney, *et al.* 1996). Such persistent shame leads to future anticipation of shame in which each new shaming experience adds to the already huge vat of shame which constantly threatens to overflow and obliterate any sense of self. The fear of being engulfed compels the individual to withdraw from others to ward off further shame. As chronic shame becomes more embedded it is no longer activated just in the presence of others but can be triggered internally through changed perceptions and beliefs about the self. This can lead to additional shame whereby individuals feel shame for feeling ashamed, which intensifies their shame and reinforces the need to withdraw to ward off further shame. The endless cascade of shame-related thoughts can become crippling, and counsellors will need to help clients to identify both external and internal triggers in order to regulate these more effectively (see Chapter 10). The tentacles of chronic shame are often associated with a range of client presentations which are likely to emerge in the therapeutic setting (see Figure 1.2).

Figure 1.2 The tentacles of shame

EXTERNAL AND INTERNAL SHAME

The differences between healthy and chronic shame highlight that shame can be externally as well as internally generated. In external shame the focus is on fulfilling the expectations of others in order to become a valued member of the group. In this it is the gaze and judgement of others that has the power to elicit feelings of shame. These external sources of shame act as powerful regulators of behaviour through sociocultural expectations mediated through significant others, peers and institutions which in turn are reinforced through the media, popular culture and social media. The public nature of external shame can lead to vicarious shame in which individuals may feel shame on behalf of someone being shamed or feeling shame. The degree to which individuals experience vicarious shame will vary from individual to individual; it is typically associated with extremely shame-vigilant or shame-prone individuals who are more likely to resonate with shame experienced by others.

Reflection

In looking at external and internal shame you might like to think about what extent your external shame experiences have been internalised and the impact, if any, this has on you.

Shame-prone individuals are more likely to have internalised their shame experiences and as a result are more susceptible to internal shame. Their sense of self has become infected by repeated shame experiences to the extent that they believe themselves to be defective, intrinsically bad and lacking in self-worth or value. Such negative beliefs and thoughts are no longer necessarily reinforced by others but are perpetrated against the self through self-hatred, self-criticism and self-annihilation. This is often accompanied by self-sabotaging behaviours to prove that they are inferior and lacking in worth. Many clients who suffer from low self-esteem will have a degree of internalised shame which needs to be unpacked and explored in order to build shame resilience.

As can be seen, feelings of shame do not just arise due to the direct experience of being shamed by others. Repeated exposure to shame can lead to shame anxiety in which individuals constantly anticipate shame and become hyper-sensitive and hyper-vigilant to potential exposure to shame. This can lead to shame-proneness, which necessitates defensive strategies such as withdrawal and avoidance to ward off shame. Paradoxically, by rendering themselves invisible both physically and psychologically in the hope of avoiding shame, they have internalised their shame and become imprisoned by it.

CONSCIOUS AND UNCONSCIOUS SHAME

Another crucial difference between healthy and unhealthy shame is the degree to which it remains a conscious experience. In milder forms of shame which are fleeting and transitory the experience is much more likely to remain in conscious awareness, while in severe or chronic shame the feelings are so intense and unbearable that they have to be pushed out of conscious awareness or hidden. Although this numbs the sense of shame and separates it from the original event, later shame will trigger the decoupled shame and intensify the feelings, leading to a spiral or vicious cycle of shame (see Chapter 2).

Conscious shame

In conscious shame the individual remains in touch with the physical sensation of shame such as increased heart rate, lowering of head, slumping of shoulders and blushing and the accompanying feelings. Despite this conscious awareness of shame there may nevertheless be a reluctance to label the experience as shame. The very word 'shame' can elicit feelings of shame and accompanying fears of further exposure to shame, making it hard to name it or talk about it. This is often seen in the therapeutic process where clients disguise or misname the feeling of shame through code words such as feeling embarrassed, awkward, stupid, weak, needy, less than or weird. You need to be aware of how these code words may act as a mask for shame and help clients to develop a language that reflects their experiences more accurately. Alternatively individuals may distance themselves from the internal felt sense of shame by projecting it outside of themselves. Thus rather than saying they felt embarrassed or shamed they might say that the situation was embarrassing or awkward (Nathanson 1992). Such avoidance of shame has to be managed sensitively as it is harder to talk about shame once activated or intensified, hence the need to regulate exposure to it in the therapeutic process.

Unconscious shame

By placing feelings of shame outside conscious awareness, individuals are able to avoid intense and unbearable feelings or could reinforce an already chronic sense of shame. While there may be some initial physiological reactions to shame the feeling is immediately split off through dissociation. Dissociation, while initially an adaptive response in numbing the feelings associated with shame, also allows the individual to deny shame experiences to self as well as others. As shame is forced out of conscious awareness and becomes increasingly more difficult to access, individuals may become shame deficient in not feeling any shame whatsoever. This can lead to an inflated sense of self, narcissism, grandiosity, arrogance and excessive or hubristic pride (see later in this chapter). The all-consuming self-centredness in shame deficiency prevents empathy and compassion for others, which can lead to shameless acts of violence, abuse and torture.

Reflection

Take a moment to reflect on what happens to the shamed parts that you hate or want to disown. Where do they go? Do they remain frozen in time, albeit deeply buried and outside conscious awareness? Do they splinter or fragment? Do they coalesce and fuse with other shamed parts? Or do they mutate? What do they look like now? How could you reclaim them?

Hidden or unacknowledged shame may also manifest as overt and undifferentiated shame (Lewis 1971) in which individuals display the feeling of shame but are not able to identify or name it as such. Instead they tend to label their experience as feeling foolish, stupid, awkward or vulnerable and ascribe it as low self-esteem (Lewis 1971; Scheff 1987). Alternatively some individuals hide shame by by-passing the feeling and switching into hyperactive, repetitive and accelerated thoughts, speech or behaviour (Lewis 1971; Nathanson 1992; Scheff 1987). In this the feeling of shame is activated but never fully experienced and thus avoided. Such by-passed shame cauterises and deadens the feeling of shame but does not quell or conquer it, trapping clients into an 'insoluble dilemma' (Lewis 1971, p.87). The escalation of obsessive thoughts can lead to rumination in replaying shame-related experiences, as in obsessive compulsive disorders and 'Pure O' (see Chapter 7). Such ruminations can lead to a spiral, or cycle, of shame in which the obsessive thoughts become proof of shame and are constantly replayed to keep the shame alive. To manage the obsessive thoughts some individuals may feel compelled to perform rituals or develop addictions which become a source of further shame. Alternatively individuals may distract themselves from shameful thoughts by generating fantasies of power, control, money, sex or fame and replacing shame with excessive pride.

When working with clients with hidden shame counsellors will need to identify what strategies are used to cover up deeply buried feelings of shame and find ways to bring split-off feelings of shame back into conscious awareness so that they can be discharged and processed. As the feelings of shame are not readily available to conscious awareness, you may need to use more non-verbal ways of accessing these through a variety of media including projective tests rather than relying on clinical scales or measures (see Chapter 10). You also need to see shame within the context of a range of other self-conscious emotions in order to help clients distinguish between these and develop a more sophisticated language of shame-related emotions.

Reflection

Take a moment to reflect on your conscious experience of shame, how this manifests and how you defend against it to by-pass the feelings.

THE FAMILY OF SHAME EMOTIONS

There are a number of other socially adaptive emotions associated with shame, in particular embarrassment, humiliation, guilt and pride. These can be seen as part of a 'family of shame emotions' (Elison and Harter 2007) which share commonalities in terms of their function, purpose and antecedents as evolutionary adaptations to threat of rejection, social exclusion or loss of face and social status. In addition they share a range of similar responses such as physiological arousal, feelings, thoughts, non-verbal cues such as body language and facial expressions, and behavioural reactions. Despite these commonalities there are also differences that are worth exploring to have a more nuanced understanding of these self-conscious emotions and their relationship to shame.

One difference is how intense and painful the elicited feelings are, and how such experiences can impact negatively on the individual. The spectrum in Figure 1.3 attempts to plot these in terms of mild to severe consequences for these emotions.

Mild	Moderate	Severe

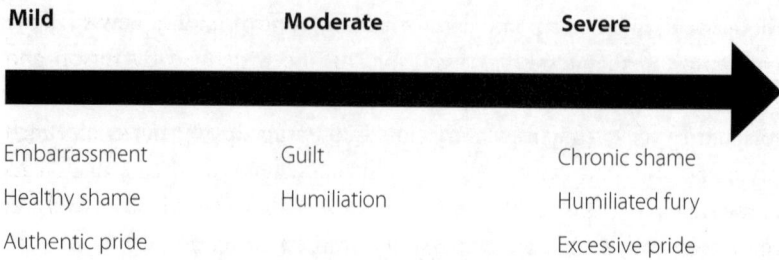

Mild	Moderate	Severe
Embarrassment	Guilt	Chronic shame
Healthy shame	Humiliation	Humiliated fury
Authentic pride		Excessive pride

Figure 1.3 Spectrum of family of shame emotions

Embarrassment

In contrast to shame which cuts more deeply and is often 'a darker, angrier, and more intense emotion' (Miller 2007, p.244), embarrassment is considered a much milder response to loss of face or failure. The feelings associated with embarrassment are typically less painful or intense and thereby promote more reparative reactions. This is in part due to the more fleeting nature of embarrassment as it is much more transitory than shame and reduces the need to hide or withdraw. This allows the person to display their embarrassment, make amends, avoid rejection and remain connected to others. The physical signs of embarrassment are very similar to those seen in shame and are often accompanied by anxious and nervous smiles and laughter which produce greater levity in self and others, thereby facilitating social bonds (Keltner and Buswell 1997).

The experience of embarrassment has been defined by Miller as a state of 'unwelcome chagrin and abashment', which in severe cases can lead to 'crushing discombobulation and mortification' (Miller 2007, p.245). It is further characterised by a sense of awkwardness, sheepishness, clumsiness and feeling conspicuous. As it is relatively short lived and does not linger, it is less corrosive than the defective sense of self associated with shame. Miller (2007) also argues that embarrassment differs from its cousin shyness, which entails a greater degree of worry, not just in the presence of embarrassment but in anticipated future events, making it hard to connect to others.

Humiliation

The *Oxford English Dictionary* definition of humiliation is 'to make low or humble in position, to be psychologically lowered by someone else'. This is echoed in the research literature wherein humiliation is seen as high-intensity embarrassment or shame (Kaufman 1992; Lewis 1987; Nathanson 1992; Tomkins 1963) and has been defined by Elison and Harter as a 'highly intense emotional reaction to the context of being lowered in the eyes of others' (Elison and Harter 2007, p.314) in which there is a loss of esteem, dignity or social status (Gilbert 1997). In its mildest form humiliation is often enacted through teasing, put-downs and mocking, and in its extreme form includes bullying, abuse and torture. This suggests that humiliation is much more goal directed in that it uses hostility in an intentional and purposeful way to harm others.

Although humiliation is often equated with shame and embarrassment it is significantly different in that it incorporates a sense of unfairness which elicits acts of aggression and a desire for revenge (Elison and Harter 2007). Gilbert (1997, p.133) distinguishes shame from humiliation by arguing that 'in shame the focus is in the self, while in humiliation the focus is in the harm done by others'. As a result humiliation is more associated with anger, rage, thoughts of violence and the humiliated fury seen in the defensive shame script 'attack other' (Nathanson 1992; see Chapter 5). When it is not possible or too dangerous to attack others as in abuse and torture, it can be turned against the self and transformed into attacks on the self, as seen in chronic sadness, depression and suicidal ideation (Gilbert 1997). While historically it was argued that attack other was more associated with males and attack self with females, Elison and Harter (2007) have found that there is no significant difference in how males and females react to humiliation – it just takes different forms.

Guilt

A common misunderstanding is in the difference between shame and guilt. Shame and guilt are often used interchangeably and sometimes fused into synonymous emotions, although they represent qualitatively different affective states (Tangney, Wagner and Gramzow 1992). In guilt the individual is able to make a conscious, cognitive distinction between the self and behaviour. As a result evaluations are focused on the act of wrongdoing while the self remains relatively unscathed and intact. In addition, in focusing on behaviours and actions, it is easier to activate reparative responses (Sanderson 2013). As such, guilt can be seen as a barometer of one's actions, which can motivate taking responsibility for one's actions and ensure we don't repeat such behaviours. More importantly, concrete reparative responses such as apologising are critical in restoring and maintaining interpersonal relationships. This is often not possible in shame where the focus is entirely on the self and the belief that the whole of the self is inferior, defective and worthless with no possibility of reparation (Sanderson 2013). As it seems to be impossible to make up for or repair the self there is no other option than to withdraw and avoid further exposure to shame, in other words to become invisible (Lewis 1971; Sanderson 2013; Tangney and Dearing 2002).

As can be seen from Table 1.1 there are significant differences between guilt and shame. The focus in guilt is 'I did something bad' rather than 'I am bad', which is the focus in shame. Guilt is typically a conscious experience in which the individual is aware of their transgression, which motivates reparation either through apology, confession of guilt or restitution. Furthermore, although guilt prompts feelings of remorse or regret, it does not necessarily affect the core identity or the whole self as it does in shame. Most importantly, in making reparation, the guilt can be discharged, which is less easy in shame as there is no direct channel to discharge the painful emotions.

Table 1.1 Guilt versus shame	
Guilt	**Shame**
• 'I did something bad'	• 'I am bad'
• Ashamed of one's actions or behaviour	• Very essence of existence can feel shameful
• Usually conscious	• Not always conscious
• Focus on transgression rather than self	• Focus on self as failure and inadequate
• Motivates restitution, confession, apology	• Pervasive and chronic
• Reparative response, remorse and regret	• Induced or reinforced by others
• Does not affect core identity	• Lacks channel for discharge
• Involves fear of punishment or retribution	• Paralysing
• Discharged through making amends	• Have to make amends for whole of self

In cases of child physical and sexual and domestic violence individuals will experience both shame and guilt as they become inextricably linked in the belief that 'I feel guilty for what I have done, and I did it because I am bad'. Survivors of abuse and complex trauma invariably feel guilty about the context and the act of abuse as well as feeling ashamed for being humiliated and violated. This is compounded by feelings of shame for feeling aroused or not doing enough to stop it. In addition, they may absorb the shame that the abuser has projected into them. When working with survivors of abuse you will need to enable clients to differentiate between guilt and shame by reallocating responsibility for the abuse and reapportioning projected feelings of guilt and shame.

Pride

According to Scheff (1988, p.399), 'We are virtually always in a state of pride or shame' as we veer between achievement and frustration, mastery and failure on a daily basis. In many respects pride is the polar opposite of shame (Gilligan 2001) in that it is an essential component in developing deep-rooted and stable self-esteem. Moreover research has shown that authentic pride promotes prosocial behaviours such as acceptance and status through social bonds and stable, harmonious relationships, while loss of pride as in shame or excessive pride can lead to antisocial behaviours such as aggression, violence and the breaking of interpersonal bonds (Tracy and Robbins 2007).

Reflection

Freely associate to the word 'pride' and reflect on your responses. Does it have positive and negative connotations? How does this link to what you learnt in your family, community or culture? How might you manage this when working with clients with a different connotation of pride?

Although pride is universal it is associated with both positive and negative connotations, often driven by religious beliefs and cultural variations. Different cultures will have divergent attitudes to the expression of pride, with some validating it as a pleasurable and joyous experience while others will find open displays of pride unacceptable or sinful. Research has shown that individualistic cultures typically see pride as a virtue and as part of the actualisation of the self, while collectivist cultures that are honour based and prioritise the group over the individual self tend to disapprove of the expression of pride and see it as a vice (Tracy and Robbins 2007).

Equally, families may have different connotations of pride and will exert considerable influence on its expression. This highlights the need to attenuate, moderate or suppress pride in different contexts, cultures and families. Given such variation in the expression of pride, you will need to be mindful of client experiences of pride and how these are responded to. This is particularly the case when building shame resilience by releasing shame and replacing it with authentic pride (see Chapter 12). Some clients may be resistant to this as it may be deemed maladaptive and reduce their likeability and social status in the eyes of their family, community or cultural milieu.

Research on the perception of pride has shown that positive views of pride emphasise the achievement, mastery and competency necessary for genuine self-esteem, self-efficacy and self-agency. In contrast, negative associations accentuate the excessive nature of pride characterised by an inflated sense of self, grandiosity and narcissism, leading to arrogance, conceit and disdain for the achievements of others (see Table 1.2). Given the positive and negative associations with pride, researchers have attempted to identify whether pride is a single, distinct emotion or whether it encompasses a range of affects (Ekman 2004; Lewis 2000; Tracy and Robbins 2007). To date, two important facets of pride have been identified, namely authentic pride and excessive, or hubristic, pride (Schimmel 1997; Tracy and Robbins 2007).

Table 1.2 Positive and negative connotations associated with pride	
Positive connotations	**Negative connotations**
• Mastery • Skill • Self-satisfaction with meeting personal goals • Personal triumph over adversity • Positive self-evaluation • Self-reflection • Sense of belongingness • Exhilarated pleasure	• Inflated sense of one's personal status or accomplishments • Vanity • Arrogance • Grandiosity • Conceit • Deadly sin • Narcissism

Authentic pride

Authentic pride has been defined as 'a pleasant, sometimes exhilarating, emotion that results from a positive self-evaluation' (Tracy and Robbins 2007, p.263) and which is based on actual accomplishments and genuine feelings of self-worth (see Figure 1.4). This implies that an essential component of authentic pride is internal attributions and the good feelings associated with success, which in turn promote positive feelings and thoughts about the self, or what Broucek (1991) calls 'competence pleasure'. Thus the emphasis is on self-acceptance and self-assurance rather than relying on the acceptance of others.

The positive feelings in authentic pride are echoed in the accompanying body language and words associated with pride. Non-verbal indicators of authentic pride display confidence and joy, as seen in the swell of pride in which the body expands and seems to grow taller, with the head tilted back, arms extended out from the body and gestures that signal 'well done'. These are usually accompanied by smiling and infectious expressions of joy or laughter. Such non-verbal cues are likely to be innate as they are also seen in visually impaired people who have not seen such expressions in others. Non-verbal cues are further reinforced by words typically used in relation to pride such as: confidence, accomplished, achieving and triumphant. These all signal feeling good about the self and wanting to share this. To help shamed clients attain such confidence and self-esteem and to restore authentic pride you need to focus on the client's achievements and successes to counterbalance their sense of failure as this is a powerful antidote to shame and leads to the path to self-acceptance (see Chapter 12).

Alongside self-acceptance, research has shown that authentic pride is necessary to maintain and enhance self-esteem, which to some extent is a social barometer, or sociometer, of self-worth and social status (Tracy and Robbins 2007). This suggests that deep-rooted and stable self-esteem is based on a sense of self-directed achievement of personal goals, success and mastery rather than merely praise received from others. Authentic pride also enhances creativity and productivity, which increases the likelihood of future achievement and success, and motivates prosocial behaviours such as helping others and altruism.

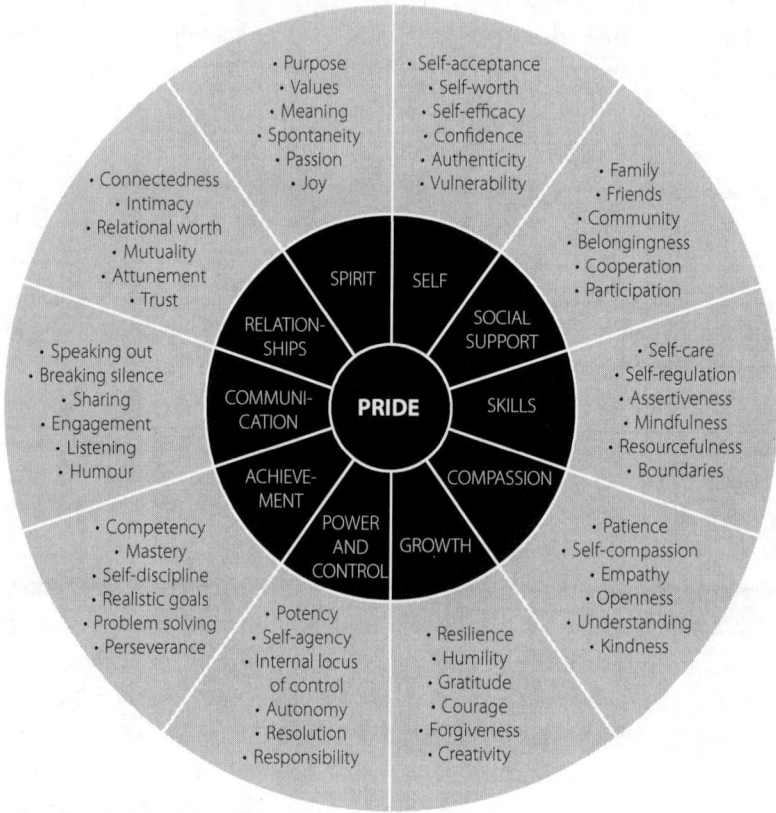

Figure 1.4 The circle of pride

★

Critical in this is the sense of achievement in attaining developmental milestones such as gaining control over the body and intentional actions which lead to a sense of self-agency and self-efficacy. The excitement, joy and pleasure in achieving these are further amplified when they are shared with others. An apposite example of this is the delight seen in toddlers when uttering their first words or taking their first steps. When this is celebrated by others there is a shared sense of pride and joy which intensifies the child's experience of achievement and pleasure in success. However, when caregivers do not resonate with this and become anxious or embarrassed by the child's accomplishments, then the expression of pride and pleasure becomes stifled and shame pervades. In order to recapture the joy and pleasure in achievements counsellors need to help clients to reclaim authentic pride and build genuine self-esteem.

Reflection

Take a moment to think about your own attainments throughout your life span (e.g. learning to ride a bike, to swim, playing an instrument or other skills) and how you felt, and how others responded to this. Did they resonate with your feelings? Did you feel you needed to suppress your exuberance? How do you feel now?

Hubristic pride

While authentic pride is adaptive and associated with deep-rooted self-esteem and positive personality traits such as agreeableness, extraversion and emotional stability, excessive or hubristic pride is largely maladaptive in terms of social bonding. Schimmel (1997) argues that excessive or hubristic pride closely matches the negative connotation of pride as sinful (Schimmel 1997). He goes on to suggest that it is hubristic pride rather than authentic pride that has historically been associated with arrogance, cruelty, evil and the deadliest of the Seven Deadly Sins. This is in part due to the fact that hubristic pride is a defensive pride activated to compensate for shame and shame-proneness. As a result it is fuelled by a damaged and narcissistically wounded self that leads to self-aggrandisement, a sense of entitlement and seemingly shameless behaviour. In this individuals seek admiration through boastfulness, competitions and superiority at the cost of interpersonal relationships.

Research has shown that hubristic pride is negatively correlated with self-esteem, agreeableness and conscientiousness, and positively related to narcissism and self-aggrandisement (Tracy and Robbins 2007).

In addition it has been linked to aggression, hostility, interpersonal problems, relationship conflict and antisocial behaviours including violence and psychopathy (Lewis 2000; Tracy and Robbins 2007). This is demonstrated by the range of words characteristically associated with hubristic pride such as arrogance, conceit, haughtiness, disdain for others' accomplishments, envy and jealousy (see Figure 1.5). Within this context one can understand how hubristic pride has become inextricably linked to negative connotations and why it must be avoided and hidden at all costs.

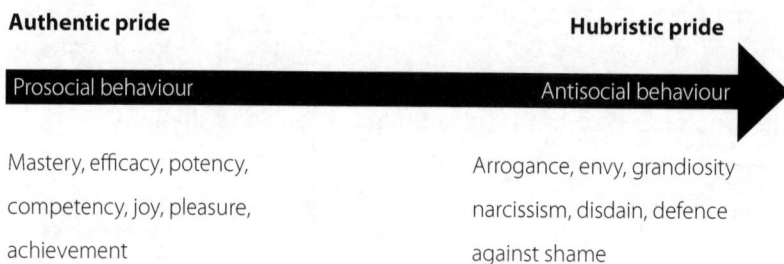

Authentic pride   **Hubristic pride**

Prosocial behaviour   Antisocial behaviour

Mastery, efficacy, potency,   Arrogance, envy, grandiosity
competency, joy, pleasure,   narcissism, disdain, defence
achievement   against shame

Figure 1.5 Authentic pride and hubristic pride

However, you will need to be mindful that hubristic pride is a powerful defence against shame, and a way to compensate for feelings of failure. You must also be mindful that for some clients the expression of authentic pride has become a source of shame. This tends to occur in families and cultures that see pride as shameful and view displays of pride in accomplishments as showing off, which needs to be stifled. It is also more likely to arise in families who are not able to resonate with the child's pride as they see striving for autonomy and self-agency as defiance, disobedience or rejection of the caregiver. Such families will judge any expression of pride and accomplishment negatively and in doing so instil a profound sense of shame. As authentic pride becomes entwined with shame, hubristic pride takes its place. This corruption and distortion of authentic pride is rarely available to conscious awareness as it typically occurs in early childhood and yet will leave indelible, internalised messages which have become decoupled from the original experiences. Such clients will benefit from exploring family responses to achievement and success and sanctions on the expression of pride.

The expression of authentic and hubristic pride is not just seen in individuals but can also be expressed by groups, communities and whole nations. Group pride is typically seen in role models, sports teams or pride in one's culture, ethnicity or nation. Supporting one's team or country can lead to national pride, which in turn enhances a sense of shared joy in successes achieved. Equally, groups can be stripped of pride and shamed for being different, as in sexual orientation, race or religious beliefs, or committing atrocities such as torture and genocide. The risk in this is that such groups may react to being shamed or humiliated by adopting hubristic pride to defend against shame.

The link between shame, authentic pride and hubristic and behavioural outcomes can be seen in Figure 1.6.

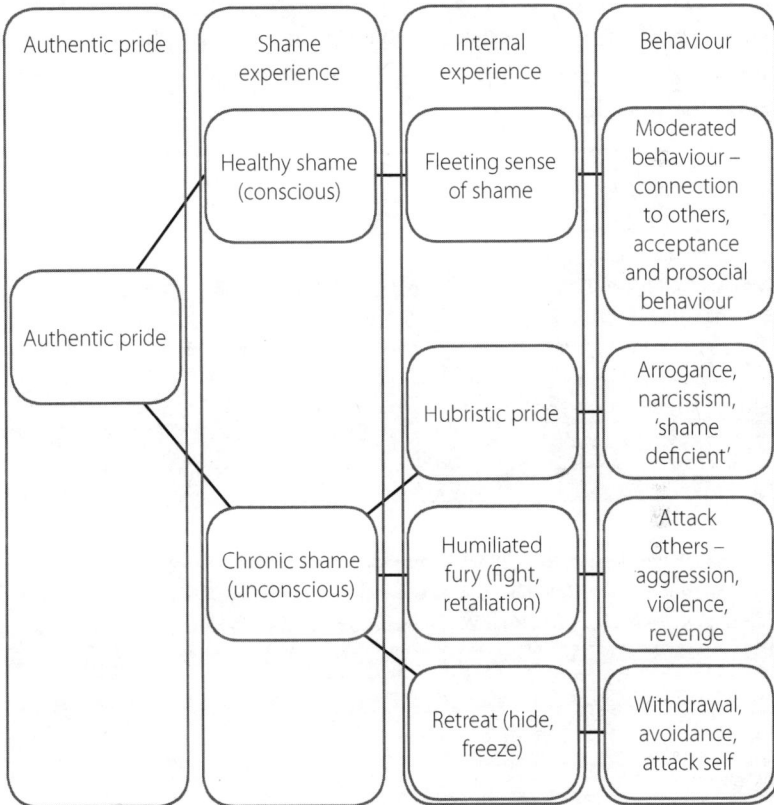

Figure 1.6 The link between shame and authentic and hubristic pride

Given the potentially negative outcomes of chronic shame, you will benefit from helping clients make the link between the range of feelings associated with shame and defences such as hubristic pride. It is only when shame has been worked through that authentic pride can emerge, embrace and flourish so that shame can be discarded. To facilitate this, you need to have a deeper understanding of the nature of shame and the role it plays in inhibiting clients from taking control over their lives and being able to accept themselves. It is only in the safety of the therapeutic relationship that the impact of shame can be explored, processed and overcome.

To aid you in this, the following chapter will elaborate on the nature of shame by focusing on the development of shame in early childhood through attachment relationships with primary caregivers, family dynamics, the intergenerational transmission of shame, and the common triggers that activate shame experiences. Alongside this, it will identify the phases of shame and examine the range of physiological, non-verbal, verbal and cognitive cues associated with each phase and how these impact on the self.

SUGGESTED READING

Dearing, R.L. and Tangney, J.P. (eds) (2011) *Shame in the Therapy Hour*. Washington, DC: American Psychological Association.

Kaufman, G. (2004) *The Psychology of Shame: Theory and Treatment of Shame Based Syndromes* 2nd edn. New York: Springer.

Lansky, M.R. and Morrison, A.P. (1997) *The Widening Scope of Shame*. Hillsdale, NJ: Analytic Press.

Lewis, H.B. (1971) *Shame and Guilt in Neurosis*. New York: International Universities Press.

Lewis, M. (1995) *Shame: The Exposed Self*. New York: The Free Press.

Morrison, A.P. (1989) *Shame: The Underside of Narcissism*. Hillsdale, NJ: Analytic Press.

Nathanson, D.L. (1992) *Shame and Pride: Affect, Sex, and the Birth of the Self*. New York: W.W. Norton.

Tangney, J.P. and Dearing, R.L. (2002) *Shame and Guilt*. New York: Guilford Press.

Tracy, J.L. and Robbins, R.W. (2011) 'The Nature of Pride.' In R.L. Dearing and J.P. Tangney (eds) *Shame in the Therapy Hour*. Washington, DC: American Psychological Association.

2

THE NATURE OF SHAME

As social animals that live in groups humans are primed for shame to ensure bonding and social cohesion. As a result everyone learns to feel shame, especially in the early years, through the attachment experiences with the primary caregivers, siblings and family members. If significant others are emotionally attuned to the needs of the child and are able to regulate shame experiences, the child will learn to manage shame in a healthy and constructive way. However, in families that are critical and hostile and where shame is applied too harshly, the child will experience humiliation and rejection and fear abandonment. This can lead to the range of presenting symptoms commonly seen in therapy such as sadness, depression, anxiety and self-destructive behaviour and personality disturbances such as narcissism and asocial behaviours.

This chapter will look at the nature of shame and how it develops in early attachment relationships and will consider the role of significant others and family dynamics in exposing the child to shame and how these impact on the regulation of shame experiences. This is most common in families with historical shame that has been passed from generation to generation. As the intergenerational transmission of shame is often unconscious it is helpful in exploring this to highlight shame-based family dynamics to have a better understanding of how early experiences of shame shape later responses and reactions to shame and how these are activated throughout the life span. In addition, shame in unparented children who are cared for by others, or sent to boarding school at a young age, will be explored with regard to impact and long-term effects. Typical triggers that reactivate shame will be examined and linked to the cycle of shame in which the recall of past shame amplifies current shame. Finally the phases of shame and common cues will be reviewed to increase awareness of non-verbal expressions of shame to help you identify these when working with clients who are not able to verbalise feelings of shame.

THE NATURE OF SHAME

Shame acts as a powerful regulator in personal and social relationships and expected ways of behaving and is a strong indicator of relational worth. In this individuals who act within expected parameters, and who express shame appropriately, are valued, loved and respected, while those who fail to do so are shunned and ostracised. In this respect shame is relationally based as it is elicited through the gaze of others. Shame is also a form of social control in which individuals learn about power, dominance, submission and compliance. These are first encountered within the family in which parents guide, or enforce, culturally acceptable behaviours which are reinforced by siblings and significant others in the child's social world. Throughout the life span these expectations become internalised and are a source of internally regulated shame. The appropriate expression of shame allows individuals to remain connected to others and avoid rejection. It is this fear of rejection, abandonment and isolation that motivates individuals to conform to social norms and engage in prosocial behaviours. For young children, who are completely dependent on others for their survival, to be abandoned feels dangerous and life threatening, and it is this terror that underpins the initial shock and physiological arousal characteristic of shame.

Remember
The appropriate expression of shame allows individuals to remain connected to others and avoid rejection.

The threat of danger triggers the alarm system, activating the release of a cascade of neuro-chemicals which start a complex chain of bodily reactions. The alarm system activates the fight, flight or freeze response via the sympathetic nervous system (SNS) and the parasympathetic nervous system (PNS). While the SNS increases heart rate and blood pressure, and releases cortisol, necessary for fight or flight, the PNS slows down the heart and metabolic rate, which results in the freeze response. These are thought to account for the non-verbal cues seen in shame such as feeling hot, reddening of the skin and blushing (SNS), and gaze aversion, lowering of the head and slumped shoulders (PNS).

While the freeze response is an important aid to survival in conserving energy until the danger is over, it is often accompanied by dissociation and a sense of shame for not having done more to ward off the threat (Sanderson 2013). In addition, if the fear and shame experience is overwhelming, the child is likely to dissociate from the experience to defend against overpowering emotions that cannot be processed. While the immediate benefit of dissociation is protection and to anaesthetise the pain, there is a long-term cost in that by pushing it outside of conscious awareness it cannot be processed or discharged and thus increases shame (Freyd and Birrell 2013; Lewis 2000; Nathanson 1992). In addition, not knowing is a good survival strategy, as 'The best way to keep a secret is not to know it in the first place; unawareness is a powerful survival technique when information is too dangerous to know' (Freyd and Birrell 2013, p.6). Thus dissociation allows the child to remain blind to betrayal by significant others especially in the face of repeated shame, humiliation and abuse (see Chapter 3). A further cost of dissociation is that it can lead to an array of mental health problems, which due to stigmatisation can be a source of further shame (Herman 2011b).

Research has shown that early childhood experiences shape babies' brains and become engraved into neural patterns of perceiving, feeling, thinking and behaving (Badenoch 2008; Gerhardt 2004) which direct behaviour, albeit outside conscious awareness. This is because early experiences are stored in the right brain where they become invisible to left brain cognitive processing, and yet exert considerable influence over bodily responses and feelings. This is why shame experiences are often implicit and not accessible to conscious awareness. As they are right brain based there is little or no language to verbalise them. You therefore need to develop a language for shame and shame experiences with your client and bring them into conscious awareness where they can be processed.

SHAME AND EARLY ATTACHMENT EXPERIENCES

The development of shame is lodged in early attachment experiences with the primary caregiver. It is these early experiences that create internal working models of relational worth and ways of relating to others which create a template for future relationships (Bowlby 1969; Gerhardt 2004). Research has shown that close bonds are critical from birth to help regulate the baby's internal states (Badenoch 2008; Gerhardt 2004; Schore 1998; Trevarthen 2005) and to establish trust that needs will be met. This is most likely to be achieved when the caregiver is responsive, attuned and able to mirror the infant's needs. Most parents are able to manage this well; however, some are not as responsive as they have developmentally inappropriate expectations of the baby such as being able to self-soothe, or feed or sleep to a schedule that best suits the parent. When the baby fails to meet these demands and the parent responds with disappointed expectation rather than 'the widened eyes...of sparkling eyed pleasure' (Schore 1994, p.144) the baby will encounter its first experience of shame. This is aptly demonstrated in Tronick's 'still face' experiments (Tronick 1989) where when the mother stops responding the baby quickly manifests non-verbal cues that are typically seen in shame.

These nascent experiences of shame will become more pronounced as the child develops self-consciousness and becomes more autonomous (Schore 1994, 1998). This is usually between 9 and 16 months of age as the child develops intentionality and self-agency and begins to move away from the parent. As the child's curiosity drive is sparked it will want to explore the world and become self-directed and goal-oriented. It is at this point that parental responses to attempts at separation and autonomy become crucial in the regulation of shame. As the baby learns to walk and explore the world independently it is likely to encounter myriad dangers which the parent needs to guard against. In order to balance the need to protect and the child's drive to explore the world, caregivers need to find a balance between acknowledging the toddler's desire to explore the dangerous or forbidden and redirecting behaviour to some other interest or joy. The more balanced the parent is in this the greater the opportunity for the child to develop self-regulation with little or no shame. More importantly, if the child is gently but firmly redirected without severing the connection, the child is likely to develop fleeting, healthy shame (see Figure 2.1).

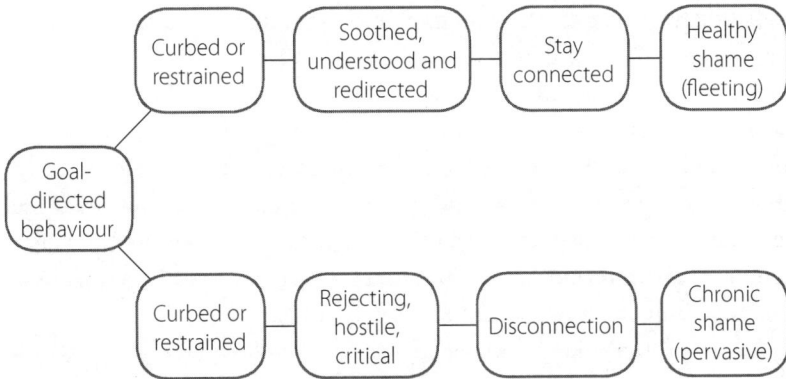

Figure 2.1 Modulation and regulation of shame

The main aim is to minimise ruptures in the relationship by staying connected, and when ruptures do occur, endeavour to reconnect and repair these as quickly as possible. When the child's desire to explore is not understood within the context of curiosity, is interpreted as acts of defiance or harshly punished, the connection between the child and caregiver will be severed. If this rupture is prolonged through further criticism or denigration, the rupture will turn into a deep fissure of chronic shame which inhibits and paralyses the child in seeking future attachments or from forming close bonds. Repeated exposure to humiliation and rejection will amplify shame to the point that 'the essence of self-definition is immutably linked to shame' (Nathanson 1992, p.30) and that shame is embedded into the personality to become an expected and accepted part of the core identity.

Remember

Shame is relationally based and is elicited when the caregiver fails to see the child, or invalidates his or her sense of self and feelings.

Shame is also elicited in the absence of accurate mirroring or attunement in which the caregiver is not able to respond to the child's feelings (Trevarthen 2005). Thus when the child says they feel sad, angry or happy and the caregiver ignores or invalidates this, the child learns that their feelings are wrong and cannot be trusted. This lack of acknowledgement or 'soul blindness of the other' (Wurmser 2013, p.4) dehumanises and objectifies the child, which serves to intensify existential angst and chronic shame. Over time and repeated exposure to inaccurate mirroring the child will stop listening to its feelings and inner experiencing and come to depend on others to define their emotions. Paradoxically this intensifies dependency needs which become a further source of shame. This can also be seen in how the caregiver responds to separation and reunion. If the child is met with excitement and delight then the child feels soothed; if it encounters disapproval, indifference or ridicule the child will feel ashamed. When this lack of emotional attunement is repeated the child will fear rejection and humiliation from the caregiver and learn that basic needs are inherently shameful (Herman 2011b).

In order to avoid ridicule or rejection the child will learn to disavow basic needs and hide these from others through a façade of self-sufficiency and fierce independence which will characterise all future relationships. Covering up dependency needs necessitates turning inward and a focus on self which can evolve into narcissism, grandiosity and hubristic pride to compensate for deeply buried narcissistic wounds (Mollon 1993). The fear of shame and humiliation means that others have to be kept at bay at all costs to hide the tender, wounded child. Ultimately intense shame deactivates the attachment system and cuts off access to empathic others through withdrawal, hostility, denigration of others or predominantly superficial relationships. In addition shame also deactivates connection to the authentic self, leading to inhibited self-expression and self-denigration (DeYoung 2015).

While these early shaming experiences are initially formed in the attachment to the primary caregiver they can be reinforced by other family members, in particular siblings. While children need to learn how to manage competition and comparison between siblings and teasing and name calling, this needs to be modulated by caregivers so that it does not descend into pervasive shame and crippling humiliation.

FAMILY DYNAMICS

Families vary enormously in terms of how attuned they are and to what extent they are able to regulate shame. Even in families where this is optimised the child may still be exposed to shaming experiences. Obvious examples of these are that the child is smaller, less knowledgeable, less skilled and much less autonomous than its parents or older siblings, which can create shame. In nurturing families this is accommodated and the child learns that it is okay to not know or be able to do everything and that they will learn over time. This allows for the development of a healthy appraisal of its abilities without feeling shame. Unfortunately some families are not able to provide such an environment and tend to shame children for not performing to their expectations, or by comparing them negatively to others such as siblings or peers. Instead of encouraging the child they may ridicule him or her for not being good enough, strong enough, grown up enough, too needy or not knowing things. These become internalised and are crucial in forming indelible shame scripts that direct feelings, thoughts and behaviour.

Reflection
Freely associate to the word 'teasing'. What feelings and thoughts arise? What role did teasing take in your family? Who teased the most? Was there ever a fine line between teasing and shaming? How did this feel? Does teasing feature in your life now?

It is worth noting that such ridicule is not always directly from the parents or primary caregivers, but may be instigated by older siblings. This is often through what is believed to be teasing, although this may easily spill over into humiliation and shame. Families will differ in where the tipping point is between teasing and shaming, and may collude with, or indeed encourage, such interactions without any recognition of how the child feels. Many children feel they have to endure this, as if they challenge such teasing they may then be shamed by being told they are a bad sport, or are overly sensitive. Such alleged teasing can be the source of crippling shame which has to be hidden and kept secret to avoid further shame or humiliation. This will increase vulnerability to further shame by peers, teachers and others in the child's social world. While many families use shame in a benign and sensitive way to encourage prosocial behaviour, humility, empathy and compassion, some families use shame to humiliate and inhibit the child's sense of self and self-agency.

Shame-based families
Some families are immersed in shame, sometimes through the intergenerational transmission of shame (see p.48), or through their own unconscious shame experiences that have not been processed. In this, families can repeat patterns of parenting that caused their own shame and which they feel compelled to repeat. Such conditioned shaming behaviours, while often not intentional, are nevertheless no less damaging or hurtful to those they shame and humiliate. Conversely some families

deliberately humiliate and shame their children because of their need to be all-powerful, or because they believe this is the most effective way to prepare the child for the adult world. Either way this can lead to shame-based family dynamics in which shame is a prominent feature.

There are several characteristic dynamics associated with shame-based families including uneven balance of power, pressure to conform to expected roles, emotional rigidity in suppressing and invalidating emotions, as well as constant comparison to others. Shame-based families typically have an uneven balance of power where one individual, usually a parent, is all-powerful and dominant while other family members are expected to be submissive and compliant. In this there will be myriad rules and regulations which have to be adhered to at all cost. These are typically non-negotiable and are enforced in order to hold the family together.

Bradshaw (2005) identifies several common rules that are inviolable such as the need to be in control of feelings and behaviour at all times, especially negative or vulnerable feelings such as anxiety, fear, loneliness, grief, anger or rejection. This is accompanied by the need to be perfect in everything one does, and never make mistakes. Furthermore, whenever anything goes wrong, someone must be blamed, whether that is the self or others. In addition, children are taught to deny freedom of thought, perception, feelings, choice and imagination and that these must remain hidden and unexpressed. Overarching all of these is the rule 'never trust anyone', even those closest to you. This can make it very difficult to enter and maintain relationships as these rules inhibit closeness and intimacy yet promote attachment to food, alcohol, sex, work or money as these are infinitely more reliable than humans.

Shame-based families also exert enormous pressure to conform to expected roles such as 'the good girl/boy', 'the bad girl/boy', 'the rebel', 'the sunny one', 'the super achiever', 'the martyr', 'the rescuer', 'the victim', 'the loser', 'the clown', 'the nurturer' or 'the scapegoat'. These are often implicit and thereby hard to challenge, which can lead to the adoption of lifelong unwanted identities (see Chapter 3). Alongside this there may be pressure to succeed and excel in certain areas such as sport, academia or high social status professions or careers with little or no consideration of the child's ability, interest or desire.

A more subtle way of conveying pressure to conform is in the comparison with others. This is usually done in comparing the child negatively to siblings, friends or peers, making them feel they are never 'good enough'. Such constant comparison can become a default setting in which the child can never accept themselves as they are and continue to compare themselves with others, and reinforcing their sense of shame no matter how accomplished or successful they are. This engenders an inflated reliance on social comparison, which is reflected in how social media is used by adolescents.

Shame-based families are also typically very rigid and absolutist with regard to what is right and wrong and good and bad, with little or no tolerance for discussion or negotiation. While these are sometimes overtly expressed, they are often implicitly enforced. This is most evident in terms of having and expressing emotions. Feelings are often taboo in a shame-based family in which being too happy or too sad or too angry are not acceptable and thus a source of shame. This can lead to the suppression and invalidation of emotions to avoid feeling shame, which can result in lifelong difficulties in expressing emotion. A by-product of this is the suppression of spontaneity, exuberance and authenticity, giving rise to the adoption of a false sense. It can also create a façade of being 'nice' in not allowing the expression of any negative, unacceptable or uncomfortable thoughts or feelings to emerge. Such families often appear as 'normal' and functional on the surface yet cover up a myriad of powerful feelings and dangerous forces which need to be hidden. As a result children learn to hide their thoughts and feelings and pretend that all is well, which further distances them from their feelings and needs.

Reflection

When have you been criticised or been seen as 'not good enough'? Where did this come from – parents, siblings? What were some of the implicit messages in your family around the expression of thoughts and feelings? How did these impact on you? Do they still reverberate now?

You can begin to explore the origins of shame by encouraging the client to talk about their family. See the following exercise for ways to do this. You will have to be mindful throughout this to contextualise any responses within a multicultural perspective.

Exercise

Identifying the origins of shame in family dynamics

1.   Invite the client to think of examples of what others said or did when they were young that made them feel 'less than' or 'not good enough'. Try to

   get the client to identify who conveyed these messages and how this
   relates to anger triggers in the present.

2. Encourage your client to reflect on the family dynamics around the
   expression of feelings, especially anger and aggression and the expression
   of needs, and on how mistakes, vulnerability, dependency, pleasure,
   failure, pride or achievement were managed. Try to get the client to link
   these to some of the messages that still direct behaviour in the present.

3. Next invite them to reflect on the spoken and unspoken 'dos and don'ts' or
   family rules and the consequences if these were violated, including how
   they could disappoint other family members or bring shame to the family,
   and encourage the client to list these in their journal.

4. Invite the client to write down the destructive life script they were given
   and identify to what extent they have enacted this script, and what they
   have done to maintain and build on it.

In exploring family dynamics and rules clients will become aware of how
these early messages have been a source of shame and to what extent
these have persisted into adulthood. What might be less clear is how
shame is passed down through the generations and the impact this has in
creating shame-based families. Clients might also find it useful to reflect
on the unwanted identities that were assigned in childhood and how
these continue to influence current relationships.

   Another common feature in shame-based families is the type of
strategies used to manage shame. A recurrent theme is the use of alcohol
or drugs to numb feelings of shame. This renders the parent(s) emotionally
unavailable, which further reinforces the child's sense of shame. Attempts
to provide some emotional support when sober usually oscillate between
chronic remorse and mawkishly sentimental apologies in which the child
needs to reassure the parent. As the child cannot depend on the parent
for consistent emotional support they often need to become self-sufficient
and deny their own needs. This leads to a role reversal in which the
child becomes the parent who reassures and takes care of the adult. This
can have long-lasting effects of feeling ashamed of their own needs yet
feeling compelled to meet the needs of others (see Chapter 3). This is
compounded if addiction is accompanied by physical or sexual abuse.
The use of violence, coercion and manipulation to ward off shame is
also commonly seen in domestic abuse in which partners and children
are humiliated and shamed (see Chapter 10). Thus defences against
shame can generate more shame, which increases vulnerability to the
intergenerational transmission of shame.

THE INTERGENERATIONAL TRANSMISSION OF SHAME

All families have secrets and go to some lengths to hide these from themselves and others, not realising that this intensifies the sense of shame. Secrets and silence are powerful incubators of shame which can be transmitted across generations. The wounds of historical shame are typically inherited unconsciously and yet weave their way into the psyche of future generations. Although invisible they exert a potent force on others, which can lead to a vulnerability to shame throughout the life span.

Reflection

Are there stories in your family about your grandparents, parents or other relatives that have been cloaked in secrecy and silence? Consider what these might be and how they brought shame onto the family. How have these been passed down in the family to the present day? To help you track these consider making a genogram (see p.52).

Typical examples of intergenerational shame seen in the therapeutic setting are illegitimacy, abandonment, adoption, being in care, mental health problems, being sectioned, addictions, rape, child sexual abuse and incest, separation, divorce and affairs. In addition, there may be family shame around parentage, religion, cultural heritage, ethnicity, race, skin colour, poverty, bankruptcy, social status and class (see Chapter 4). To make intergenerational shame more manageable it is important to identify the shame skeletons in the cupboard and give voice to them so that clients can be released from their hold.

As the intergenerational transmission of shame is largely unconscious it can be difficult to unravel. To enable clients to identify to what extent shame has been passed down through the generations it is helpful to construct a visual document such as a shame genogram. A shame genogram can track the history of shame throughout the family over multiple generations by charting family relationships, major events and the dynamics of a family. To begin a genogram clients will need to decide how many generations they wish to include and who in the family has access to information that they feel they can talk to. As they gather information they can begin to create a genogram either from a standard template, which can be sourced from the internet, or make one of their own design.

⚙ **Exercise**
Shame genogram

1. To start their shame genogram the client will need to decide how many generations they wish to represent in the genogram.

2. Once they have decided this ask them to write down everything they know about the family history.

3. Tell them that when they have exhausted their own knowledge they may need to talk to other family members and ask questions about family relationships and significant events. They need to be mindful that these discussions may be difficult for some family members and they may not feel comfortable with this.

4. Make the client aware that they will need to be prepared to listen to lots of stories. Encourage them to do this as attentively as they can and to remember to ask open-ended questions that motivate the person to share more information.

5. Once the client has gathered information they will need to design their shame genogram by using either a standard genogram template which can either be found and completed online or downloaded and filled out by hand. Alternatively they can design their own using the templates as a guide.

6. They can organise the family history of shame beginning with the oldest generation they want to represent (e.g. grandparents or great grandparents).

7. Once completed the client can identify shame patterns with you, the counsellor, and how these have been transmitted to their parents and to them and their siblings. This will help the client to identify the shame that they have absorbed through the family history.

Clients who have experienced cultural or national shame will find it helpful to include this on the genogram as this can be transferred intergenerationally. For instance, some individuals who are of German heritage and had a family member who was actively involved in the Holocaust may feel shame for the actions of their forebears which they have absorbed and which have inhibited them in some way. This is equally true of clients from other cultures whose ancestors have been involved in mass genocide, torture or religious persecution. In becoming more aware of the shame they carry for past atrocities they will be able to identify intergenerational shame to allow them to shed their sense of responsibility in this and relinquish the burden of ancestral shame.

Top tip

Remind your client he or she was not responsible for what happened in the family past and that they are responsible for trying to make sense of aspects of their history and trying to do things differently.

SHAME IN UNPARENTED CHILDREN

Shame is increased in unparented or looked after children who already feel shame for having been abused, abandoned or rejected by their biological parent(s). In trying to make sense of their experiences they typically blame themselves for their abuse or rejection, which compounds their feelings of being unlovable, unwanted, not valued and worthless. Sadly this is all too often reinforced by prevailing attitudes that there must be something wrong with looked after children and that they are in care because they are difficult to manage or defective in some way. This has a long tradition where children are blamed or shamed for their misfortune, as seen in the Irish laundries and Magdalene homes. As a result looked after children are vulnerable to chronic shame, which they tend to manage through defensive or compensatory behaviours such as excessive dependency, self-sufficiency, grandiosity, narcissism, aggression or violence.

Traumatised or unloved children who are dependent on hostile or aggressive caregivers are also more vulnerable to shame as they are conditioned to associate fear and abandonment with closeness and caregiving. Rather than learning that relationships are a source of safety, protection and security they learn that they are dangerous and punishing. As the child cannot afford to see the parent as bad they come to believe that 'I am bad' in order to maintain love and connection. This conflation leads to the incorporation of shame into the sense of self in which the parent is idealised and the self is vilified. As this begins to form part of the child's core identity it can resonate throughout life with the individual associating close relationships with a source of pain and shame rather than love or comfort. As a result some will either feel compelled to re-enact this through becoming trapped in abusive relationships, or avoid close relationships in order to avoid shame and maintain a separate and autonomous sense of self.

Shame is also a prominent feature in socially privileged children who are sent to boarding schools from a young age where vulnerability and dependency has no place, or in which bullying and abuse are endemic. The experience of boarding school is a complex mix of privilege, abandonment and neglect, making it difficult to acknowledge the damaging effects this can have on some children. While some are able to navigate the boarding experience well and emerge from it relatively unscathed, many do not. In his work with boarding school survivors, Duffell argues that privileged abandonment, which ridicules emotionality and vulnerability while emphasising rationality and self-sufficiency, leads to 'a defensively-organised personality that is durable, if brittle' (Duffell 2014, p.iii). Such children learn that they cannot show sadness or hurt in being separated from their parents for fear of being shamed or humiliated by their peers, older pupils and staff, or indeed their parents, for making a fuss (Duffell 2000, 2014). They also learn to remain silent about any physical or sexual abuse for fear of the consequences of disclosure and the need to 'man up'. Such secrecy and denial highlight the demands on boarding school children to be self-reliant, stoical and grown up. Paradoxically such pseudo-adult behaviour prevents emotional maturation as dependency needs are pushed outside of conscious awareness, where they bind with feelings of shame, humiliation and rage.

Moreover, such feelings have to be quelled and silenced as the children have been told that being able to go to boarding school is a privilege to be valued, especially when parents have made innumerable sacrifices to afford such a privilege. This prevents the expression of feelings of vulnerability, rejection, abandonment or shame, as any implied criticism is regarded as ungrateful and a further source of shame. As adults the shame associated with vulnerability and dependency will threaten to emerge in intimate relationships and result in a range of relational difficulties, including lack of trust and constant fear of abandonment. As the negative aspects of the boarding school experience are disavowed the adult will recollect their experience as positive and 'the making of them', fuelling the desire to provide the same privileged experience to their own children (Duffell 2000). You need to be mindful that while many, but by no means all, clients who have experienced privileged abandonment will have severed the link between shame, rejection, vulnerability and dependency from these early experiences, they will find it difficult to explore this and risk more shame.

Shame will also be seen in children who are in residential care due to physical or cognitive disabilities. Not only do they have a sense of shame by being less physically or cognitively able than others, they also have to manage their sense of abandonment and rejection. Similar to boarding school children, they may not be able to express this either due to their disability, or because they feel guilty for being a burden on their family. This renders them voiceless in their shame, with no outlet to discharge unbearable pent-up feelings.

The fear of abandonment and rejection and dependency needs feature prominently in early attachment experiences and the emergence of shame, as when children:

> suffer the loss of love from others, by being rejected or abandoned, assaulted or insulted, slighted or demeaned, humiliated or ridiculed, dishonoured or disrespected is to be shamed by them...and without a certain minimal amount of self-respect the self collapses and the soul dies. (Gilligan 2000, p.51)

SHAME TRIGGERS

Shame triggers will vary between individuals and be unique to each depending on past experiences of shame. Tomkins (1963) argues that triggers to shame activate associated experiences of shame. These will not include every single experience of shame but represent a summation of accumulated shame experiences that are compressed into a pattern, or shame-related scripts. Over time these shame-related scripts are embedded and will be reactivated in the presence of any future shame experiences. The individual thus becomes sensitised to shame that is reminiscent of earlier experiences and will react with a range of defensive strategies to mitigate the feeling or experience of shame (see Chapter 5).

Although all shame experiences are unique they typically share the same ancestry, which is reflected in a degree of commonality in the triggers that activate shame. You will find it helpful to have these common triggers in mind and ensure that, in identifying these, clients can link these to their unique experiences of shame, especially if these have been disavowed. Some of the most common triggers are given in Table 2.1. While each of these might trigger shame you will need to explore each client's individual narrative to make sense of how these experiences have coalesced into shame-based patterns of behaviour and defences.

Table 2.1 Common triggers to shame	
Trigger	**Association**
Ridicule	Being laughed at, teased, humiliated
Comparison to others	Being compared to others, less than – height, weight, strength, skills, abilities
Judgement	Being judged by others, not living up to expectations
Invalidation	Ignored, dismissed
Inadequacy	Sense of failure, incompetent, not good enough
Self-blame	Taking on the blame and shame of others, self-hatred, self-contempt
Negative thoughts	Negative messages about self, inner voices, negative thoughts and feelings, negative self-talk
Vulnerability and dependency needs	Invalidation of needs, contempt for having needs
Abandonment and rejection	Being pushed away, excluded or isolated
Exposure of shame	Discovery of hidden shame, making shame conscious

Shame can also be represented in dreams, especially those that feature public toilets and bodily ablutions such as urination and defecation, or nakedness. Such dreams often denote a fear of being exposed and found to be lacking alongside feelings of being dirty, undesirable, repulsive and unworthy. This is especially true in the case of recurring dreams and nightmares. These need to be understood within the context of shame and linked to actual shame experiences to fully process them. A further trigger is the discovery or exposure of shame which individuals have denied or hidden. To have this made conscious and witnessed by others will intensify the sense of shame and be perceived as being re-shamed. This is a particular challenge for counsellors and you will need to balance exposure to shame with minimising the potential of re-shaming the client (see Chapter 11).

In addition, there is some evidence that there is a gender difference in terms of shame triggers. Brené Brown (2007b) found that generally males have one primary trigger under which a number of factors are subsumed, while females may have a number of triggers. The main trigger for men is being perceived as being weak on a variety of dimensions such as physical strength, sexual prowess, access to resources and emotional stoicism. This is in contrast to females whose shame is attached to physical attractiveness, desirability, relationship skills and mothering.

THE CYCLE OF SHAME

The experience of shame is a complex interaction between feelings, thoughts and behaviours which are inextricably linked in an endless cycle of shame. This cycle is characterised by three phases consisting of physiological responses, cognitive processes and behaviour. The initial reaction to shame is one of shock or panic, which is usually accompanied by a range of physiological reactions which trigger the fight–flight–freeze response. In response to perceived danger the body is flooded with a cascade of neurochemicals which inhibit cognitive processing and the capacity to think or speak. This is accompanied by chest constriction, heart palpitations, loud rushing in the ears, dizziness, nausea, perceptual distortions and an upsurge in body heat and perspiration. This shifts the focus on to overwhelming internal states which prompt the need to hide and withdraw to safety and protection from further shame. If it is not possible to physically flee, the individual will cover the face with their hands, look down and avoid eye contact in a state of frozen watchfulness and self-consciousness. In becoming invisible the individual avoids further scrutiny and minimises the possibility of further shame. Alternatively some individuals will attack the source of shame through aggression or violence and thereby triumph over their shame.

Reflection

Reflect on how you know you feel shame. It might help to recall a time when you felt smaller, looked at, looked through or exposed. Try to identify feelings and sensations. Where did your eyes look? What did your hands do? How did your face feel, your stomach? Were you warm or cool? Breathe and write down physical, cognitive, behavioural and spiritual manifestations.

As the initial shock and physiological responses subside a range of cognitive processes are activated that search for any previously stored memories of shame. This will activate further associations to shame such as powerlessness, helplessness, defeat, inadequacy and self-blame. In turn, these associations will trigger cognitive processes such as rumination, negative self-evaluations, negative thoughts and negative self-talk. These are often reflected in language such as 'I am stupid', 'I am an idiot', 'I am useless' or 'I am a failure', which reinforces the sense of shame. To ward off and protect against such feelings and thoughts, defence strategies such as withdrawal, attack self, avoidance or attack other are elicited. These in turn activate a range of self-destructive behaviours such as self-harm, alcohol or drug misuse, or behaviours that are harmful to others such as rage and violence, and are a further source of shame. This complex interaction can be summarised in an endless cycle of shame in which the individual becomes imprisoned, with no hope of escape (see Figure 2.2).

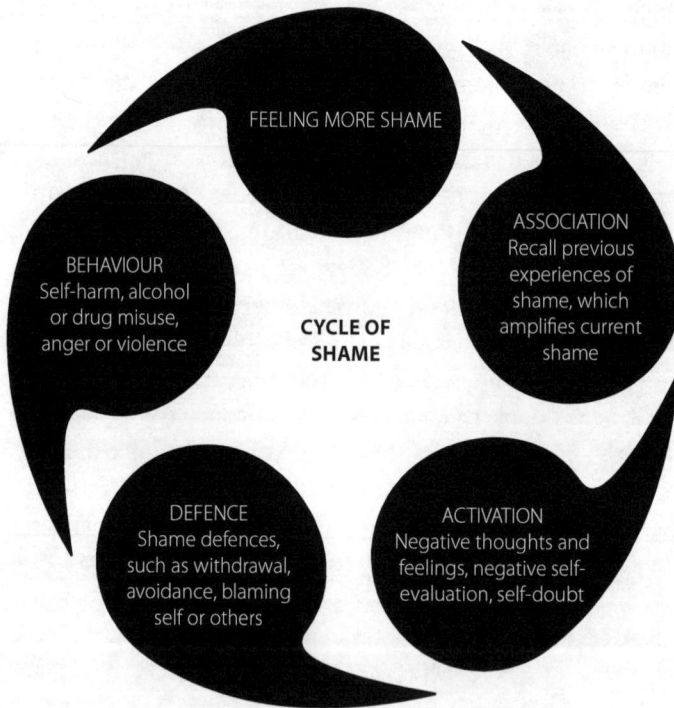

FEELING MORE SHAME

BEHAVIOUR
Self-harm, alcohol
or drug misuse,
anger or violence

CYCLE OF
SHAME

ASSOCIATION
Recall previous
experiences of
shame, which
amplifies current
shame

DEFENCE
Shame defences,
such as withdrawal,
avoidance, blaming
self or others

ACTIVATION
Negative thoughts and
feelings, negative self-
evaluation, self-doubt

Figure 2.2 The Cycle of Shame

To prevent full activation of the Cycle of Shame it is imperative that clients are able to find a way of interrupting it before it takes hold and overwhelms the client. The following exercise is a useful technique to help clients identify shame images, associated feelings, thoughts and defences.

⚙️ **Exercise**
Interrupting the Cycle of Shame

1. Invite the client to make a list of shame-based images and rank order these.

2. As soon as any one of the shame images is activated tell the client to try to stop the image from taking hold or activating the Cycle of Shame.

3. To facilitate this you need to build a repertoire of distraction and grounding techniques that involve neutral or positive thoughts or activities.

4. Remind your client to practise using these whenever the shame cycle is activated.

Another creative way of managing shame is to make a shame box in which to place shame-based thoughts, feelings or experiences as soon as they arise so that clients do not get entrapped in the Cycle of Shame. In storing these shame-based thoughts and feelings they can be contained and prevent clients from having to replay them in their minds and activating the shame cycle.

⚙️ **Exercise**
Shame box

Encourage your client to find a box (either wooden, cardboard or plastic) which they can decorate and customise. Tell the client that whenever shame-based feelings, messages, thoughts or experiences threaten to overwhelm them they should write these down on paper and then cut the paper into separate strips, each with a feeling or message, etc. Each strip of paper should be folded and placed inside the box. Once these are contained in the box, they should close the lid. These can be stored until the client is ready to look at them or share them with a trusted friend or counsellor. It helps to schedule a specific period of time such as 20–30 minutes to look at one or two of the strips and allow shame feelings to arise. It can be a help for the client to set a timer to remind them when the specified time is up, and then close the box and put the shame thoughts or feelings away. This can be done daily or whenever necessary as a way to interrupt the shame cycle and tolerate shame-based thoughts or feelings.

THE RELATIONAL CYCLE OF SHAME

The Cycle of Shame can also be enacted in relationships, especially ones that are predicated on shaming dynamics and shame-based communication. This might be with a partner or a member of the family such as a parent or sibling, or a boss or work colleague. It is useful for clients to be able to identify shame cycles that are perpetuated in relationships. The following exercise is a helpful way of identifying relational shame cycles.

Exercise
Interrupting relational shame cycles

1. Invite your client to list any shame cycles that are enacted with significant relationships by someone who persistently shames them.

2. Ask them to explore and list three ways in which they could interrupt this cycle without shaming the other person.

3. Ask them to agree to try at least one of these alternatives next time the shame cycle is activated and check how effective these are.

4. Your client can use these in the future to interrupt the relational cycle of shame.

CLUES TO SHAME

Accompanying the cycle and phases of shame are a number of clues indicating that the person is experiencing shame, which are summarised in Table 2.2. You will find these a useful guide to the felt sense of shame, particularly with those clients who have disavowed their shame and have no conscious awareness of it. Many of these clues are not under voluntary control and as such provide more accurate indicators of shame than purely verbal or cognitive expressions. If the shame defence is to attack others then the opposite would occur in enlargement and swelling of the body, erect posture and direct eye contact to intimidate the source of shame.

Paralanguage and language are powerful indicators of shame. Further clues are in tempo and irregular rhythm in speech, or a change in pitch or tone of voice such as a sing-song lilt to signify ridicule, or staccato, monotone and robotic speech. These are accompanied by verbal descriptions of the self with adjectives such as stupid, silly, needy, pathetic, ridiculous, weak or worthless which reflect the degree of self-hatred and self-contempt. These are often so deeply embedded that any challenge to these is resisted and any praise rejected.

While there are many powerful overt and visible clues to shame, you need to be reminded that some clients will try to compensate or hide their shame through arrogance and grandiosity. This will manifest in an overinflated sense of self with glowing self-descriptions to signal how wonderful, successful and attractive they are. This will be accompanied by impressionistic speech and language, narcissism, hubristic pride and the tendency to over-value the self while denigrating others. Those clients who use attacks on others as a defence may hide their shame by being loud, brash, bombastic, hostile, aggressive, threatening and full of rage, making it hard to connect to them.

Clues to the discharge of the crippling effects of shame are seen in restored eye contact, more erect body posture, the ability to share humour or laughter and a more empathic and compassionate perception of self. The exploration of shame in the therapeutic process allows these to emerge, which is critical in building shame resilience. To facilitate this, you will need to link early experiences of shame to how they have impacted on the client. This will be addressed in the next chapter, which will look at the impact of chronic shame on clients and how shame is perpetuated and kept alive.

Table 2.2 Typical clues to shame

Non-verbal	Paralinguistic	Verbal	Cognitive	Behaviour
• Gaze aversion • Downcast eyes • Bowed head • Blushing • Slumped or hunched shoulders • Covering all or part of the face • Squirming • Fidgeting • Biting or licking lips • Biting tongue • False smiling • Contraction of the body • 'Shrivelling' or collapse in body posture • Restless shifts of posture or gesticulation	• Hesitation • Soft speech • Mumbling • Silences • Stammering • Long pauses • Rapid speech • Tensely laughed words • Vocal retreat • Disorganisation of thought • Over-use of qualifiers • Self-interruption • Self-censorship	• Negative language directed at self • Use of adjectives such as needy, ridiculous, silly, idiotic, stupid, dumb, weak, pathetic, inept, worthless • Confused • Inadequate • Angry • Inferior • Unworthy • Vulnerable	• Confusion of thought • Negative self-thoughts • Humiliated fury • Rumination • Memory of other shame experiences • Negative self-talk	• Hide • Shrink • Paralysis • Inhibition • Hostility • Rage • Violence • Shaming others • Appeasement behaviour – submission, compliance, helplessness

SUGGESTED READING

Badenoch, B. (2008) *Being a Brain-Wise Therapist: A Practical Guide to Interpersonal Neurobiology.* New York: W.W. Norton.

Duffell, N. (2000) *The Making of Them: The British Attitude to Children and the Boarding School System.* London: Lone Arrow Press.

Duffell, N. (2014) *Wounded Leaders: British Elitism and the Entitlement Illusion – A Psychohistory.* London: Lone Arrow Press.

Fonagy, P., Gergely, G., Jurist, E.L. and Target, M. (2002) *Affect Regulation, Mentalization and the Development of the Self.* New York: Other Press.

Gerhardt, S. (2004) *Why Love Matters: How Affection Shapes the Baby's Brain.* London: Brunner-Routledge.

Kaufman, G. (2004) *The Psychology of Shame: Theory and Treatment of Shame Based Syndromes.* 2nd edn. New York: Springer.

Nathanson, D.L. (1992) *Shame and Pride: Affect, Sex, and the Birth of the Self.* New York: W.W. Norton.

Schore, A.N. (1994) *Affect Regulation and the Origin of the Self: The Neurobiology of Emotional Development.* Hillsdale, NJ: Lawrence Erlbaum.

Schore, A.N. (1998) 'Early Shame Experiences and Infant Brain Development.' In P. Gilbert and B. Andrews (eds) *Shame: Interpersonal Behavior, Psychopathology and Culture.* New York: Oxford.

Trevarthen, C. (2005) 'Stepping Away from the Mirror. Pride and Shame in Adventures of Companionship: Reflections on the Nature and Emotional Needs of Infant Intersubjectivity.' In C.S. Carter, L. Ahnert, K. E. Grossmann, S. B. Hrdy, M. E. Lamb, S. W.Porges, and N. Sachser. (eds) *The 92nd Dahlem Workshop Report. Attachment and Bonding: A New Synthesis.* Cambridge, MA: MIT Press.

3

THE IMPACT OF SHAME

The nature of shame is highly complex and can generate both positive and negative outcomes. While most individuals have experienced primarily healthy shame, there are many who have been crippled by chronic shame and frequently end up in the consulting room. To help you identify the impact chronic shame can have, this chapter will explore some of the most common effects. The intention is not to provide a comprehensive 'shopping list' of shame but rather a guide to what is typically seen in clients who have experienced crippling shame. Shame will impact on individuals in a variety of ways and you need to explore and assess the unique impact it has had on clients rather than assume that they are all affected in the same way.

In order to provide a general guide to the impact of chronic shame the chapter will examine shame anxiety and how this elicits shame-proneness. It also highlights how shame-prone individuals get trapped into a spiral of shame, or a recursive shame loop, which intensifies their shame experience. To manage the overwhelming feelings of shame clients will adopt a range of defensive strategies, or shame scripts, which can form part of their self-identity. The chapter will unpack some of the ways shame impacts on the self by exploring a range of identity scripts such as diminished sense of self and low self-esteem, self-blame, social comparison, negative thoughts and negative self-talk, perfectionism, the need for control and how chronic shame can lead to grandiosity, narcissism, anger and violence.

SHAME ANXIETY

In response to repeated shaming experiences clients can develop shame anxiety in which they anticipate shame through pre-empting threats of being exposed, humiliated, belittled or rejected (Wurmser 1995). This can lead to a heightened sensitivity to shame, making them hypervigilant to both external and internal potential sources of shame. Such hypervigilance is exhausting as the client is preoccupied by the terror of shame, which can deplete already limited resources to manage shame when it is experienced. Underpinning shame anxiety is self-consciousness and concern about how they will be seen by others. The assumption is that they will not measure up to expectations or that they will be perceived as less than. In addition they fear exposure of their shameful feelings of inadequacy, defectiveness and worthlessness. In trying to hide their secret shame they invariably feel more shame, which reinforces the anxiety and distress. This is compounded by the assumption that should their shame be discovered they will become an object of ridicule or humiliation and will be socially ostracised and excluded.

To avoid the potential of external shame and to manage the accompanying anxiety clients will tend to hide away and withdraw from others. This can manifest as chronic shyness, depression and social anxiety disorder and avoidance of all social interactions. While this protects clients from exposure to shame it comes at a cost, as they become socially isolated and more vulnerable to chronic loneliness, which in turn is a further source of shame. Such social withdrawal confirms their lack of relational worth and deficiencies, making it harder to break out of the cycle of shame. On the occasions when social interaction cannot be avoided, the anxiety around being shamed will elicit people-pleasing behaviours such as malleability, compliance or submissiveness in order to avoid ridicule or rejection. This entails relinquishing any sense of self and becoming chameleon-like in being whatever others want them to be and adopting whatever mask is necessary to hide their shame.

SHAME-PRONENESS

The constant preoccupation with shame and shame anxiety leads to the internalisation of shame (Kaufman 1989) in which the client becomes more and more enmeshed in shame anxiety. This inner focus on shame can lead to shame-proneness in which clients are engulfed by shame until it becomes a prison with no escape. As a result shame activation is no longer dependent on external sources but is triggered by internal feelings and thoughts and the reliving of past experiences of shame in an endless cycle of shame (see Chapter 2). In this, feelings and thoughts of shame are fused with previous and unrelated experiences of shame which become embedded into the core identity, spreading shame through the personality like a viral infection. This creates a shame-based identity that continuously absorbs, maintains and amplifies shame irrespective of actual defeats or failures. In addition any minor everyday mistakes or setbacks become shame-bound, thereby increasing the need to cover up and keep it secret from others by living in a 'shell and a façade' (Wurmser 1995) in which authenticity cannot be risked. Ultimately 'shame-prone' individuals are emotionally extremely fragile as they are not able to make themselves feel good enough and rely on others to do so.

Top tip

The antidote to shame is to break the silence and secrecy that surround it and to acknowledge its source openly and honestly.

Having to pretend and keep up the façade is exhausting and depletes already-limited energy resources and is often the cause of the enervation felt by many clients who feel paralysed by chronic shame. This immobilisation also accounts for the lack of spontaneity in thinking and behaviour which limits the ability to take positive risks and reinforces the sense of helplessness and feeling trapped in the cycle of shame. The more shame is internalised and unacknowledged with no opportunity for discharge, the more clients get trapped into a recursive emotional feedback loop, or feeling trap (Lewis 1971), of self-perpetuating shame (see Figure 3.1). In extreme cases this can lead to chain reactions such as explosive episodes of extreme panic, resentment, anger, humiliated fury and guilt (Scheff 1997). The only escape from this never-ending loop of shame and destructive explosions of aggression or violence is to acknowledge and discharge the shame in the presence of someone who will not re-shame or judge.

When shame-prone clients are not able to discharge the shame they are vulnerable to developing chronic shame in which they develop a mind-set that is permanently ready to feel shame. They feel overly responsible for what happens in their personal and social world and attribute all negative outcomes of events and interactions as their fault due to their personal defects. In this any misunderstanding, mistake or error is seen as proof of inadequacy rather than a normal part of learning and development. As the sense of worthlessness and defectiveness gets embedded shame-prone clients begin to surrender to their prison of shame and believe that they are beyond help. This can be challenging in the counselling process where any attempts to discharge the shame and reverse shame-based beliefs are fiercely resisted by the client (see Chapter 12).

Figure 3.1 The shame loop
(Adapted from Scheff 1990)

In many respects chronic shame dehumanises individuals in not allowing them to be human, to make mistakes and fail. This dehumanisation is often projected onto others, making it even harder to connect to them in case they do not live up to expectations or let them down (Broucek 1991). As the individual becomes more and more dehumanised they begin to question their very existence and their right to exist. This often manifests as feeling dead inside with no vitality or zest for life. This can result in robot-like behaviours in the pursuit of needing to prove themselves, to get things right and be perfect. When they fail in this they become highly critical of themselves, which reinforces their existential angst and sense of shame. To manage such overwhelming chronic shame clients will develop a number of defensive strategies to either mask or ward off feelings of shame.

DEFENCES AGAINST SHAME

As chronic shame becomes more unbearable a number of defences such as dissociation and anger are activated to facilitate survival. Research has shown that dissociation is an adaptive strategy to defend against overwhelming pain especially during initial exposure to fear and terror (Budden 2009; Freyd and Birrell 2013; Kluft 1992; Lewis 1992; Nathanson 1992; Platt and Freyd 2012). However, while it anaesthetises and numbs the feeling of shame, it does not process or discharge it; it merely disrupts the experience of shame (Nathanson 1992) by pushing it outside of conscious awareness. In this, shame is sealed off, allowing it to grow to corrosive levels, which contaminates the sense of self and contributes to a range of mental health difficulties such as post-traumatic stress disorder (Fisher, Appiah-Kusi and Grant 2012; Herman 2011a), dissociative disorders (Freyd and Birrell 2013; Kluft 1992), self-harming behaviours and suicidal ideation (see Chapter 8).

Alongside this clients will try to hide or avoid shame from themselves and others. This results in unacknowledged or hidden shame which is characterised by overt or undifferentiated shame or by-passed shame (Lewis 1971; Nathanson 1992; Scheff 1987). In overt and undifferentiated shame clients display the feeling of shame but are unable to identify or name it. Instead they tend to label their experience in a more diffuse way as feeling foolish, stupid, inadequate or awkward (Lewis 1971). This is in contrast to by-passed shame, which is experienced but cauterised through rapid and repetitive thoughts, speech and behaviour to avoid and distract from the full intensity of shame. As in dissociation this does not resolve and discharge feelings of shame; it merely covers them up so that shame can remain hidden. This condemns individuals to re-enacting and reliving shame through shame scripts, which can lead to disintegration and fragmentation of the self, or the emergence of shame-based parts such as the needy self or the angry self. Over time these become autonomous parts of the self which are decoupled from experiences of shame.

This is commonly seen in explosive episodes of anger or rage. Shame and anger are often fused as individuals may feel angry about their shame or being shamed and yet may not be able to express this as it may elicit further shame and sever connection to others. As the associated anger is incorporated into the shame loop it intensifies to volcanic levels of incandescent rage, which becomes a further source of shame (Lewis 1971; Miller 1985). This leads to further suppression and the creation of humiliated fury, which when unleased can result in a cascade of aggression and violence (Gilligan 2001).

STRATEGIES TO MANAGE SHAME

In addition to dissociation and the disavowal of shame there are a number of other defensive strategies that are commonly activated. These tend to coalesce into either defensive shame scripts or identity scripts in which shame becomes the organising principle of the core identity (Kaufman 1989).

Defensive shame scripts

Nathanson (1992) proposes that defences against shame are necessary to avoid exposure to shame and to guard the hidden shame within. This can be achieved in a variety of ways, although they cluster around four distinct strategies – withdrawal, attack self, avoidance and attack other – which form the four points of the Compass of Shame (Nathanson 1992). While all of these strategies may be used at different times and in different contexts, there is a tendency for one to predominate and become the default setting (see Chapter 5 for a full discussion).

In withdrawal individuals tend to display shame through classic behaviours associated with shame such as hiding, gaze aversion, lowered head and slumped shoulders. Such displays of shame serve to signal that shame has been acknowledged in order to maintain the connection to others rather than risk further ridicule or rejection. The physical signs of shame may also be accompanied with internal retreat, emotional unavailability and negative self-thoughts which can result in a sense of isolation and loneliness. In attack self the experience of shame is made more manageable and controllable through constant self-aggression, self-ridicule and self-disgust. This can be relatively mild, as in expressions of modesty and humility, humour, self-effacement, shyness and deference, but can evolve into more active attacks on the self such as self-neglect, self-sabotage, self-debasement, self-humiliation, masochism and self-injury (Nathanson 1992).

The primary strategy in avoidance is the deception of self and others. This is predicated on covering up shame at all costs through a range of cognitive distortions and behaviours ranging from self-deprecating charm, focusing on achievement and perfectionism. This is often accompanied by a need to numb the pain of shame through dissociation, or attempts to forget through the pursuit of pleasure to deaden the pain or fill the void of emptiness. Typically this is sought through alcohol, drugs, food, sex, consumer goods, work, exercise or the adrenaline rush in risk taking. This can lead to compulsive and addictive behaviours which paradoxically reinforce shame rather than fill the void. The emphasis is on covering up shame through deflection and displays of success and achievement, which can range from pathological lying, arrogance and grandiosity to narcissism. This differs from attack other where distance from shame is achieved by shaming and humiliating others and treating them with shame and contempt. This can be enacted through good-natured banter, teasing, put-downs or criticism which can spill over into hostility, rage, aggression or bullying and culminate in physical or sexual violence, abuse and in extreme cases murder (Nathanson 1992).

Shame-based identity

In contrast to defensive shame scripts, shame identity scripts serve to erode the self-identity, which can impact negatively on the sense of self. Kaufman (1989) proposes that this is mediated by annihilation of the self through self-blame, constant comparison to others, self-contempt, inner voices and re-enactment of shame, or by disowning or splitting the self to induce a shame-based identity which is stripped of any value, worth or esteem. Shame identity scripts typically replay early attachment experiences and reflect shame-based family dynamics which have been internalised and yet direct behaviour and exert a powerful influence on the sense of self.

The most commonly repeated shame-based dynamics include blame and self-blame, over-responsibility, preoccupation with performance and perfection, not being able to take pleasure in activities and fear of making mistakes (see Table 3.1). In addition the need to suppress and invalidate feelings and needs leads to inhibited emotional expression through coded messages that need to be unravelled by others (DeYoung 2015; Kaufman 1989). These often send mixed messages such as 'I want to be close' and 'I need to push you away', making it difficult to know which needs to respond to. Alternatively needs are sacrificed through focusing on helping others and denying one's own needs. This is often accompanied by martyr-like behaviour in which compliment or praise cannot be accepted. In this the self is denied or disowned as individuals turn against 'or invade the self' (Kaufmann 1989, p.106) to dissolve the core identity and replace it with a false self.

Reflection

Take a moment to reflect on how shame has impacted on your sense of self, your self-esteem and how you relate to others. Think about how shame has affected your beliefs about yourself and how these have impacted on your relationships with others.

The preoccupation with self-blame serves to moderate behaviours that may be disapproved of or punished by others (Fisher 2013) and also provides a semblance of control. In blaming the self it shifts responsibility onto the self rather than holding others to account for their behaviour. However, constant self-accusations prevent the reparation of mistakes as the focus is primarily on determining fault and accountability. This can lead to repeated self-denigration and self-humiliation for real or imagined faults with no room for self-compassion or empathy for the self, only relentless self-blame. To reinforce distorted beliefs about the defectiveness of the self, individuals will engage in endless internal comparisons of the self to others. Rather than acknowledging that everyone is different with varying strengths, talents and abilities, the focus is on 'I am less than' and any difference is interpreted as evidence of deficiency, which in turn fuels and reproduces shame. Such internal comparison typically represents early childhood experiences of being compared to others by parents, siblings, peers or teachers and magnifies the shame identity.

Diminished sense of self and low self-esteem

The diminished sense of self leads to low self-esteem, in which 'the essence of self-definition is immutably linked to shame' (Nathanson 1992, p.30), leading to an increasingly negative view of the self. This is supported by inner voices and self-critical language consisting of self-definitions such as stupid, ugly, foolish, weak, pathetic or needy. These commonly represent early messages from parents or others about the self which have become internalised and are perceived as belonging to the self. As the original shame experiences are pushed out of conscious awareness only the voice remains as a reflection of feelings and thoughts about the self. These negative thoughts and language, along with comparison to others, have an insidious impact on the erosion of self-esteem. As self-esteem is linked to feelings about how we compare and relate to others, our relational worth becomes enmeshed with shame (Scheff 1990). Low self-esteem is further supported by a rejection of the self through self-contempt and punishing anger for never being 'good enough'. This can lead to overly compliant and submissive, and at times masochistic, behaviour in order to be liked and accepted by others and remain connected.

Paradoxically, chronic low self-esteem and self-contempt create a barrier between self and others which turns people away. When this is combined with lack of trust, fear of dependency needs, rejection or abandonment, connecting to others becomes a source of terror. As a result the individual is condemned to a seemingly lifelong sentence of disaffection and alienation from others and feelings of loneliness, dejection and despair. In the absence of supportive relationships distorted and negative beliefs flourish as there are no reality checks or positive reinforcement from others to challenge these. As the negative thoughts take hold and the sense of powerlessness and helplessness increases, the willingness to make changes is eroded. As a result resignation and defeat set in, which amplifies shame and negative beliefs.

The diminished sense of self that underpins low self-esteem can lead some individuals to over-identify with others, especially those who they admire – such as stars of stage or screen, musical or sporting heroes or celebrities – in the hope of acquiring some of their qualities. As a result they may adopt the persona of the role model in order to replace the defective self. This is often extremely hollow, as this identified or borrowed self can never be fully owned and will always remain illusory, which can become a further source of shame.

Idealisation and over-identification with others is in part a search for perfection, which is a prominent feature in shame-based individuals and low self-esteem. Paradoxically, in the endless pursuit of perfection, individuals are only ever one step away from shame due to the polarisation of perfection and shame. The drive in perfectionism is the need to prove to self and others that they are capable and competent in all they do. This puts pressure on individuals to achieve and do well in everything, as any failure will reveal their sense of inadequacy and shame. As a result, perfectionists set impossibly high standards and expectations which are unattainable and thereby destined to fail. This catapults them back into shame, as any failure is perceived as total failure, only to repeat the cycle by setting even higher expectations. In the desperation to appear perfect, individuals are ensnared in an endless cycle of needing to perform and prove their worth rather than allow themselves to just be. Ultimately, perfectionists dehumanise themselves by never allowing themselves to make mistakes or fail in order to hide their shame and diminished sense of self.

Need for control

One way to conceal and deflect from deeply embedded shame is to control the self, others and the environment. This is most evident in distorted core beliefs about the self, and rigid rules and regulations with regard to acceptable behaviour especially in relation to others. In this there is a tendency to control interactions with others by limiting self-expression, inflexibility in thinking and ritualised patterns of behaviour. Some individuals control the expression of feelings by immersing themselves in excessive work schedules, exercise routines or frenetic activities so that there is no time to feel or reflect. Alternatively they will inhibit emotional expression by suppressing or dissociating from feelings, allowing them to project a calm exterior.

A by-product of controlling emotional expression is that it restricts the degree of self-revelation or self-disclosure and controls others in redirecting the focus of attention to see only what is carefully orchestrated. Some individuals will control this by revealing very little about themselves other than superficiality, while others will deflect and dissemble. Individuals who dissemble often appear to reveal a lot but in a highly controlled way by filtering, or editing, personal information. This is often seen in carefully crafted self-narratives in which shame masquerades as pride by emphasising only positive aspects of the self, such as achievements and success. However, this is rarely authentic pride as the self is excessively over-inflated and accompanied by arrogance, grandiosity and narcissism.

Table 3.1 Summary of the impact of shame on the self	
Diminished sense of self	Low self-esteem, negative self-concept, self-contempt
Negative thoughts	Distorted core beliefs about the self, inflexibility in thinking, rumination
Negative self-talk	Inner voices, self-criticism
Social comparison	Constant comparison to others, idealisation of others
Need for control	Rigid rules and regulations, inflexibility, ritualised patterns of behaviour, lack of spontaneity, what is revealed to others
Inhibited emotional expression	Suppression and invalidation of feelings and needs, especially dependency, vulnerability, lack of emotional expression
Perfectionism	Unrealistic standards and expectations, preoccupation with performance
Grandiosity and narcissism	Overinflated sense of self, hubristic pride, focus and preoccupation with the self
Over-responsibility	Self-blame
Unwanted identities	Roles imposed by others, perceptions of others, false self
Anger and rage	Turned against self or others, humiliated fury, violence
Lack of empathy and compassion	Shame inhibits empathy through excessive negative focus on self, lack of compassion for self or others

Grandiosity and narcissism

One way to control others is to manipulate and beguile them by directing the focus away from shameful aspects of the self onto positive attributes and displays of success and achievement. This is a central feature in grandiosity and narcissism in which the exaggerated self 'draws attention away from centrally damaged self-concept' (Nathanson 1992, p.348). By inflating self-worth, shame-based individuals replace inferiority with superiority and put themselves on a pedestal to be admired by others. However, this comes at a cost, as individuals become increasingly arrogant in their belief that they are better than others and yet are entirely dependent on them for their admiration. To ensure that they continue to captivate the admiration of others they become exhibitionistic in constantly focusing attention on themselves through ostentatious tales of their success and achievements, or through the way they dress or behave.

This is typically supported by excessive and overt displays of worth such as luxury consumer goods and status symbols such as jewellery, cars, houses or holidays to compensate for lack of inner worth. While the hope is to elicit admiration from others, this can often backfire, as they are more likely to arouse envy and jealousy. Moreover, in setting themselves apart from others through arrogance and grandiosity, they become alienated and have difficulty forming close bonds or relationships.

Anger, rage and violence

In order to protect damaged self-esteem shame can be converted into anger or rage which is either unleashed onto the self or is directed at others. Research has shown that anger and rage are emotional substitutes for shame (Gilligan 2001; Lewis 1992) in which feelings of helplessness and powerlessness are transformed into self-confidence, power and force. Anger is a survival response to threat and is activated in a number of ways in relation to shame. It may be elicited in response to the threat of abandonment or rejection, or as a reaction to being humiliated or feeling impotent (Potter-Efron 2007). Anger turned against the self typically manifests in negative thoughts and beliefs about the self and a stream of negative self-talk.

When anger is directed at others it commonly manifests as aggression, hostility or violence. This is fuelled by self-hatred, which is projected onto others as a way to deflect from our own inadequacy. In this others are objectified and dehumanised in order to unleash humiliated fury, aggression and violence and to allow individuals to 'ward off or eliminate the feeling of shame or humiliation…and replace it with its opposite, the feeling of power and pride' (Gilligan 2001, p.29). This is also an attempt to take back power and control, although this is always somewhat hollow as it is predicated on dominance and power over others, rather than power that is shared with others. Moreover, as it is not authentic, it must be consistently reinforced to retain dominance and status, which can lead to a cycle of shame and rage characteristic of abusive relationships, in particular domestic abuse (see Chapter 10). Ultimately anger, rage and violence are attempts to expunge or hide shame through hostility in which others are kept at bay and intimacy is avoided.

Unwanted identities

One advantage of avoiding close relationships is that this decreases the risk of exposure to shame and minimises others' expectations of the self and the imposition of roles or unwanted identities. Roles are expected patterns of behaviour imposed by others, usually in early childhood, which can become life scripts. These are typically shaped by the roles children are assigned within the family and which become ingrained patterns of behaviour. As these roles are absorbed with no conscious awareness of their origin they are adopted as one's own identity. Unless challenged they typically persist into adulthood and continue to direct feelings, thoughts and behaviour. The most common roles associated with shame are the good girl or boy, the naughty one, the difficult one, the crazy one, the rebel, the super-achiever, the scapegoat, the rescuer, the victim, the responsible one, the clever one, the dumb one or the clown (Potter-Efron 2007). These scripts serve to determine how individuals should be rather than who they really are, which can inhibit self-definition and access to the ideal or authentic self.

Reflection

Take a moment to consider one of the sources of shame and think about how you wish to be perceived by others and how you do not want to be perceived. Reflect on these to identify their origin, what messages and beliefs fuel these, and how these direct your behaviour.

While many of these roles are imposed by others they may also be self-imposed. Brené Brown (2007a) suggests that unwanted identities are imposed expectations of self, others and society which undermine the ideal self and are 'quintessential elicitors of shame' (Ferguson, Eyre and Ashbaker 2000). Unwanted identities consist of the traits that are associated with culturally expected ways of feeling, thinking and behaving which are often learnt in childhood and reinforced through the media and cultural norms. The emphasis is on how others perceive us and whether or not we are living up to those expectations. When we fail to do so our value and worth is undermined and shame is evoked. In order to challenge these unwanted identities counsellors will need to help clients identify these and critically evaluate them in order to restore self-definition.

Clients can benefit from challenging unwanted identities that they have either adopted or feel others perceive in them. To do this, the following exercise is helpful.

Exercise
Challenging unwanted identities
(Adapted from Brown 2009)
Invite the client to list their unwanted identities and replace these with ideal identities that they wish others to perceive.

Unwanted identities	Ideal identities
I don't want to be perceived as	I want to be perceived as
1. _____	1. _____
2. _____	2. _____
3. _____	3. _____
4. _____	4. _____
5. _____	5. _____

Empathy and compassion

One of the most damaging effects of shame is the loss of empathy and compassion for self as well as others, as the excessive negative focus on the self prevents engagement with others. As the self is seen as unacceptable, defective and worthless and deserving to be punished there is no place for empathy or self-compassion. Similarly, empathy and compassion for others is difficult to evoke as they are perceived as a source of fear, judgement and shame. This makes it hard to allow empathy or compassion to intrude despite being an antidote to shame. You need to help clients become aware of how the absence of empathy and self-compassion cultivates shame and infects and erodes the self. To truly release shame and restore authentic pride it is essential that clients are encouraged to develop empathy and self-compassion and build shame resilience (see Chapter 12). In this they will be able to reconnect to the authentic self and become who they want to become rather than be crippled by shame.

To help clients understand the impact shame has had on them and how this links to the myriad sources of shame, the next chapter will look at the sources and focus of shame and where it is most likely to manifest. Through the Circle of Shame practitioners and clients will be able to identify more specifically the arenas in which they have experienced shame and how these trigger shame in the present.

SUGGESTED READING

Freyd, J.J. and Birrell, P.J. (2013) *Blind to Betrayal: Why We Fool Ourselves We Aren't Being Fooled.* Hoboken, NJ: Wiley.

Kaufman, G. (2004) *The Psychology of Shame: Theory and Treatment of Shame Based Syndromes* 2nd edn. New York: Springer.

Lansky, M.R. and Morrison, A.P. (1997) *The Widening Scope of Shame.* Hillsdale, NJ: Analytic Press.

Lewis, H.B. (1971) *Shame and Guilt in Neurosis.* New York: International Universities Press.

Lewis, M. (1995) *Shame: The Exposed Self.* New York: The Free Press.

Mollon, P. (2002) *Shame and Jealousy: The Hidden Turmoils.* London: Karnac Books.

Nathanson, D.L. (1992) *Shame and Pride: Affect, Sex, and the Birth of the Self.* New York: W.W. Norton.

Sanderson, C. (2013) *Counselling Skills for Working with Trauma: Healing from Child Sexual Abuse, Sexual Violence and Domestic Abuse.* London: Jessica Kingsley Publishers.

4
SOURCES OF SHAME

As a self-conscious emotion shame is focused on aspects of the self that are visible to others and whether these are socially acceptable. To ensure social approval and avoid rejection emphasis is placed on conforming to social norms and fitting in. Individuals who are perceived as being different stand out from the crowd and are subject to greater scrutiny, and thus exposure to shame. The gaze of others is often initially focused on the body in terms of appearance, as well as performance. This occurs alongside scrutiny of achievement, attaining expected standards of behaviour, and status and position in society. Measures of these will include wealth, access to resources, ability to sustain stable relationships, parenting and relational worth.

To ensure social cohesion individuals are expected to engage in gender-appropriate behaviour, and to regulate their sexuality and sexual behaviour. Shame, loss of face or status and social exclusion are the costs of transgressing socially approved behaviour. Pressure is placed on individuals by dominant groups, culture, society and religion to uphold expected values and principles. When individuals deviate from these they risk being ridiculed, shamed or humiliated. While much of the pressure stems from being shamed by others, expected ways of being and behaving are internalised to become an inner source of shame. This is most commonly seen in a shame-prone sense of self due to the humiliation associated with abuse, ageing and mental health.

This chapter will explore the sources of shame in all of these dimensions and identify areas on which the spotlight of shame is most concentrated. It will look at how shame arises in these contexts and how they might be identified. With this in mind, a Circle of Shame is presented that highlights the many sources of shame. It will propose that this Circle of Shame can be used to help both you and your clients to identify their own shame and become more aware of how shame in the past impacts on the present, and how to build shame resilience.

CATEGORIES OF SHAME

According to Nathanson (1992) shame has two primary components. One is the shame induced by the gaze and assessment of others – external shame – and the other by scrutiny and assessment of the self through self-assessment – internal shame. In addition shame is not solely focused on individuals but can include group shame in which groups are judged and shamed. This can be small groups of individuals such as families, a group of professionals, institutions, faith communities and minority groups through to whole societies and cultures. Group shame is often the source of racism, sexism, prejudice, stigmatisation, religious persecution and the execution of violence ranging from rape to honour killings and genocide. Such shame in turn can incubate humiliated fury, which is then turned on others in a desire for revenge.

Research on shame has identified a number of areas in which shame is focused (Andrews 1995; Gilbert and Mills 2002) which primarily concentrate around bodily shame and interpersonal experiences of shame. Based on her research, Brené Brown (2007a) formulated the range of shame experiences into 12 distinct categories. These consist of appearance and body image; money and work; motherhood or fatherhood; family; parenting; mental and physical health; sex; ageing; religion; speaking out; surviving trauma; and being stereotyped and labelled. These identified areas of shame have been encapsulated in the Circle of Shame (see Figure 4.1) to provide an accessible tool for use with clients in facilitating a dialogue about shame and to determine areas where shame is focused in individual clients.

Figure 4.1 The Circle of Shame

THE CIRCLE OF SHAME

Figure 4.1 shows the sources of shame. The very nature of shame is that it is hidden, not only from others but also from self. The fear of exposure of shameful experiences, and the potential for further shame, makes it extremely hard for clients to talk about shame. This is often also the case in the therapeutic process where they might use analogous words such as guilt, embarrassment or self-blame. The Circle of Shame can be used to open an initial discussion of the nature of shame, which can then help the client to identify sources of shame in the past and present and to clarify areas for therapeutic exploration. Most importantly, it can determine target areas for building shame resilience.

Underpinning all of the categories in the Circle of Shame is the fear of exposure and of being laughed at, ridiculed or rejected. As shame is so crippling many people fear asking for help in case they are seen as dependent or needy, or because they feel that they do not deserve to be shame-free. They may also fear revealing the full range of their emotions, especially unacceptable ones such as self-hatred, anger, murderous rage, contempt or self-destructive feelings. In addition individuals often feel ashamed for feeling ashamed, making it hard to be authentic and congruent.

Talking about shame can trigger past experiences of shame and accompanying negative thoughts and feelings which intensify feelings of shame to unbearable levels. This can activate a cycle of shame (see the Cycle of Shame, Chapter 2) which you and your client may find it hard to manage. Thus you must be careful to avoid the escalation of shame to such overwhelming levels that the client withdraws. To this effect you must be mindful of regulating the exposure to shame in session to render it more manageable (see Chapter 12).

Top tip

You need to regulate exposure to shame in session so that this does not become unbearable for either you or your clients.

While each segment in the Circle of Shame represents a source of shame, these are by no means comprehensive in covering all shame experiences. It is a guide to the common areas of shame and is merely a tool to develop greater awareness of the focus of shame. We will now look at each source of shame in turn.

Mind

The focus of shame in the mind category is either on mental capacity or mental health. Intelligence is highly valued in most cultures, and individuals who are not as intellectually able are subject to ridicule, humiliation and shame. Thus in cultures where intelligence is valued and constantly tested, those who have learning difficulties, low IQ and reduced mental capacity are seen as 'stupid' and as 'less than'. This can be a huge source of shame especially if such individuals are marginalised and stigmatised.

A further source of shame in this category is mental health. There is considerable research that indicates a strong correlation between mental health and shame (Andrews 1995; Covert *et al.* 2003; Dorahy 2010; Herman 2011a, Leskala, Dieperink and Thuras 2002; Matos and Pinto-Gouveia 2010; Robinaugh and McNally 2010; Sanderson 2013). The role of shame seems to be most prominent in depression (Andrews 1995; Leskala *et al.* 2002; Matos and Pinto-Gouveia 2010); negative alterations in cognition and mood (Dorahy 2010); post-traumatic stress disorder (Herman 2011; Robinaugh and McNally 2010; Sanderson 2013); addictions (Potter-Efron 2001); self-harm (Motz 2001); eating disorders (Sanftner and Tantillo 2011); and personality disorders, in particular borderline personality disorder and narcissistic personality disorder (Ritzi *et. al.* 2011). Shame is also a characteristic feature of obsessive compulsive disorders, especially in what is commonly referred to as 'Pure O', in which sufferers have persistent, unwanted shame-based thoughts which they are compelled to repeat through unseen mental rituals. In addition shame contributes to a range of anxiety disorders including phobias, social anxiety disorder and chronic shyness (see Chapter 6).

As mental health disorders are often poorly understood and feared by people, they often shun those with mental health difficulties, which is a further source of shame. This is further reinforced through labelling and stigmatisation by health professionals and society. As a result people with mental health problems are reluctant to speak for fear of being shamed. Having to keep their mental health difficulties secret from others serves to amplify shame as they are unable to be authentic in expressing themselves. This can lead to chronic shame whereby the individual withdraws physically and psychologically and becomes socially isolated, increasing the risk of chronic loneliness and ultimately suicide.

Body

In contrast to the mind, the body is highly visible and, as such, a powerful source of shame. Different cultures and societies will have different attitudes towards the body, and those that do not fit a prevailing social norm may be ridiculed or stigmatised. It is not uncommon in some cultures for people with physical disabilities to be hidden away from public gaze or places of worship to avoid shame to the individual and their family. Such shame may also be experienced by individuals who do not fit into cultural norms of physical attractiveness. This can make individuals highly self-conscious about their appearance and body image.

There is typically a gender difference in terms of body shame wherein the focus for females is invariably on attractiveness, facial features, weight, body shape and size, breast or buttock size and body hair. While body shape and size are also a focus for shame in males, it is directed more on height, muscularity, physical strength and loss of hair. Both males and females will experience shame in these areas, which in extreme cases can lead to body dysmorphic disorder or muscle dysmorphia. The emphasis for individuals experiencing either disorder is to reduce feelings of shame by changing or modifying their appearance through diet, excessive exercise, steroids or cosmetic surgery.

In an increasingly digital world dominated by social media and the distribution of visual images, physical appearance is now under constant scrutiny, which has increased the potential for shame. This has led to an increase in cosmetic surgery for both men and women. While this is often focused on procedures that change facial features such as the nose, mouth, cheekbones, jaw-line or wrinkles, it also includes breast augmentation or reduction, buttock augmentation, liposuction and more defined chests for men. The desire for the perfect body that is hairless, smooth, unwrinkled and blemish and acne-free is not just confined to visible parts of the body.

Body shame has also increased in more private areas of the body that are normally hidden and not subject to public scrutiny due to the accessibility of online pornography. The body objectification inherent in pornography elicits shameful feelings about the body and appearance, and what Orbach (2009) calls 'body dis-ease'. Such shame has contributed to an increase in vaginal and clitoral cosmetic surgery (Orbach 2009). In addition, shame associated with loss of vaginal muscle tone after childbirth, or loss of virginity in unmarried women, has further contributed to the high level of vaginal cosmetic surgery. Males have also been impacted by the proliferation of pornography in feeling shame around penis size and sexual performance, leading to an increase in penis augmentation and the use of Viagra.

Social norms of beauty, attractiveness and desirability vary from culture to culture. However, with the increase in global media, these may conflate into a unified standard of what is deemed attractive and the erosion of individuality and difference. Moreover, the relentless pursuit of body perfection does not necessarily eradicate shame but merely covers it up with narcissism.

The body as a source of shame is also focused on the body in action. This includes how the body performs through movement, coordination and physical activity. This is usually associated with physical skills needed for walking, talking, eating, sporting activities, dancing and sexual performance. To achieve this necessitates a degree of control over the body. This is instilled in early childhood through gaining control over muscles to facilitate walking but also control over the bladder and bowel. A huge source of shame is lack of control over bodily functions such as the elimination of wind, urinating and defecation. Children who wet the bed, or soil themselves beyond what is deemed socially acceptable, are often the target for ridicule and humiliation by their peers and other adults. Similarly adults who suffer from poor bladder or bowel control due to medical conditions such as irritable bowel syndrome, colitis or Crohn's disease experience excruciating and paralysing shame in not having control over their bodily functions. Such shame can also be experienced with involuntary erections, erectile dysfunction, nocturnal emissions or premature ejaculation (see Chapter 6 on sex and sexuality).

Body shame is also associated with other sensory channels, in particular smell. While the body can be a powerful sexual attractant it can also repel and in that be a source of shame. Similarly the texture and the feel of the skin can attract or repel. Many people are repulsed by the texture of old, wrinkled or mottled skin and find it difficult to reach out to touch or stroke the elderly, not realising that tactile stimulation for them is as important as it is to a young baby. This can lead to tactile hunger in which the yearning for touch is never satisfied, leading to feelings of shame and rejection. Bodily sensations can also be a source of shame in which feelings of pleasure, arousal or spontaneity are seen as shameful and needing to be hidden or curbed. This is often the case with people who were sexually or physically abused in childhood and can lead to dissociating from the body to ward off any feelings or sensations.

Achievement

Authentic pride is associated with achievement, mastery and competency, while achievement failure is associated with shame. Opportunities for achievement and attainment are present throughout the life span, from early childhood when learning to communicate, to walk, to run and to read or write, through to adolescence to gain vocational or academic success to improve access to employment, and into adulthood in acquiring interpersonal skills to form stable and fulfilling relationships. This process is characterised by innumerable challenges which need to be faced and conquered to gain mastery. When some of the expected achievements are suffused with failure then shame ensues.

Sources of shame due to achievement failure include illiteracy, innumeracy and poor educational attainment, which in turn reduce employability. Adults who have not learned how to read and write feel acute shame over their deficiency and go to great lengths to avoid situations in which they might be exposed (Kaufman 1992). The accompanying shame can be crippling, necessitating a desperate need to cover up.

Low literacy and innumeracy rates are typically seen in prison populations, with 48 per cent of offenders in the UK with literacy skills at or below the age of 11, and 65 per cent with a numeracy rate at or below age 11 (CIVITAS 2010). In addition one in three offenders has a reading age below 11 while 75 per cent have writing skills below age 11 (CIVITAS 2010). Furthermore, 49 per cent of prisoners were excluded from school, and 52 per cent of male and 71 per cent of female offenders have no qualifications at all (CIVITAS 2010). Not surprisingly, 62 per cent of offenders were unemployed at the time of imprisonment (CIVITAS 2010). According to Gilligan (2001) the shame associated with not being able to read or write underpins the defensive reactions seen in violent and aggressive prisoners.

Shame associated with achievement can include the acquisition of a wide variety of skills in a range of activities, be they ball skills, sporting skills, the skills needed to drive, speak a new language and use technology, or those aquired when becoming a parent. The degree of shame will depend on what is expected of self and others. The greater the expectation to achieve or master a skill, the more likely shame will ensue when there is failure.

Status

A powerful function of shame is the regulation of social rank and social status which is necessary in hierarchically structured groups or societies. As social animals humans depend on the acceptance of others, and fear rejection. To be accepted by a group will depend on a variety of factors such as dominance and submission, attractiveness, access to resources, desirability or being valued by the group (Gilbert and McGuire 1998). Thus social acceptance has become entwined with cues that signal social status. While the signs of social status and what is valued and socially accepted will vary from culture to culture there are some – such as beauty, wealth, access to resources or valued skills and power – which appear to be universal.

These ancestral patterns of social behaviour that regulate social status and the signals of acceptance have evolved over time to include displays of wealth through money, high-status employment, luxury consumer-goods, property, jewellery and travel. Social status can also be conveyed through dress, adornment, accent, the area in which the individual lives, what school or university they attended, career and the degree of control they have over their lives. Those individuals who have access to, or are in possession of, these will be more likely to be accepted and accorded a higher status than those who are poor, lack resources or are deemed unattractive. Furthermore, those who are accorded a lower status are more likely to be rejected and shamed for being inadequate or 'less than'.

Gender

In order to be accepted by the dominant social group it is necessary to conform to social norms with regard to gender. All cultures differentiate between the two genders, although they vary in terms of what is expected of them in those gender roles. Invariably there are strict rules with regard to how males and females are expected to behave, dress or express themselves. Transgressions of socially approved stereotypes of male and female gender roles are often punished through ridicule, humiliation and shame. Thus individuals who do not conform to culturally prescribed gender roles or who do not display typical masculine or feminine traits, or who are androgynous or transgendered, will face exclusion and rejection and an increase in shame and humiliation.

Sex and sexuality

Due to the range of cultural and religious sanctions around sexual behaviour, sex and sexuality are extremely common sources of shame. This is often reinforced by cultural norms of what is seen as acceptable. These direct appropriate sexual behaviours and underpin sexual scripts (Gagnon and Simon 1973) with regard to *whom* we can have sex with (age, class, religion, gender, ethnicity), *what* is considered sexual (feelings, thoughts, behaviour), what we *do* sexually (acts, behaviour), *when* to have sex (age, frequency, how many times, what time of day/night), *where* we can have sex (location, indoors, outdoors, private, public) and *why* we have sex (reasons, procreation, fun, pleasure, justifications). Any deviations from these are seen as a violation of sexual norms and can become a source of shame.

Common anxieties around sexual norms cluster around masturbation, involuntary erections, nocturnal emission, nudity, sexual modesty, sexual orientation, virginity, frequency of having sex, pregnancy (as an overt signal of having been sexual), abortions, sexual promiscuity, sexually transmitted infections (STIs), prostitution, celibacy, lack of sexual conquests, male circumcision, female circumcision and genital mutilation (FGM), premature sexualisation, child sexual abuse, rape, sexual preferences, variant sexual behaviour and paraphilias (see Chapter 6 for a fuller discussion).

More internal sources of sexual shame focus on performance anxieties such as erectile dysfunction, premature ejaculation, anorgasmia, vaginismus, degree of sexual arousal and expression of pleasure. A lot of sexual shame is also focused on penis or breast size, erection size, degree of lubrication, how much or little partners have enjoyed sex and overt expressions of this (making too little or too much noise) and whether they have been able to bring their partner to orgasm. Shame around sexual performance and the fear of being ridiculed can promote extreme stereotypical male and female behaviours such as male sexual machismo, female modesty or sexual temptress. Sadly, the focus on performance all too often reduces intimacy, mutuality and sexual connection, which can be a further source of shame as partners feel objectified when body parts are fetishised.

The degree of sexual shame experienced will depend on gender, with females conditioned to be modest and discreet, and not being allowed to admit to sexual pleasure or arousal, while males often feel shame about their sexual prowess in terms of performance and number of sexual conquests. As sex and sexuality is such a powerful source of shame, many clients will find it difficult to talk about sexual intimacy. Equally, practitioners may also experience sexual shame, which may add to any difficulties in developing an open and shame-free dialogue (see Chapter 6).

Sense of self

Repeated experiences of being shamed can become internalised and affect the sense of worth. Nathanson (1992) argues that 'shame guards the boundaries of the self' and yet it can also infect the sense of self and pollute it with external conditions of worth. In the presence of invalidation, abuse, humiliation and pervasive or chronic shame experiences, individuals become dehumanised, which corrodes any sense of self-worth and replaces it with self-loathing, self-hatred, self-criticism and an inauthentic self. The sense of self is further eroded through feelings and thoughts that are perceived to be unacceptable. Thus feelings of vulnerability, dependency, anxiety, anger, rage, contempt, excitement or envy must be covered up or split off to ward off unbearable feelings of shame. This can result in a range of defensive strategies such as withdrawal, perfectionism and narcissism and self-destructive behaviours such as self-harm, addictions, humiliated fury, rage and violence against others.

To avoid experiencing shame associated with perceived weakness and inadequacy individuals will attempt to become invisible, both physically and emotionally. In this they become voiceless in not being able to talk about their shame or their defective sense of self, which further isolates them to the point of chronic loneliness. In working with such clients, you need to provide a safe environment in which deeply embedded shame can be explored and in which conditions of worth are transformed, secrets are revealed and vulnerability is validated as courage. In this clients are given a voice and autonomy and self-efficacy is restored.

Values

Values, beliefs and attitudes are highly correlated with sense of self and self-identity. When these differ from social norms individuals may be humiliated by others and excluded from the group. In extreme cases, if these different beliefs are perceived to be threatening to the dominant culture, they will be punished, imprisoned or destroyed. This is particularly pertinent with regard to religion, which all too often has been associated with inhumane treatment and mass genocide. Similarly people who hold different political views, ethical principles or attitudes to human rights may be persecuted, excluded, marginalised or rendered voiceless to protect the norm. Humiliation and shame are powerful weapons to regulate such differences and ensure that the status quo is not undermined. They are also ways to maintain culturally sanctioned morality which is essential to social cohesion.

Relationships

The origin of shame is usually located in early childhood when infants begin to develop self-consciousness and become more mobile and separate from the caregivers. In families where the child's striving for autonomy and separateness is valued the child will experience authentic pride which is shared by the caregiver. However, all too often children are shamed in their endeavour to be separate or autonomous. These shaming experiences will contribute to an internal working model (Bowlby 1969) of relational worth and how to navigate relationships. These relational templates often persist into adulthood and direct personal relationships, especially with regard to responsiveness, mutuality, intimacy, dependency, acknowledgement of needs, and mutual respect – all of which contribute to a caring and loving environment in which individuals can thrive and grow (see Chapter 6).

When relationships are fraught with abuse, fear of abandonment and rejection, humiliation, ridicule and shame, children and adults seek protection from unbearable inner states by withdrawing, submitting or disconnecting from others. This reduces opportunities for love, care, affection or intimacy. The absence of stable, healthy relationships is a further source of shame in cultures that value and promote intimate partnerships. As social animals we need to feel connected to others and that we belong, and when this is compromised shame will ensue. This is why friendships with peers are important to children and adolescents, as they are a measure of not just popularity but social status in which a lack of friends implies social exclusion and rejection. In contrast popularity suggests social desirability and social status. This is aptly demonstrated in social media such as Facebook and Twitter which is predicated on how many friends or followers one has. Children who are brought up in care often feel rejected by their parents and find it hard to trust others.

This makes it hard to form social or romantic bonds, which further intensifies the sense of shame.

Individuals who have difficult or abusive relationships or who are single may also be shamed for not being able to find or keep a partner. There is still considerable stigmatisation of victims of domestic abuse who are often made to feel that they contribute to their abuse or are masochistic for enduring it. Shame may also arise when individuals perceive themselves or are judged to be too dependent or needy, or when relationships fail or end in separation or divorce.

A further source of shame in relationships and families is reproductive success and parenting. Shame may arise when children are born out of wedlock, as a result of rape or sexual abuse, or when unwanted pregnancies are carried to term. This is often accompanied by fears of capacity to parent effectively. Couples who are not able to have children often feel shame at not being able to procreate. Both males and females may feel shame for their infertility or inability to conceive and as a result feel 'less than'.

Fears around parenting can also be a source of shame. The family acts as a microcosm in which children are socialised to be accepted in the macrocosm of society and culture. How children are parented is often the focus of scrutiny and judgement by the dominant culture to ensure that they adhere to social norms not just in childhood but also in adulthood. As a result parenting can become a source of shame if they are found to be lacking in providing moral guidance through discipline and control, or are not able to provide for their family. This includes such factors as clean and tidy living conditions, adequate personal hygiene, health and social care, as well as diet, nutrition and exercise. When any of these are lacking parents may be judged and shamed and labelled as bad parents.

Research has shown that early experiences of parenting can influence the capacity to parent one's own children (Gerhardt 2004). Some but by no means all children who were abused, humiliated or shamed in childhood may initially lack the necessary parenting skills to instil a sense of authentic pride in their children. This can lead to the intergenerational transmission of abuse or shame. In addition, families that have experienced shame over generations may become shame-prone and are compelled to carry the burden of shame into future generations. Common examples of intergenerational shame include poverty, criminality, violence, domestic abuse, incest, illegitimacy, being in care, single parenthood and sexual orientation (see Chapter 2). Clients who carry the burden of intergenerational shame can benefit from exploring this through genograms so that they can become more aware of carried shame and how to relinquish it (see Chapter 10).

Abuse

Abuse, whether physical abuse, emotional abuse, sexual abuse or neglect, is a pernicious source of shame. In order to commit abuse, victims are objectified, dehumanised and stripped of any dignity, value or worth. Such brutalisation and degradation, alongside demands for submission and compliance, increases feelings of humiliation and shame. This is compounded by the shame felt for not being able to stop the abuse, passive compliance and lack of self-agency. As a result, many victims blame themselves for their abuse in order to feel some sense of control. However, blaming themselves only serves to amplify feelings of shame and humiliation. This is further increased when victims are compelled to absorb the split-off shame of the abuser. The absorption of abuser shame and self-blame is typically seen in all forms of interpersonal abuse such as child physical or sexual abuse, domestic abuse, rape, sexual exploitation and sexual trafficking, as well as abuse in residential settings such as children's homes, care homes for the elderly and prisons (Sanderson 2010). When such abuse is enacted by professionals such as doctors or therapists, victims may feel too humiliated to seek help and thereby reduce opportunities to recover from their shame (see Chapter 10).

Shame is also seen in people who have been traumatised or who suffer from post-traumatic stress disorder (Herman 2011b). Autonomic survival mechanisms undermine a sense of control and self-agency, which can be a source of shame. Thus people who have been traumatised may blame themselves for not fighting back or freezing, not realising that these neurobiological survival strategies are outside of voluntary control. In addition, submission, compliance and secrecy not only ensure survival but also protect from further shame by reducing exposure to others. This is what makes it hard for clients to talk about their traumatic experiences as they fear a return of the shame that is inextricably linked to their abuse.

Culture

Society and culture serve to regulate social norms and acceptable forms of behaviour through shame and social exclusion to ensure conformity and social cohesion. This is achieved through a range of social systems that reward and accord status to those who conform and excludes or rejects those who do not. In hierarchical social structures this is achieved through systems that divide people into different social strata by means of class or caste, dominant religion or ethnicity. To support these honour systems ensure that people behave in ways that do not besmirch the honour of the community or through losing face.

While the focus of shame is primarily on individuals it can also be applied to groups, communities and whole nations. This is seen in the marginalisation and shaming of minority groups on the basis of their ethnicity, race or religion. Religious persecution, ethnic cleansing and genocide are potent ways to wield power over others and thereby shame and humiliate them. Such atrocities have led to national shame, most notably in Germany, Rwanda, Bosnia and South Africa. Shame has also become associated with communities such as the Orkney Islands for alleged ritual and satanic abuse, and institutions such as the Catholic Church in their handling of the sexual abuse of children by priests. It can also become attached to professional groups like bankers who are perceived to be the architects of the global economic downturn.

Ageing

Different cultures and societies will have different attitudes towards ageing, with some cultures valuing the ageing process while others emphasise youth. Those cultures that do not value the ageing process will render their ageing population invisible by hiding them away in residential settings, reducing their status and infantalising them. This can be a source of shame as the aged feel socially excluded and marginalised. Many elderly people feel that they no longer have a valued role in society and end up feeling worthless. This is exacerbated when they are ridiculed for not being as mobile or as quick witted as they once were, ignored, or not worth engaging in conversation. The lack of human contact and stimulation often leads to chronic loneliness. This is compounded when there is little or no affection or physical comfort or reassurance in an increasingly bewildering world.

Shame in the ageing process is also felt internally as mental and physical capacities such as strength, energy, vigour, sexual potency and mental prowess become compromised. This in turn may increase dependence on others, which can be a further source of shame. The deterioration in one's faculties such as vision, hearing, cognition and memory, as well as physical agility, can also contribute to feelings of inadequacy as memory is lost and the capacity to recognise loved ones is reduced. As the aged become increasingly isolated they become more vulnerable to mental health problems such as chronic depression and suicidal ideation. These are often not responded to, leading to further shame.

IDENTIFYING SOURCES OF SHAME

As can be seen from the Circle of Shame there are myriad sources of shame. Clients will experience some but not all of these and present with varying degrees of shame. You need to help clients to identify their particular sources of shame and explore how these have impacted on them and how they continue to affect them. To facilitate this you can use the following exercise with clients.

Exercise
Identifying sources of shame
Copy the Circle of Shame (see Figure 4.2) and ask the client to fill in the blank areas in which they have or still experience shame. Remember this is merely a guide and not all the segments will apply. Tell your client that this is a working document and they may add or subtract as they work through their shame, completing it over time as shame is explored in greater depth. The exercise can be helpful to both you and your client.

Top tip
To avoid the client being overwhelmed and activating a cycle of shame it is important to work through this at a manageable pace.

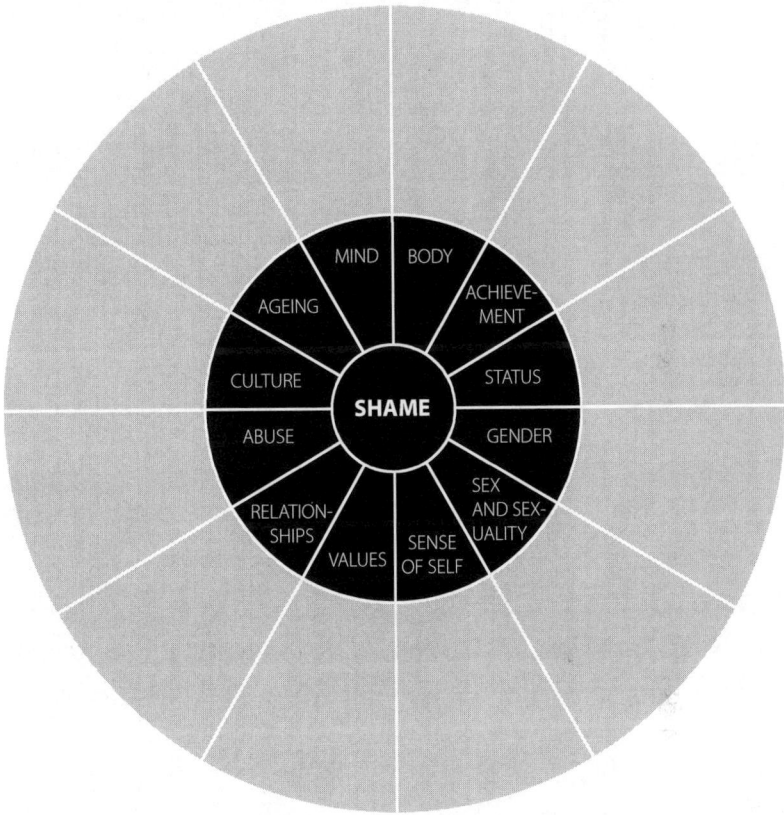

Figure 4.2 Circle of Shame

★

SHAME THROUGHOUT THE LIFE SPAN

Having identified the sources of shame it is useful to track how these have evolved over the life span. Early childhood experiences of shame may have dissipated as the client has acquired and mastered more skills, while others who have not achieved their full potential may still be limited by early experiences of shame. Knowing how shame can dissipate and transform into authentic pride will provide concrete evidence to the client that it is possible to heal and recover from shame. For those who are still imprisoned in their shame, the following exercise can identify areas that need to be worked through in order to redistribute and reapportion shame and build shame resilience.

Exercise
Shame throughout the life span

1. Encourage the client to look at their personalised Circle of Shame and reflect on how shame manifested at different periods in their life.

2. Provide a sheet of paper divided into three columns headed 'Childhood', 'Adolescence' and 'Adulthood' and ask your client to fill these in.

3. Encourage them to reflect on these and highlight which have dissipated and which have persisted.

4. Together make a list of those that have been resistant to change and encourage your client to make a commitment to work through these.

Having identified the sources and focus of shame and how these have manifested throughout the life span, the next chapter will look at the dynamics of shame and how these impact on clients to facilitate a deeper understanding and awareness of their responses to and defences against shame.

SUGGESTED READING

Brown, B. (2007) *I Thought It Was Just Me: Women Reclaiming Power and Courage in a Culture of Shame.* New York: Penguin Group.

Dearing, R.L. and Tangney, J.P. (eds) (2011) *Shame in the Therapy Hour.* Washington, DC: American Psychological Association.

Herman, J.L. (2007) 'Shattered shame states and their repair.' From the John Bowlby Memorial Lecture 10 March, Department of Psychiatry, Harvard University School.

Nathanson, D.L. (1992) *Shame and Pride: Affect, Sex, and the Birth of the Self.* New York: W.W. Norton.

Sanderson, C. (2013) *Counselling Skills for Working with Trauma: Healing from Child Sexual Abuse, Sexual Violence and Domestic Abuse.* London: Jessica Kingsley Publishers.

5

DEFENCES AGAINST SHAME

The unbearable nature of shame elicits a range of defences. These are often initially adaptive survival strategies to enable the child to manage the more toxic components of shame. This chapter will look at shame reactions as a survival strategy that elicits a range of protective mechanisms. It will explore a number of shame screens or 'masks' that are used to cover up shame, and how these lead to the development of shame defences or shame scripts. These may include: withdrawal, attacking the self, avoidance or attacking others (Nathanson 1992). It will look at the function and purposes of these defences and how they commonly manifest in everyday encounters and the therapeutic process. Equipped with a deeper awareness of these, you will be able to understand clients better and remain connected to them.

The fear of exposure that underpins shame means that it has to be hidden, not just from others but also from the self. This means that shame, and some of the defences to manage shame, are often sealed off or disowned and remain largely unconscious. In this process feelings of shame in the present are decoupled from shame experiences in the past. Uncovering these hidden faces of shame is an essential part of the therapeutic process in which clients can become more aware of how they react in the presence of shame. Such awareness will enable them to develop more adaptive responses and become more resilient to shame experiences. As uncovering shame can intensify shame experiences, you must manage this process sensitively so as not to re-shame the client (see Chapter 12).

Remember

The detoxification of toxic shame is a painful process and needs to be managed sensitively to avoid re-shaming the client.

You need to be aware that individuals adopt a range of different strategies to manage shame, and that these will have a different impact on the self and others. Some individuals will consistently devalue themselves and idealise others, while others will develop a grandiose sense of self and devalue others. In addition, defensive strategies are not always fixed, with some individuals fluctuating between defensive scripts. This is commonly seen in borderline personality disorder and abusive relationships where individuals swing between devaluing themselves to the point of submission, and being narcissistic bullies (Broucek 1991). Defences may also vary in different contexts where at times it might be expedient to blame others to gain a sense of power, while at other times it may be advantageous to attack the self in order to remain connected to others.

It helps to be mindful that some shame defences such as mild withdrawal and mild avoidance of shame are healthy and normal and should not be pathologised. Conversely, chronically shame-prone clients who consistently disown their shame through withdrawal, attack self, avoidance or attack other may benefit from becoming more aware of how shame has shaped their behaviour and interaction with others. Such shame awareness will enable them to tolerate their shame rather than resorting to futile defensive strategies that often reinforce or stamp in shame.

SHAME AS A SURVIVAL STRATEGY

The experience of unbearable shame is often perceived as a threat or a signal of danger which can trigger the body's alarm system, leading to withdrawal (flight), attack others (fight) or avoidance (freeze) responses (see Table 5.1). These strategies are often mediated outside of conscious awareness and direct behaviour which is not always under voluntary control, therefore becoming a further source of shame.

Table 5.1 Shame and alarm reactions		
Alarm reactions	**Shame reactions**	**Behaviour**
Flight	Withdrawal	Hide, cover up
Fight	Attack other	Rage, humiliated fury, reactive violence
Freeze	Avoidance	Denial, dissociation

PROTECTIVE STRATEGIES TO MANAGE SHAME

According to Wurmser (1995), shame is a 'layered emotion' which co-exists alongside a number of other powerful emotions such as humiliation, fear, threat or rage. This can make it difficult to decipher the origins of shame and the range of concomitant emotions. As some of these emotions can be so overwhelming they activate a number of behaviours that propel the individual into adopting protective strategies to avoid the experience of shame. In healthy shame which is usually fleeting, most individuals are able to recognise and accept the experiences of shame and see it as a signal that something is wrong, prompting change in behaviour. However, when shame is chronic or toxic, individuals are more likely to defend against it through habitual patterns of behaviour, strategies, excuses or justifications. These reactions are often so instantaneous that they by-pass the feeling of shame and occur outside of conscious awareness, so the link with shame is lost.

SHAME SCREENS

The very nature of shame demands that it is hidden, which results in the development of a number of smokescreens to cover up shame, which Nathanson (1992) calls 'shame screens'. These strategies are ways of disconnecting from the experience of shame and can either amplify the intensity of shame, or minimise it through dissociation or shame vigilance. Shame screens commonly cluster around core defensive strategies such as moving away, moving towards or moving against others (see Table 5.2) (Hartling *et. al.* 2000; Horney 1945; Nathanson 1992).

Table 5.2 Protective strategies to manage shame	
Protective Strategy	**Behaviour**
Moving away	Withdrawal, hiding, silencing self, keeping secrets, isolation, borrowed pride
Moving towards	Compliant, seek to appease and please, looking for approval, submissive to stay connected
Moving against	Rage, violence, hostility, anger, envy, harm others in order to gain power over others through aggression, shame to fight shame (counter-shame)
Compensation	Compensate through perfectionism, grandiosity, arrogance, narcissism, self-sufficiency, repudiation of needs

In moving away individuals withdraw physically, psychologically or emotionally from others. The focus is on becoming invisible, silent, secretive and isolated. In moving towards, individuals try to appease others, become compliant and submissive and seek constant approval in their attempt to please others. This strategy is driven by the primitive need to preserve attachments and affiliations which render individuals vulnerable to becoming entrapped in unhealthy relationships wherein the need to stay connected outweighs being humiliated or abused. In contrast, in moving against others, individuals become aggressive and try to overpower others to make themselves feel more powerful and to escape their sense of shame. This often comes at a cost as their hostility pushes people away and creates a barrier to closeness and intimacy.

Another effective way to cover up shame is to adopt a range of compensatory strategies such as perfectionism, arrogance or grandiosity. In combination, these defences are designed to protect the individual from further experiences of shame, and keep them out of contact with self and others. These strategies consist of primitive responses which are learned in early childhood and form habitual patterns of behaviour that become embedded and activated in any future experiences of shame. As these are often triggered autonomically, the link to early experiences of shame is severed and not available to conscious awareness. Thus a crucial component of healing and recovery from shame is to become aware of how we react in the presence of shame so that more positive responses can be adopted.

Reflection

To identify your reactions to shame reflect on your experiences of shame and how you react in the presence of shame. Do you tend to move away from feeling shame and hide, or do you move towards others who shame you to remain connected to them? Do you move against those who elicit shame by attacking or shaming them? What other compensatory strategies do you use and are these people or situation specific? Which of these might arise in therapeutic encounters?

You can also get clients to identify the protective strategies that they use in the presence of shame by encouraging them to complete the statements in the following exercise. This will help them to understand which strategies they use with different people, and in different circumstances, including the therapeutic process.

Exercise

Identifying protective shame strategies

I use the strategy 'moving away' when _____
_____

I am most likely to 'move away' with _____
_____

I use the strategy 'moving toward' when _____
_____

I am most likely to use 'moving toward' with _____
_____

I use the strategy of 'moving against' when _____
_____

I use the strategy 'moving against' with _____
_____

SHAME SCRIPTS

The healthy, adaptive way to deal with shame that has occurred as a result of a mistake or transgression is to admit the error or offence and discharge the shame by making amends for harm caused. However, in some cases the experience of shame is so overwhelmingly toxic that individuals have to defend against the corrosive effects of shame. In order to minimise the swathe of negative feelings unleashed by shame individuals tend to avoid experiencing it so that 'almost any affect feels better than shame' (Nathanson 1992 p.312). This allows them to disown the experience of shame, detoxify it and defend against any future experiences of shame. Defences against shame are typically learnt in early childhood as creative solutions against unbearable feeling states. Over time these develop into a storehouse of habitual patterns of thinking, acting and behaving whenever in the presence of shame. With repeated exposure to shame these coalesce into defensive scripts which become activated whenever shame threatens.

Nathanson (1992) proposes that there are four core defensive scripts against shame: withdrawal, attack self, avoidance and attack other (see Table 5.3). These represent patterns of physiological, emotional and cognitive responses which when triggered direct behaviour. These defensive scripts are not seen as separate entities but as habitual patterns of responses which can be used at different times in response to different shaming experiences and whoever bears witness to the shame. For example, someone who has been exposed for having an affair may acknowledge their shame in public by hanging their head in disgrace (withdrawal), may use self-deprecating humour among friends (attack self), plead to their partner that they were falsely accused (avoidance through denial), or blame their transgression on the person they had the affair with (attack other). While all four strategies can be used in different situations, there is a tendency to prefer one over others and this often becomes the default setting (Nathanson 1992).

Table 5.3 Summary of strategies to manage shame

Shame strategy	Internal	Behaviour	In therapy
Withdrawal	• Awareness of shame • Shame prone • Isolated • Chronic loneliness	• Hide, blush, lowered gaze, submissive stance • Retreat to private space for shame to run its course • Isolation	• Depressed • Dissociated • Emotionally disengaged to avoid re-shaming • Unreachable
Attack self	• Acceptance of shame • Shame prone • Controlling amount of shame by inflicting self-shame to control external shame • Fear of abandonment and rejection • 'I don't deserve better'	• Deference so as to remain affiliated • Clowning • Self-deprecating humour • Modesty • Self-neglect • Masochism • Self-sabotage • Self-mortification • Shyness	• Self-sabotage • Refusing help or medication • Doomed to failure • Humour to deflect • Submissive • Masochistic • Self-harming behaviour

			• Suicidal ideation • Abusive relationships • Appease and please • Looking for approval • Compliant
Avoidance	• Intolerant of shame • Disowned shame • Covered up by inflated self-esteem • Grandiosity and narcissism • Inner emptiness • Imposter syndrome	• Distract attention away from perceived defect • Cover up defects through striving for perfection • Arrogance • Grandiosity • Narcissism	• Narcissistic • Grandiose • Perfectionist • Hubristic pride • Denial of shame or problem to hide behind the mask of 'everything is perfect'
Attack other	• Disowned and by-passed shame • Anger/rage/humiliated fury which needs to be expunged by projecting it into others	• Shaming others through contempt and humiliation, verbal and physical threats or assaults • Devaluing and objectifying others • Sexual violence • Murder • Cost is rejection by others	• Externalise shame by shaming the practitioner • Devaluing them and the therapeutic process through personal attacks, physical threats, sabotage and deskilling the practitioner • Highly resistant and non-compliant rejection of empathy and compassion

THE COMPASS OF SHAME

In order to understand the range of shame scripts Nathanson (1992) categorised the four defensive patterns into what he calls the 'Compass of Shame'. This provides a framework in which to identify the range of shame reactions and make their manifestation in everyday life more visible. Given that few people are unable or reluctant to acknowledge or talk about their shame, the Compass of Shame becomes a handy tool to navigate the broad range of defences against shame. In addition, highlighting and recognising shame scripts enables you to identify these in the therapeutic process. As can be seen in Figure 5.1, Nathanson places withdrawal at the North point of the compass with avoidance at the South point, while at the Eastern point lies attack self and on the Western point lies attack other.

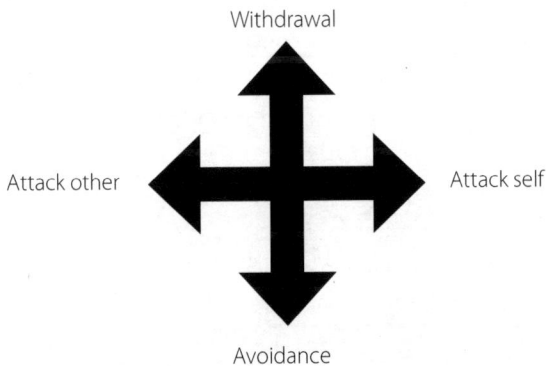

Withdrawal

Attack other

Attack self

Avoidance

Figure 5.1 The Compass of Shame
(Adapted from Nathanson 1992, p.312)

When identifying shame scripts it is helpful to view these on a continuum from mild, momentary or fleeting reactions through to very extreme, persistent behaviours. You need to be aware that the duration and intensity of defensive reactions will vary from individual to individual and cause varying amounts of distress. For example, in withdrawal the defence is to withdraw to safety by removing the person from the glare of others and avoid scrutiny and judgement. This breach in contact can range from a momentary break in eye contact to prolonged isolation and chronic depression. In attack self the spectrum can range from relatively healthy responses such as humility and self-deprecating humour, through to chronic self-destructive behaviours such as ritual humiliation, self-harm and suicidal behaviour. These strategies allow individuals to have a semblance of control over shame through self-condemnation and humour and still remain connected to others.

While withdrawal and attack self strategies are often conscious and relatively healthy ways of managing shame, avoidance and attack other are associated with unconscious, denied or split-off shame experiences. In avoidance the person draws attention away from shame and redirects the focus on to some aspect of self that is not defective in order to restore status. Commonly this redirection is related to things that are a source of hubristic pride such as enhanced body image, possessions or competence, all of which display a more positive image of self. Alternatively, individuals may turn to alcohol, drugs and addictions to numb the pain, or compulsively seek excitement through thrill-seeking and risk-taking behaviours in order to avoid a sense of inner emptiness. In attack other the pain of shame is lessened by making someone else the target of shame, enhancing one's own status and thereby eliciting a sense of superiority. This can range from harmless banter and good-natured teasing through to malicious hurtful insults, physical aggression, sexual assault or even murder.

WITHDRAWAL

In shame-induced withdrawal individuals willingly take on the experience of shame and display reactions that are typically associated with shame, for example, looking down, slumped shoulders and blushing. This is mediated by the release of a cascade of bio-chemicals that flood the body and result in an increase in body temperature and loss of muscle tone in the neck and shoulders. These physiological responses provide escape from the intolerable experience of shame, allowing the person to break their connection with others and become invisible. Paradoxically these reactions to shame, especially blushing, make the person even more conspicuous in their shame, which intensifies the need to hide.

Continuum of withdrawal

Withdrawal strategies are best seen on a continuum (see Figure 5.2). In their desire for invisibility the individual loses all connection to others and mutuality and ends up becoming imprisoned in their shame. This can lead to paralysing depression, agoraphobia and chronic loneliness.

Mild	Extreme
Gaze aversion	Emotionally unavailable
Lowered head	Isolation
Slumped shoulders	Depression
Chronic loneliness	Negative thoughts
Blushing	Internal Retreat
Silence	Chronic loneliness
Biting of lower lip	
Hand to lips	
Stuttering	

Figure 5.2 Continuum of withdrawal

By withdrawing physically, emotionally and cognitively individuals avoid all interpersonal interactions in which shame might be evoked such as social situations, conversation, eating in public, or new experiences in which they are unsure how to be. Through internal withdrawing individuals retreat deeper inside until the real self becomes sealed away with only a superficial, false self left visible to the world. Over time individuals become more and more isolated, leading to chronic loneliness which further reinforces shame. People who use withdrawal as a defence strategy are often highly shame-vigilant and anticipate negative, shaming reactions from others. In addition, they are hyper-sensitive to rejection and any perceived shameful actions, faults, failures or character flaws.

Withdrawal in therapy

Clients who use withdrawal to defend against shame are often most willing to engage in the therapeutic process as they already have quite a high awareness of shame. The focus of the work is to provide a safe and secure relational base in which shame can be uncovered. This requires an empathic and compassionate stance in which you remain sensitive to the safety strategy of withdrawal that has rendered the client invisible. Through unconditional positive regard you need to build an interpersonal bridge in which clients can become visible and be released from the prison of shame. This can be challenging as clients are highly shame vigilant and will constantly scrutinise you for any signs of rejection or re-shaming. You need to adopt a counter shaming stance in which they stay connected and enable the client to reconnect to self, others and the world (see Chapter 12 for skills to facilitate this).

Remember

Withdrawal is a retreat from the shaming gaze of others which can lead to disconnection from others, isolation, chronic loneliness and depression.

ATTACK SELF

Attack self in its mildest form can be both a useful and healthy response to shame, especially when the response is brief or fleeting. Accepting some shame, not too little and not too much, is healthy and is usually viewed by others positively and, in the case of humour, with affection. To this effect it fosters connection and affiliation. On the mild end of the attack self continuum (see Figure 5.3) appropriate responses to shame such as modesty, humility or deference are respected and valued. This is especially the case when humour or laughter is used to dissipate shame, especially when it is directed at the self as in self-deprecating humour. Nathanson argues that 'shame can power all forms of humour' (Nathanson 1992, p.19) as it deflects shame while retaining a sense of efficacy and power over self and others. Humour and laughter tend to connect people and so, in laughing at the self, close bonds can be maintained and attachment is assured. However, when humour is used to humiliate others, it can increase the toxicity of shame.

A positive aspect of attack self is that it engenders deference and conformity, which allow for acceptance by others. In addition, in order to tolerate attack self strategies, individuals must have a certain degree of self-esteem which inoculates against shame. The ability to tolerate shaming put-downs is most commonly seen in teenagers who trade compliments and put-downs in good-natured banter (Nathanson 1992). However, it is critical to have a balance between healthy deference and good-natured banter and erosive self-debasement and submission in order to retain a degree of self-esteem.

Mild   **Extreme**

Modesty	Self-effacement	Self-debasement
Shyness	Self-humiliation	Masochism
Deference	Self-neglect	Self-injury
Humour	Self-sabotage	Suicidal behaviour

Figure 5.3 Continuum of attack self

While controlled displays of shame can evoke respect from and affinity with others, if it is overused as in self-abnegation, docility, obsequiousness, subservience or masochism it can provoke disgust and loss of respect. The positive aspects of attack self strategies can be undermined when these become habitual and destructive through ritual self-mutilation, self-debasement and masochistic tendencies. In this context masochism needs to be understood as an initially adaptive solution to remaining attached to shaming or persecutory figures, such as parents in early childhood. To young children the fear of abandonment and the threat of annihilation is so terrifying that they need to remain attached at all costs, even in the presence of excruciating humiliation and shame. If the intensity of attachment hunger is not assuaged and persists into adulthood it can ensnare individuals into abusive relationships (Montgomery and Greif 1989) in which they endure shame and humiliation in order to obtain love and respect (Wurmser 1995, p.xviii).

Central to the attack self script is the acceptance of shame and willingness to let it enter into conscious awareness, which has a number of positive components such as motivation to change, to fit in and conform to expected social norms. It also allows individuals to exchange the overwhelming experience of external shame for more manageable portions of internal shame through constant self-aggression, self-ridicule and self-disgust. Furthermore, self-controlled amounts of shame allow individuals to pre-empt shaming experiences and direct them against the self, thereby depriving others from shaming them. In this process external attacks of shame become less corrosive than the inner attacks on the self. In addition taking control over self-harming behaviours such as self-injury and self-mutilation is a way of regulating unbearable inner states associated with shame.

In extreme self-attacking behaviours, anger, contempt, disgust and self-hatred are turned inward against the self. This leads to negative beliefs about self which are used to belittle the self through self-criticism and self-punishment for perceived failures, faults or negative characteristics. Invariably these will consist of internalised messages from significant others in childhood which are replayed outside of conscious awareness of their origins (see Chapter 4). Left unchecked these can develop into compulsive behaviours such as replaying shame-based messages in obsessive thoughts as seen in Pure O, self-harming behaviours to numb feelings of shame, through to self-injury and ultimately suicide.

Such self-destructive behaviours are driven by self-mortification in which the individual attempts to deaden, or murder, the offending, inadequate self and thereby annihilate shame.

Attempts to subdue, control and perfect the self through self-denial and self-control can also lead to severe self-neglect (Kinston 1987; Morrison 1987). In self-neglect individuals ignore their own needs such as setting healthy boundaries, neglecting appetitive behaviours such as eating, sleep and rest, and losing interest in personal hygiene and their appearance. This self-neglect can spiral into self-harming behaviours such as eating disorders, substance misuse or refusing medication. Accompanying this may be elements of self-sabotage in which all offers of help are refused so as to undermine any chance of success or happiness. In therapy this script manifests as 'I don't deserve help', and any attempts to provide help or sustenance are doomed to failure.

A milder, more subtle form of defence against shame is shyness. According to Nathanson shyness 'is a form of shame avoidance by which we accept one portion of the shame experience in order to prevent the emergence of the whole' (Nathanson 1992, p.329). Shyness allows a degree of invisibility by keeping a low profile and becoming so unobtrusive that the individual is barely detected on the shame radar, and does not risk exposure. Individuals who suffer from shyness may not necessarily lack self-worth; they are merely willing to fade into the background to avoid being seen. This reduces the likelihood of them being shamed or rejected and maximises affiliation as they are seen as non-threatening. In essence shyness says 'there is no need to reduce me because I am already lower than you, despite that I have not shown a fraction of my real self' (Nathanson 1992, p.330).

Remember
Attack self prevents the helplessness of abandonment and isolation and promotes bonding and affiliation with others.

In combination, attacking the self is a way of taking control over and regulating shame internally whilst remaining attached and connected to others. In essence it provides an illusion of control over shame which makes it appear less annihilating. Acceptance of shame, especially self-inflicted shame, also promotes the belief that it can be repaired by constant striving to improve the self, although nothing is ever good enough, which plunges the individual back into shame. Paradoxically, in attack self the individual perpetuates shame against the self, albeit without risking abandonment or rejection.

Attack self in therapy

Clients whose defensive shame script clusters around attack self can be challenging in therapy, especially those who have masochistic tendencies. This is due to their deeply embedded belief that 'to feel bad is good and to feel good is bad'. They may be reluctant to relinquish tried and tested self-attacking strategies as they believe that they do not deserve to get better and fear the abandonment of strategies that have sustained them in the past. This is especially the case in self-harming behaviours such as substance misuse, addictions and self-injury. Counsellors must be patient, compassionate and empathic in supporting clients to relinquish defensive scripts as from attacking self to expressing and tolerating their shame. They also need to understand how attacking the self has come to feel better than having someone else do it (Nathanson 1992, p.330) and how the cost of seeking affiliation through self-abasement can lead to the destruction of self.

AVOIDANCE

The primary strategy in the avoidance script is the need to cover up the defective self at all costs so that it can never be exposed. To achieve this, individuals need to deceive themselves and others about their true self by weaving a web of intricate lies to such an extent that 'their very identity is a lie…with a sense of self so false that they may be seen as imposters' (Nathanson 1992, p.350). The energy that is needed to control the pervasive inner chaos and worthlessness and to sustain the façade of self-worth is exhausting and psychologically costly. To achieve this individuals adopt a number of avoidance strategies, from denial, numbing the experience of shame through alcohol, sex or thrill seeking, to perfectionism, pathological lying, arrogance, narcissism and grandiosity to support this false identity.

Continuum of avoidance

Individuals who adopt the avoidance script to defend against shame are condemned to find any way to avoid the inner experiences, feelings or thoughts that may evoke shame (see Figure 5.4). The message is that shame has to be denied, disowned or split off and overridden with distracting activities such as thrill seeking, excitement or joy. This allows individuals to fool themselves and others by 'blinding the eye of the mind' (Wurmser 1989 p.175) and deflecting shame by directing attention to a sanitised version of the self: 'Look at me but only where I tell you to look' (Nathanson 1992, p.351).

As the motivation is to minimise the conscious experience of shame many individuals will also try to deaden or numb the experience through a range of addictive behaviours such as alcohol, drugs, sex, consumer goods, food, work, exercise, mystical religious movements and therapy to try to fill the void.

On the extreme end of the continuum they may develop psychological strategies that can coalesce into personality traits such as grandiosity, arrogance and narcissism designed to prove that they do not feel shame. The constant self-surveillance and need to hide a sense of inferiority leads to inner emptiness that resembles a body without a soul (Kaufman 1989; Nathanson 1992).

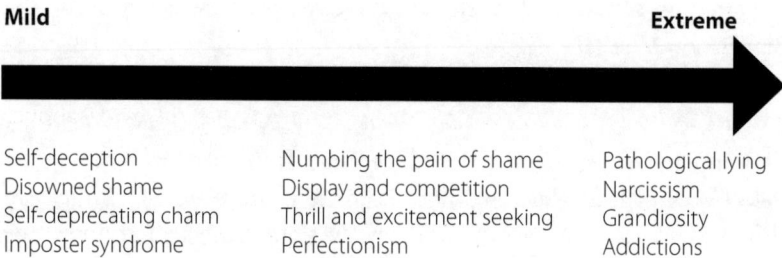

Mild   **Extreme**

Self-deception	Numbing the pain of shame	Pathological lying
Disowned shame	Display and competition	Narcissism
Self-deprecating charm	Thrill and excitement seeking	Grandiosity
Imposter syndrome	Perfectionism	Addictions

Figure 5.4 Continuum of avoidance

Avoidance promotes a degree of self-deception and the deception of others by displaying positive attributes to distract the gaze of others away from inadequacies or defects, or what may lie beneath the surface. As in attack self strategies this can be done on a relatively healthy level through openness, modesty and unexaggerated self-esteem alongside self-deprecating charm and humour. In some cases the defective self becomes so sanitised that the individual loses all contact with the true self, replacing it with a fraudulent self. If left unchecked this can develop into imposter syndrome in which the individual is unable to internalise their achievements or competencies (Clance and Imes 1978).

Another way to avoid unbearable states of shame is to override the pervasive inner sense of emptiness through relentless seeking of thrills and excitement. In their hedonism and pleasure seeking, individuals endeavour to distract from a blighted inner world. Typically this is associated with high-adrenaline activities such as dangerous or extreme sports, joy riding, taking risks, high-octane, stressful work environments, or a constant diet of sexual excitement through sex addiction. This is often accompanied by numbing experiences such as alcohol or drug misuse, which if left unchecked can lead into full-blown addictions.

Perfectionism

Another way of diverting attention away from a general sense of inadequacy is to focus on convenient imperfections such as appearance (facial features, hair, muscles, body tone) and to re-sculpt these. This propels individuals into an endless cycle, designed to perfect their physical appearance through over-exercising, starvation, body building or cosmetic surgery to erase defects and present a constantly new, photo-shopped self to the world. This quest for perfectionism is often employed in other arenas such as work, relationships and the social world. This ferocious pursuit of exaggerated levels of ability, competence, wealth and possessions is in essence a barricade to cover up the inner sense of inadequacy and shame (Nathanson 1992, p.345). A classic example of this are workaholics who are driven to succeed and yet have no time to enjoy the fruits of their labour or take pleasure in their success. Paradoxically the pursuit of perfectionism is inevitably doomed to failure either due to unrealistic expectations which are too high and thus can never be achieved, or that whatever is achieved is deemed never good enough to fully compensate for the feeling of being inherently flawed.

Displays of worth

Another potent way to distract attention away from any imperfection is through exaggerated displays of achievements, triumphs and successes. This can involve the acquisition of trophies, be they luxury goods, clothes, jewellery, home, car, holidays, school, art, antiques or upward mobility. Each of these is designed to shift the spotlight away from deeply embedded shame onto overt examples of success and status. Such brittle and superficial displays of status never really assuage the hidden shame lurking deep inside, and only reinforce the need to acquire ever more symbols of success in an endless cycle of consumerism. The acquisition and display of trophies represent a wished-for shame-free self who is powerful and potent. This is often accompanied by exhibitionism in which individuals act as though they have nothing to hide by flaunting themselves, their wealth, their attire or their sexuality. In essence such publicly flamboyant displays are attempts to provide evidence and proof that they have not been compromised by shame experiences. However, such avoidance of shame comes at a price, as the gnawing sense of shame is never quelled and prevents real engagement with others, leading to increased isolation from others and the world (Nathanson 1992).

Comparison and competition

Rather than being released from shame, the avoidance of shame makes individuals more shame vigilant in constantly comparing themselves with others to verify their status and competence. This leads to highly competitive behaviour which is characterised by endless efforts to prove their status and worth. This is designed to gain attention and approval from others. A by-product of comparison and competition is arrogance in which inferiority is traded for superiority, grandiosity and an inflated sense of self-worth. This is accompanied by a belief that they are better than others and a sense of entitlement as proof of their worth. To maintain this false self, individuals need to consistently ensure their superiority by putting other people down by making them feel weak, incompetent and ashamed. Despite these endeavours the avoided shame remains within the core of the self and continues to eat away at self-worth, setting up a vicious cycle and spiral of shame.

Narcissism

In combination, perfectionism, displays of achievement and competition underpin the narcissism characteristic of avoidance. In essence narcissism 'is the system through which personal attributes are exaggerated in order to avoid shame' (Nathanson 1992, p.348) and a way for individuals to avoid conscious awareness, or '"knowing" anything that might increase an already unbearable amount of shame' (Nathanson 1992, p.348). Thus narcissism protects against shame through an exaggerated sense of self, or self-aggrandisement, which covers up a deeply damaged sense of self. To support such self-aggrandisement, inflated sense of self and hubristic pride individuals seize every opportunity to display their achievements even if it means erasing or re-writing their narrative. This is seen in their manipulation of their history, their name, their accent and their lifestyle through the use of social media in which they control their profiles and censor what is seen by, or known to, others.

Ironically some people cover up deeply ingrained narcissism through counterfeit altruistic or charitable acts. To offset the inner emptiness that underpins narcissistic tendencies, individuals seek to take care of others or adopt worthy causes to increase their self-worth. In this they objectify others and use them to fulfil their own needs. This is commonly seen in the exploitation and sexual abuse of children in which abuse masquerades as love, affection and care. Classic examples of these are seen in sexual abuse by priests and 'secular saints' such as Jimmy Savile (Sanderson 2010 2013).

On a more everyday level the cover up of narcissistic tendencies is seen in those who try to escape their depleted inner selves by taking care of others. Despite their efforts they often make poor caretakers as they are not really interested in the needs of others but are solely preoccupied with meeting their own needs to be admired or needed. In pretending to take care of others they are able to cover up the fact that others are seen merely as objects to be sacrificed and used in whatever way necessary to meet insatiable needs for aggrandisement. The roots of such behaviour are laid down in early childhood where the child's needs were not met as they had to care for others. Through this they learned that the only way their needs could be met was to meet the needs of others, and to be needed (Nathanson 1992).

⚑ Remember

Avoidance is characterised by the denial of shame and deception of self and others, leading to perfectionism, addictions, self-aggrandisement and narcissism to fill an inner void and emptiness.

Avoidance in therapy

Clients who adopt avoidance as a defence against shame can be particularly challenging in therapy as they have dissociated from their experience of shame and have difficulty linking their current behaviour to shaming experiences in the past. In addition, their level of self-aggrandisement can make them appear arrogant and grandiose, and their sense of entitlement and constant need to use their achievements and success as a barricade to real engagement makes it hard to establish an authentic relationship. Crucially they will find it especially challenging to relinquish their narcissistic tendencies until enough inner resources have been developed to build authentic pride and shame resilience. This can only be achieved through empathic understanding of the link between shame and narcissism rather than re-shaming the client. A further consideration is to address any addictions that are used to numb the pain of shame and enable the client to relinquish these.

ATTACK OTHER

Like avoidance, the defence script of attack other is an attempt to dissociate from the experience of shame. This is motivated by the desire to improve one's own self-image and projecting shame into, and onto others. The emphasis is on 'turning the tables' (Wurmser 1995, p.302) by making others feel ashamed and inferior while allowing the self to appear shame free and thus superior. To achieve this individuals engage in a range of hostile behaviours such as put-downs, teasing, bullying, violence and rape to produce shame in others. This comes at a cost as such hostility and violence keeps others at bay and interferes with developing healthy relationships.

The continuum of attack other strategies ranges from verbal and physical assaults such as teasing, good-natured banter, overt put-downs, ridicule and public humiliation to antisocial behaviours such as graffiti, vandalism, bullying, humiliated fury and explosive rage, to violence, rape and ultimately murder (see Figure 5.5). The goal is that 'someone must be made to feel less than I do' (Nathanson 1992, p.367). In addition, the projected self-hatred allows for the objectification of others so that they can be violated or attacked without impunity. While the attack other script is usually used in relation to other individuals it can also be used in creating a culture of contempt where whole classes of individuals are humiliated or shamed for their gender, race, ethnicity or religion.

Mild   **Extreme**

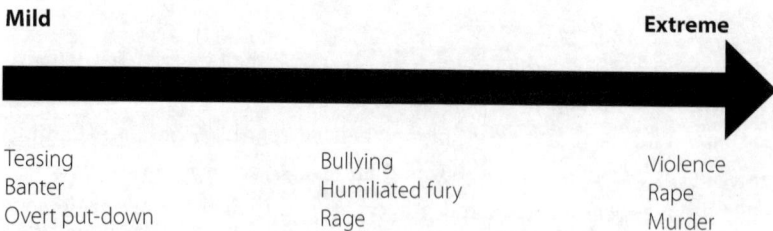

Teasing	Bullying	Violence
Banter	Humiliated fury	Rape
Overt put-down	Rage	Murder

Figure 5.5 Continuum of attack other

Attack other scripts can be enacted non-verbally, verbally or physically through acts of violence or aggression. Non-verbal examples of attack other can be seen in facial expressions such as a contemptuous sneer, barely raised eyebrow, one corner of lip curled, or angry facial tension, as well as in dismissive actions such as the refusal to acknowledge a greeting, exclusion from social interaction through snubbing or shunning someone from one's social circle. This is typically designed to belittle others through sarcasm, scorn, derision, mockery, disdain, criticism, superciliousness or verbal insults. These are often strategically reinforced by demands for total compliance, intimidation, bullying, coercion, threats of physical violence or the use of weapons. Sometimes the humiliation is enacted through defiling the other by urinating or defecating on them, or the smearing of faeces to strip away any glimmer of self-respect (see Chapter 8).

The purpose of deflected shame is to 'erase the sting of weakness and disgrace' (Nathanson 1992, p.368) and elevate depleted self-esteem by shaming others in order to feel more powerful than them. In essence it allows individuals to by-pass their own shame and humiliation by diverting attention away from the shamed self and redirecting the spotlight of shame onto others. By-passed shame also reduces the capacity for empathy or compassion, which allows individuals to dehumanise others by objectifying them and avoiding closeness, mutuality or intimacy. In humiliating others, self-hatred and self-contempt are evacuated from the self and projected into others. This externalisation of shame is often seen in sexual assault and rape in which the victim is blamed for their rape. In some cases the rape victim is murdered in an attempt to annihilate the object of shame (the victim) altogether and expunge the projected shame of the rapist.

Rage and humiliated fury

The attack other script is often the most primitive of the defences against shame and is often triggered by shame around physical size or strength, proficiency, competence, mastery over skills, limited verbal skills, stupidity, weakness, vulnerability and dependency needs. When any of these are evoked they can trigger silent rage or humiliated fury, which compel individuals to annihilate those who have exposed them in their shame. The elicited humiliated fury unleashes reactive attacks of anger and rage including verbal and physical violence. The intensity of such attacks is typically directly proportional to the original unbearable shame experiences that gave rise to humiliated fury.

To expunge this fury, individuals use cold-dissecting anger, rage or hostility as weapons to diminish others and reduce their status (Gilligan 2001; Nathanson 1992) and gain power over them. However, this power over others is somewhat hollow as it is not authentic power and as such must be consistently enforced to retain dominance and status. Most importantly it does not detoxify shame but reinforces it in the commission of shameless acts of violence. In addition, rage and hostility keep others at bay and prevent opportunities for connection, closeness or developing trusting relationships with others. This can lead to isolation and loneliness, which can become a further source of shame.

Remember

Attack other is a way to expunge shame by projecting it onto, or into, others by shaming them to gain power or dominance over them. It is also a way of keeping others at bay which reduces opportunities for connection and mutuality.

Attack other in therapy

The attack other script in therapy is often used by individuals to reduce shame due to an unequal power dynamic in the therapeutic relationship. This is commonly characterised by devaluing you, the counsellor, or the therapeutic process through hostility, resistance, silent anger, humiliated fury or direct verbal assaults or physical threats of violence. More subtle versions cluster around consistent attempts to shame or deskill the counsellor through overt criticism, refusal to engage in the therapeutic process or undermining opportunities for change. Often such clients find it hard to take responsibility for their actions by blaming and shaming others for their actions and lack of success in their recovery from shame. You need to be empathic and sensitive to the underlying shame that fuels the attack other script and not personalise such attacks (see Chapter 12).

The next two exercises are useful in helping clients to identify their shame screens. The second uses a more non-verbal approach, encouraging the client to make a mask to represent how they cover up their shame.

⚙ **Exercise**
Identifying shame screens

1. Discuss the Compass of Shame and help the client to identify which defensive scripts they use to defend against shame, and which one represents their default setting.

2. Encourage the client to reflect on these and make a list of the advantages and disadvantages of these reactions to shame, and how they impact on empathy, compassion and connection.

3. From this discuss with the client how the least effective ones could be changed and consider alternative, more adaptive ways of managing shame.

4. Encourage the client to practise these in session until they feel confident to use these new skills outside of the counselling session.

⚙ **Exercise**
Shame masks

Using the mask template as a guide (see Figure 5.6) ask your client to draw the masks they use to cover shame. They might emphasise a smile, or make it ornate to emphasise value and worth…

★ *Figure 5.6 Shame mask template*

Given that many of these defensive scripts fail to undo shame it is critical that you facilitate greater shame awareness to enable clients to tolerate unbearable feelings of shame. This is most effective through identifying shame screens and scripts and enabling clients to move towards acceptance of self. You must be mindful that the best antidote to shame is to uncover the masks that hide it and this is best achieved through openness, compassion and empathy. In the presence of an accepting, non-judgemental counsellor it is possible to recover from shame and begin to connect to self and others with a sense of mutuality. To ensure more mutually satisfying relationships the next chapter explores how sexual shame impacts on relationships.

SUGGESTED READING

Dearing, R.L. and Tangney, J.P. (eds) (2011) *Shame in the Therapy Hour.* Washington, DC: American Psychological Association.

DeYoung, P.A. (2015) Understanding and Treating Chronic Shame: A Relational/ Neurobiological Approach. Hove: Routledge.

Mollon, P. (2002) *Shame and Jealousy: The Hidden Turmoils.* London: Karnac Books.

Nathanson, D.L. (1992) *Shame and Pride: Affect, Sex, and the Birth of the Self.* New York: W.W. Norton.

Sanderson, C. (2013) *Counselling Skills for Working with Trauma: Healing from Child Sexual Abuse, Sexual Violence and Domestic Abuse.* London: Jessica Kingsley Publishers.

6

SHAME IN SEX AND SEXUALITY

The potent mix of desire, excitement and arousal can be both a source of pride and shame. Sex and sexuality can be a powerful source of pride in terms of success in finding sexual partners and the demonstration of sexual prowess and sexual performance. However, it can also be a source of anxieties, fears and crippling shame when this is not achieved, or sex has been used to humiliate or violate. The extent to which sex becomes a source of pride or shame is determined from early childhood through a complex interplay of biological factors and socially constructed messages about sex and sexuality which shape later sexual behaviour. Thus while sex can be a form of adult play it can also be drenched in shame, as it 'hovers everywhere in the bed of lust' (Nathanson 1992, p.300).

This chapter will explore how the relationship between sex and shame is forged from early childhood in the construction of a sexual script and a sexual arousal template that influences how we feel and think about sex and sexuality. It will look at the development of sexual shame in early childhood development and adolescence and how this shapes later adult sexual behaviour. Particular attention will be focused on the different sources of shame in males and females in terms of arousal, performance and relational dynamics, as well as cultural and religious sanctions that can intensify shame. In addition, it will examine defensive reactions to sexual shame and how these link to sexual compulsions and addictions and variant sexual behaviour. The emphasis throughout is to enhance awareness of sexual shame and how this impacts on sexual behaviour and the range of sexual difficulties that present in clinical practice.

SOURCES OF SEXUAL SHAME

Sex and sexuality are biologically based drives which are necessary for the survival of the species and consist of powerful innate affects which seek release and expression through sexual behaviour. However, throughout our evolutionary past, the cost of sexual arousal is that it exposes us to potential dangers. As we become submersed in sexual arousal we lose ourselves through disinhibition and are less aware of our surroundings, making us more vulnerable to predators. This need to make ourselves less visible and hide is manifest in sexual behaviour, which is often conducted in the dark with closed eyes rather than in full daylight and sustained eye contact. This suggests that there is a biological imperative in linking sex and sexuality with shame in order to protect us from the scrutiny of others who could cause harm. As a result, sexuality is often hidden, and sexual behaviour is conducted in private or even in the dark to avoid the shaming gaze of others.

The biological basis of sex and sexuality can also be a powerful source of anxieties and fears which become entwined with early childhood sanctions against sexual expression and behaviour which are imposed by family and society. While some of the messages about sex may be largely unconscious, they do wield a large impact on sexual feelings, thoughts and behaviours. These become more pronounced during the upsurge of sexual hormones during puberty and can be replayed in sexual behaviours throughout adulthood. This is exacerbated if sexual arousal is in opposition to cultural mores or expectations and cannot quell sexual desire or excitement. The ensuing battle between sexual arousal and societal expectations becomes the crucible for unbearable shame. If the sexual arousal cannot be controlled or managed the individual risks engaging in activities that are perceived by others as perverted or criminal. This intensifies the shame, which in severe cases can lead to suicidal ideation or suicide attempts, shameless acts of compulsive sexual activity or eroticised rage and sexual violence (see Chapter 8).

As much of the shame in sex and sexuality is driven by physical sensations and arousal, the body becomes a repository of sexual shame. When this is combined with shame around the body, as well as performance anxiety or lack of relational worth, sexual shame becomes a turbulent cauldron of fear, humiliation and shame. This can lead to defences against sexual shame in which sex is avoided at all costs as in sexual anorexia, or through hidden, solitary sexual activities such as masturbation to extreme sexual fantasies, pornography or anonymous sex. Alternatively it can lead to hyper-sexuality as a way to mask sexual shame which manifests in promiscuity, multiple sexual partners and a range of sexual compulsions and addictions. These in turn can compromise sexual health and increase the risk of sexually transmitted infections such as chlamydia, gonorrhoea, herpes and HIV, all of which are a powerful source of shame. This is exacerbated by having to inform ex and prospective partners of the infection, which intensifies the sense of shame and can be particularly distressing for survivors of CSA who already feel dirty and shamed by their abuse.

The influence of cultural and religious sanctions that regulate sexuality can exert a powerful and insidious influence on sexual behaviour, sexual orientation and sexual modesty. In some cultures and religions these injunctions serve to pathologise or criminalise certain sexual activities such as homosexuality, or restrain sexual pleasure and behaviour in females through female genital mutilation. Cultures vary enormously in the way they regulate sexuality and sexual behaviour, with some being highly tolerant and others extremely intolerant. Irrespective of degree of tolerance, most cultures attempt to regulate sexuality through injunctions around sexual orientation, sexual modesty, virginity, circumcision and appropriate sexual behaviour. Both genders face approbation with regard to sexual orientation, especially male homosexuality, which is seen in many cultures as a sexual deviancy or perversion which is punishable by castration or death. This not only induces fear and shame but also results in stigmatisation and internalised homophobia. To be gay in such societies attracts taunts, verbal and physical abuse, ostracism, rejection, same-sex rape and abuse by legal systems in criminalising and demonising homosexuality. This leads to secrecy and isolation, which only reinforces sexual shame. The shame associated with breaking these cultural expectations can be internalised, leading to internalised homophobia or self-loathing about one's gender.

Many cultures also seek to control sexual impulses, especially in females, by restricting sexual pleasure through circumcision or FGM and injunctions against sexual immodesty, overt sexual behaviour and promiscuity. Many of the cultural sanctions are supported and maintained through religious beliefs which regard sex and sexual pleasure as sinful. Such messages can have a devastating effect on individuals who seek to disavow their sexuality through sexual abstinence or celibacy only to find that when this fails the overwhelming sense of shame can lead to obsessive sexual thoughts and sexual compulsions such as compulsive masturbation (Sanderson 2011).

Early experiences of sexual seduction or childhood sexual abuse can also induce shame in which the child blames themselves for the abuse, and internalises not only their own shame but also the by-passed or projected shame of the abuser. All of these influence and shape sex and sexuality and concomitant shame that can lead to a range of sexual dysfunctions and disorders, which in turn become a further source of shame (see Table 6.1).

Table 6.1 Summary of sources of sexual shame

Sources of shame	Examples
Body	Body shape and size of breasts, buttocks, penis or erection. Body secretions such as semen, perspiration or menstrual blood. Body odours, noises, cues to sexual arousal
Sexual arousal	Loss of control, over-aroused, lack of arousal, fantasies or foci of desire
Performance	Sexual prowess, failure, erectile dysfunction, premature ejaculation, degree of lubrication, orgasm
Sexual behaviours	Masturbation, fetishes, bondage and sado-masochism, paraphilias, sexual compulsions, sex addictions, eroticised rage
Sexual dysfunctions	Erectile dysfunction, premature ejaculation, sexual anorexia, sexual desire disorder, vaginismus, dyspareunia
Sexual orientation	Heterosexual, homosexual, bisexual
Relationships	Mutuality, connection, how much sex was enjoyed
Sexual compulsions and addictions	Compulsive masturbation, online pornography use, sex addiction
Sexual health	Sexually transmitted infections, HIV, AIDS
Cultural and religious sanctions	Sexual modesty, virginity, virility, fertility, circumcision, female genital mutilation

Given the range of sources of sexual shame it is essential to develop a deeper awareness of the relationship between shame and sex and sexuality and how the interaction of biological factors and social construction shapes sexuality and sexual behaviour. This can be facilitated by identifying the client's sexual script and arousal template (see the following sections). As talking about sex can be a source of shame for both you and the client it is important that you feel comfortable doing this without triggering your own shame. It is crucial that you have awareness about your own sexuality and any sexual shame you may have so that you can fully engage when talking about sex and sexuality without being embarrassed or drenched in your own shame, as this intensifies the client's shame. With this in mind you may find it useful to reflect on your own sexuality and do the exercises in the following two sections.

SEXUAL SCRIPT

The complex interplay of biology and social construction forms the basis of what Gagnon and Simon (1973) referred to as the 'sexual script' and Carnes (2001) called the 'sexual arousal template'. The sexual script is comprised of learnt behaviour, cultural and religious sanctions and messages received from family, peers and the media with a particular historical time, all of which determine what are considered to be acceptable forms of sexuality. In addition, the sexual script will also be influenced by early experiences of sexual arousal, including CSA. In essence, the sexual script is a culmination of our learning experience in terms of *whom* we can have sex with (age, class, religion, gender or ethnicity), *what* is sexual (sensations, feelings, thoughts or behaviour), what we *do* sexually (activities or behaviour), *when* we have sex (age, frequency, what time of day/night or month), *where* we can have sex (location, inside, outside, private, public), and *why* we have sex (reasons, justifications). To identify the various components of your sexual script the exercise below can be completed by yourself or your client.

Exercise
Sexual script
Take a moment to reflect on your learning experiences around sex and sexuality and how these have informed your sexual script by completing the statements below:

1. I am allowed to have sex with _____

2. Sexual feelings are _____

3. When having sex I am allowed to do_____

4. I am allowed to have sex when _____

5. The places I am allowed to have sex are _____

6. I have sex because _____

SEXUAL AROUSAL TEMPLATE

Carnes (2001) expands on this by focusing on sexual arousal cues which are conditioned from early childhood and which coalesce into what he calls the 'sexual arousal template'. As anything can be eroticised, this can become a powerful source of shame, especially if it is in opposition to prevailing societal norms or mores. As these sexual arousal cues are usually conditioned in early childhood they are often unconscious and yet exert a powerful influence on sexual fantasy and behaviour, and are particularly pronounced in sexual compulsions and sex addictions. These arousal cues will vary enormously and be dependent on each individual's experience and beliefs but can be grouped into distinct categories consisting of sensations, feelings, body types or parts, partner characteristics, courtship, processes, behaviours, objects, places or scenarios and beliefs (see Table 6.2).

Table 6.2 Sexual arousal template (Adapted from Carnes 2001)	
Sources of arousal	**Examples**
Sensations	• Smells (perfumes, body odour, massage oil, incense, alcohol, cigarette smoke) • Sounds (music, talking, radio) • Touch (feel of skin, fabric, fur, skin) • Taste (food, lipstick, gum, breath mints) • Visual images
Feelings	Fear, sadness, shame, loneliness, anger, pain
Body types or parts	Physique, build, shape, muscles, breasts, buttocks, feet, hair colour, wrinkles, stretch marks, teeth, moles, armpits, feet, pregnancy, anorexic, loss of limb, disabled
Partner characteristics	Age, same sex, opposite sex, transgendered, marital status, personality factors, specific careers (teacher, emergency workers, stockbroker, actor, footballer, sex workers, body builder, priests), wealthy, impoverished, successful, inexperienced, virginal, promiscuous, specific types (vulnerable, hurting women, unobtainable males or females, bad boy, abused, ethnicity)

Courtship processes	Flirting, seduction, thrill of the chase, rollercoaster of break up and make up, abandonment, rejection
Behaviours	Smoking, taking drugs, urination, violence, degradation, humiliation, driving, stealing, burglary, fire setting
Objects	Cars, computer keyboard, sex toys, clothing, uniform (firefighter, police, military, doctor, nurse), lingerie, high heels, sex toys, whips, snakes, insects
Places or scenarios	Bars, clubs, dancing, baths, massage parlours, parks, beaches, forests, hotel rooms, aeroplanes, parts of town, crowded spaces, shopping centres
Beliefs	Females tease, are unreliable and capricious, say 'no' when they mean 'yes', only want gifts and money, sex has to be bought Males only want sex and can't be trusted

All of these sexual arousal cues can be imbued with shame, especially if they are in opposition to societal and cultural norms or familial expectations. Many of these cues are conditioned in childhood and remain largely unconscious, although they exert a powerful influence on sexual behaviour and fantasy. When exploring sexual arousal cues it is helpful to make these more conscious to gain awareness of how these are linked to shame and how they influence sexual behaviour, especially sex addictions. A useful way for you (and your clients) to identify your arousal template is to do the exercise below and try to link the arousal cues to any felt sense of sexual shame. Remember that as anything can be eroticised it is critical not to judge clients and to focus on linking their sexual behaviour to sexual shame and how these have become conditioned.

Exercise
Reflection on sexual arousal cues
Take a sheet of paper and draw nine columns for each of the categories in Table 6.2 (sensations, feelings, body types or parts, partner characteristics, courtship processes, behaviours, objects, places or scenarios and beliefs). Reflect on each heading and list your arousal cues and how you feel about these, and note how these influence your sexual life, both in terms of fantasy and behaviour. In reflecting on these try to identify any associated feelings of shame.

Remember
Anything can be eroticised and can be a source of shame.

RANGE OF SEXUAL BEHAVIOUR

The range of sexual behaviour occurs on a continuum from hyper-sexuality such as satyriasis in men or nymphomania in women, through to sexual aversion as seen in sexual anorexia. In addition, people engage in sexual activity for many reasons, some of which are more acceptable in our society than others. Each individual evaluates sexual behaviour according to their own morals and values. Thus, it is difficult to decide objectively which expressions of sexual activity and purposes are 'right' and which ones are 'wrong'. To enhance your awareness of your own sexual behaviour it is helpful to reflect on how you have used sex and sexuality in relationships. The following exercise can be used by both counsellor and client.

Exercise
Reflection on the uses of sex
Take a moment to brainstorm how people use sex and list these. Common examples include to procreate, to have pleasure, to play or have fun, to assert the self, to gain a sense of pride, to feel free or to feel close and connected. Some people also use sex to shame, humiliate, dominate or degrade others or to obtain power and control over them, or exploit or violate them through eroticised rage. Reflect on your list and tick those that you have used in the past and how you feel about your use of sex. Remember, these can all be used in different ways at different times, and providing they are consensual may not be a source of shame.

SOURCES OF SEXUAL SHAME IN CHILDHOOD

There has been much debate about to what extent children are sexual from birth (Sanderson 2004). They are certainly in possession of an innate sexual drive which is shaped throughout their early experiences to form the sexual script. From as young as 18–24 months children experience waves of physical sensations, thoughts, ideas and fantasies that can consist of nascent sexual affects. While these are initially fragmented they begin to coalesce into the sexual script or arousal template. At this early stage these affects are a source of pride rather than shame as they represent free-flowing sexual energy that is life enhancing. The family or cultural environment in which the child is raised will determine whether the child continues to take pleasure and pride in these affects or becomes drenched in shame.

Some families and cultures will share the child's pride while others will react negatively by punishing or shaming the child. A common example is when a young boy has an erection; he might be praised for his prowess while another boy might be made to feel shamed for this. Similarly a child who experiences obvious pleasure while touching their genitals may have this acknowledged and gently guided to restrict such touching in public, or be punished or shamed (Sanderson 2004). Whichever way this is managed will send a strong message to the child about whether to feel pride or shame in their sexual arousal, which can direct the way they will feel about sexual pleasure.

Young children look to their primary caregivers to help them understand their sensations and feelings by acknowledging and labelling them. If this is done in a positive way the child is more likely to interpret sexual arousal as a source of pleasure and pride which will shape later sexuality and sexual behaviour. If, however, the reactions are overtly, or covertly, punitive and shaming, the child will associate sexual arousal with shame, fear and anxiety. It is for this reason that caregivers need to be aware of their own sexual shame when talking to or guiding their children so as not to perpetuate an intergenerational cycle of sexual shame. In talking to their children about sex parents need to feel comfortable about sex so as not to transmit their anxieties or shame (Sanderson 2004), as young children typically attend to the non-verbal aspects of the communication more than the verbal message.

Sexual shame can be exacerbated in the presence of early sexualisation either through inappropriate seductive behaviour by primary caregivers or childhood sexual abuse by adults, siblings or peers. The secrecy and silence associated with CSA have the capacity to elicit shame as 'where there is secrecy we will find the potential for shame' (Nathanson 1992, p.292). Alongside this the sexual acts and confusing sexual arousal will invariably lead to self-blame and the child feeling that they caused this to happen. This is particularly the case when the child experiences sexual pleasure and the abuser blames the child for their own arousal (Sanderson 2006). As the young child is unable to manage the intensity of sexual excitation they are unable to regulate it and stop the flow of sexual excitation. This leads to a constant flow of sexual excitation which cannot be quelled or calmed, leading to confusion and shame. In addition, the child will not only feel their own shame but is likely to absorb the by-passed or projected shame of the abuser (Sanderson 2011, 2013). This has a powerful impact on the sexual script and sexual arousal template, which can be the source of a range of sexual behaviours, including sexual anorexia, hyper-sexuality, sexual compulsions and sex addiction.

SOURCES OF SEXUAL SHAME IN ADOLESCENCE

As the child moves towards puberty they will already have acquired some of the components of their nascent sexual script. The upsurge of sex hormones during puberty will not only activate the development of secondary sex characteristics but also increase sexual arousal and desire. If the teenager has experienced sexual arousal as a source of pride they have the opportunity to navigate the sexual maturation of the body and intense sexual arousal with delight as they embark on their journey into adulthood. However, if early sexual shaming experiences prevail, these might be amplified by the upsurge of sex hormones and their impact. This is a difficult period for many adolescents who may have internalised strong sanctions around the expression of sexuality, which are in stark conflict with what is arousing to them.

The sexual arousal may be so intense that they are unable to control their physiological reactions or desire. Thus a young male might become sexually aroused and not be able to control his erection in the presence of the desired person and feel ashamed, especially if the source of his sexual attraction is perceived as inappropriate such as sexual attraction to other males, or when hugging female caregivers or siblings. Similarly an adolescent girl may be overwhelmed by her sexual desire and arousal which she feels unable to control and which compels her to act even if it means violating cultural or religious injunctions around modesty and virginity. These can be powerful sources of shame and humiliation.

The lack of control in sexual arousal and bodily changes during puberty can become a further source of shame. As children develop, considerable emphasis is placed on learning to control their impulses and bodily functions, which seem to become unmanageable as sex hormones take over. Thus the adolescent will find it hard to control signs of sexual excitation such as erections, erect nipples, lubrication or flushing through sexual excitement. In addition the need to release sexual arousal through masturbation can be a source of shame especially if there are strong religious or cultural injunctions against this practice. The lack of control also includes bodily secretions such as semen during nocturnal emissions and menstrual blood which cannot be hidden as they stain bed linen or underwear. The shame felt by many young people knowing that their caregivers will see evidence of their sexual arousal or sexual maturation is palpable and can persist into adulthood.

Bodily changes associated with puberty can also be a potent source of shame. Right at the time when sexual arousal and sexual desire are at their most potent bodily changes occur which can be confusing and embarrassing. Young males' voices change, they grow facial, body and pubic hair, their body changes and they may go through a rapid growth spurt in height. Females' bodies also change and become more rounded, with an increase in body shape and breast size as well as body hair, especially in the pubic area and under the armpits. The increased sex hormones will cause changes in both genders with regard to pheromones and accompanying body odour. In addition elevated levels of testosterone can lead into increased sebum and the development of acne on the face and in severe cases the back, shoulders and buttocks. This can lead to pimples, pustules, nodules and reddening of the skin. As acne is most commonly on the face it is highly visible and impossible to hide, which can lead to crippling shame. In addition, severe acne can leave scarring which is also difficult to hide post-puberty, prolonging the shame long after hormonal changes have settled down.

These changes can be particularly difficult for teenagers to manage especially as they live in the highly visible world of social media in which photographs are shared on Facebook and Instagram. If the adolescent doesn't fit in with the currently desirable body shape or blemish-free skin they will fear rejection and retreat into isolation to avoid humiliation or shame. This withdrawal reduces opportunities to engage with others and develop the necessary social skills to start dating, which in turn creates another source of shame, especially in males who risk ridicule for their lack of sexual experience and virginity. Fear of being shunned or humiliated may induce social anxiety in which the adolescent withdraws from peer interaction and becomes more and more isolated. As a result of being isolated they are limited in managing their sexual arousal and either avoid all sexual expression or resort to secretive sexual activities such as masturbation to online pornography. If this is the primary source of sexual expression the adolescent risks becoming dependent on solitary sexual gratification, making it harder to develop mutually satisfying sexual relationships in adulthood.

SOURCES OF SEXUAL SHAME IN ADULTS

Sexual arousal starts as a murmur, rising in intensity as excitement builds, and increased excitement creates more arousal and increased positive affect. The aim of increased intensity in excitement and arousal is to push towards orgasm and the concomitant release. In this, sexual arousal makes us feel alive, vital and energised and is a potent source of pleasure and healthy pride. However, if sexual arousal is accompanied by fears, anxieties and a sense of inadequacy, it can elicit shame and switch off sexual excitement, replacing it with shame-based feelings, thoughts or experiences. If this is repeated it can lead to deeply embedded shame and avoidance of sexual contact or it can metastasise into eroticised rage, sexual aggression and sexual violence (see Chapter 8). An example of this is when males blame women for their arousal or sexual failure rather than acknowledge their sexual shame. In reliving past sexual failures or humiliation and the accompanying shame they seek retribution by belittling or degrading their sexual partner in order to release their dis-avowed shame.

While both adult males and females experience sexual arousal it manifests differently. A high sex drive is a source of pride in males and a source of shame in females. While women are expected to be sexually responsive they are also required to moderate their libido so as not to be viewed as immodest or sexually promiscuous. This is reflected in men's ambivalence to the use of female equivalents of Viagra to enhance sexual arousal. In contrast male sexual arousal is applauded, in part due to its visibility and focus on the penis and accompanying erection. The public display of sexual arousal can be a source of pride or shame depending on the appropriateness of the stimuli or context. This is often most shaming for young males who have not learnt to control such involuntary erections. Conversely the lack of erection in the presence of sexual stimulation is equally shaming as it is seen as indicating sexual inadequacy or failure. In contrast sexual arousal in females is much more private and hidden despite being distributed throughout the body, not just in the genital area. The hidden nature of female sexual arousal demands that females need to monitor their sexual arousal more for fear of being overwhelmed by sexual excitement and compromising sexual modesty. Female sexual arousal is much more subtle and can be discerned through changes in skin coloration, especially on the upper part of the body such as the lips, neck and breasts, as well as through erect nipples and vaginal lubrication. Due to the less obvious cues of sexual arousal it is not surprising that there is greater demand on females in many cultures to produce overt displays of sexual modesty through reduced eye gaze, appropriate language, dress and behaviour that provide evidence that they are not sexually aroused.

Another source of shame is degree of sexual libido, the quality of sexual performance and achievement. Any failure in sexual potency such as lack of libido, sexual arousal, erectile dysfunction, premature ejaculation or lack of orgasm can be perceived as failure and sexual inadequacy. A sense of inadequacy can also arise if we fail to please or satisfy the other person or are not able to match their arousal pattern. This can elicit shame and trigger shame-based feelings and thoughts which can inhibit future sexual arousal and create performance anxiety. As the pressure builds to be fully attuned to the partner and perfectly match their arousal, anxiety will increase, which can impede sexual performance. This can be a tremendous source of shame especially when self-esteem is primarily sought through sexual prowess and success. You will need to remind clients that it is not always possible to perfectly match a partner's arousal pattern and that this need not be evidence for sexual inadequacy or shame.

SOURCES OF SEXUAL SHAME IN MEN

A major source of sexual shame in males involves the penis. Due to the visibility of sexual arousal through erections the penis demands considerable attention by males in terms of controlling erections. In addition the engorgement of the penis causes powerful throbbing sensations which are not only distracting but demand attention, if nothing else to dampen sexual arousal and reduce the erection. The visibility of the penis renders penis size vulnerable to comparison in urinals, at the gym and when wearing certain clothing. While penises come in all shapes and sizes there is a myth that the length and girth of the penis is central to sexual performance and sexual satisfaction. This is exacerbated by the fact that some males have very small penises which only reach a substantial size when erect, while others have relatively large penises that do not necessarily increase in size when erect. Either way, penis size is a source of anxiety for many males, and if they feel that they are lacking in comparison to other males they may feel inadequate and fear being ridiculed or rejected by potential sexual partners. Males who feel ashamed of the size of their penis as being either too small or inordinately large may avoid open urinals, swimming pools or gyms in order to minimise exposure to shame. Arguably some males with large penises may seek out such places in order to gain a sense of pride through the admiration or envy of other males. A further source of shame may be whether the male has been circumcised or not. Some cultures and religions regard male circumcision as a puberty rite that heralds the young male's entry into adulthood. In the absence of that he could be regarded as less than in the eyes of those who have been circumcised.

Some males can become overly preoccupied with penis size, controllability of erections and tumescence, intensity of sexual arousal and their ability to satisfy a partner so that it impedes their performance and reinforces shame. The uncontrollability of the penis in terms of ejaculation, nocturnal emissions and semen-stained sheets, underpants or handkerchiefs can also lead to shame as this is evidence of sexual arousal and sexual expression. This is most likely when the sexual activity is conducted in secret or through masturbation, especially if there are strict cultural or religious injunctions against masturbation. In many respects males are more vulnerable to sexual shame due to the visibility and apparent uncontrollability of their penises and the increased risk of rejection. Many cultures expect males to be the sexual initiators, and as such are much more likely to be rejected, which can be a source of shame and humiliation. If this is not managed it can lead to eroticised rage and sexual violence.

! Warning

In some males rejection, humiliation and sexual shame can lead to eroticised rage and sexual violence.

SOURCES OF SEXUAL SHAME IN WOMEN

In contrast to men female sexual excitement is much more hidden, as much of the arousal is internal and not easily visible. However, when there is visible evidence of female sexuality in lubrication or menstrual blood, this can become a source of shame. This is especially the case as fluids such as menstrual blood come with an odour which can invoke dissmell in others and shame and self-disgust in the female. This may be reinforced in some cultures and religions that regard females as unclean during menstruation and restrict them from performing certain activities and rituals. Being made to feel unclean and the accompanying shame can be internalised and lead to self-loathing. Stains that occur through vaginal secretions and menstrual blood are reminiscent of urinary dyscontrol or poor hygiene, which become another source of shame.

Another source of shame is body shape and breast size. If this does not fit with cultural ideals or norms females tend to feel 'less female', inadequate and defective. Breast, and in some cultures buttock, size can be either a source of pride or anxiety for many females. If the breasts are too large they become a source of scrutiny by the male and female gaze. Males who are preoccupied by breasts may objectify these and be mesmerised by them to the exclusion of any other attribute. Breast size can also invoke envy or shame from other women as comparisons of attractiveness and sexual success are made. In addition changes in breast size from puberty through to pregnancy and old age can elicit either pride or shame, hence the increase in breast implants and breast reductions. One other source of shame involving the breasts is in breast removal through mastectomy either as a result of, or to prevent, breast cancer. For many women (and men) breasts epitomise femaleness, and to have these removed can lead to a loss of female identity.

Increasingly the focus of sexual shame has become the vagina, which although covered and hidden by clothing has become a source of scrutiny and comparison as a result of pornography. This has led to certain expectations by both males and females as to how the vagina should look, which is often in opposition to how they actually look. Like penises, vaginas and clitorises come in all shapes and sizes and yet pornography implies there is an ideal or perfect shape and size. This has fuelled both the removal of pubic hair and an increase in vaginal cosmetic surgery in which the clitoris or labia can be enlarged or reduced, and the elasticity of the vagina is restored after giving birth.

Cosmetic surgery is also used to restore the hymen in women whose culture or religion demand that females should be virgins until they marry. This reduces the shame associated with pre-marital sex and ensures marriageability. A further source of shame is female genital mutilation (FGM). Some women from cultures that practise FGM to ensure virginity and marriageability view it as a source of pride and sexual modesty, while for others it is a source of shame. Paradoxically some females who have not been cut are often made to feel ashamed and not considered chaste by either males or females and are seen as objects of pity or humiliation.

Pride and shame are also seen in virginity, pregnancy and fertility. Cultures who value virginity may instil a sense of pride in females who remain virgins until marriage. Similarly pregnancy and fertility are seen as a source of pride as they epitomise what it means to be female. Conversely, lack of fertility, childlessness or abortions can be a source of shame for many females as they are made to feel inadequate and less than. The ability to reproduce is highly valued by males and females, and when this diminishes through the menopause and ageing, older females become increasingly invisible and less desired, which can be a source of shame. The visibility and attractiveness of females, while a source of pride, can also be a source of shame as some males blame their sexual arousal on females and view them as temptresses and sexual seducers. When they are then rejected they become enraged and seek to punish the source of their shame through aggression or sexual violence, or through obliterating their beauty, for example through acid attacks. It is for this reason that it is critical to uncover hidden sexual shame in males and enable them to take responsibility for it without projecting it onto females.

SOURCES OF RELATIONAL SEXUAL SHAME

Sexual pride or shame can be activated in sexual relationships depending on the degree of sexual success or failure. The intensity of sexual arousal and excitement can be so all consuming that it leads to lack of control. This can be disconcerting as being in control of our feelings, thoughts and impulses is expected by others in society and our culture. With such expectations, the loss of control in the presence of another can be extremely shaming as we cannot be certain that they will accept us, especially when in the throes of sexual pleasure. As sex is so exposing it can make it hard for some males and females to be both intimate and sexual at the same time. The intensity of sexual arousal can feel a little like being in a dissociative or autistic state in which the other is screened out while pursuing sexual satisfaction. In filtering out the other it can give free rein to the full expression of sexual pleasure. In addition, as sexual arousal decreases, excitement abates and the orgasm is released, interest in the partner may wane and be replaced by shame. This accounts for the post-coital shame in which any sexual stimuli or associated arousal cues are avoided as they act as reminders of the sexual abandon and loss of control.

Not all couples are able to attain the ideal connection or mutuality that they would like to achieve through sexual intimacy. While the desire is there to give pleasure and satisfy the partner it is not always possible to match sexual arousal. In addition the degree of exposure during sexual intimacy can create shame in both partners, which can be so overwhelming that it cannot be contained within the relationship. This can lead to a lack of attunement and a range of sexual difficulties in which, rather than feeling connected, partners can feel violated, shamed or humiliated. As mutuality and connection are severed they are replaced by a need to perform, which can result in performance anxiety and fears of failure.

Mutuality and sexual intimacy can also be compromised through a mismatch in libido with one partner wanting to be more sexual than the other, which can become a source of conflict and resentment and accusations of frigidity or hyper-sexuality. The sense of rejection, inadequacy and lack of mutuality can evoke shame-making intimacy and make sexual contact even more shameful. This is often replicated in the counselling setting, and you need to be aware of how shame around intimacy and connection can be replayed in the therapeutic relationship.

DEFENCES AGAINST SEXUAL SHAME

When the intense affects in sex and shame become intertwined potent and powerful feelings are created that become so overwhelming they need to be defended against. While the defences against sexual shame can include all those in the Compass of Shame (Nathanson 1992) the most common ones are withdrawal and attack.

Withdrawal as a defence against sexual shame

Withdrawal as a defence against sexual shame can be seen on a spectrum from a healthy reticence and sexual modesty through to impotence and frigidity. In withdrawal shame impedes sexual excitement and arousal in relation to others, as the shame destroys the 'interpersonal bridge' (Kaufman 2004) and closeness and intimacy are avoided. This can lead to the pursuit of pleasure to deaden the pain and to fill the void of emptiness and depletion. To manage feelings of shame refuge is sought in sexual fantasy, pornography or emotionally detached sexual encounters characteristically seen in sex addiction in which comfort and control are sought externally. All of these allow the individual to be in total control of the sexual arousal hidden from the gaze of the other. This allows them to pursue sexual gratification through sex without the humiliation of connection and exposure to shame.

Attack other as a defence against sexual shame

Attack other as a defence against shame also falls on a spectrum from sexual abusers, violating boundaries, mild hostility and aggression through to sexual violence, rape and sadistic murder. Underpinning the attack other defence is eroticised anger or rage which is unleashed in response to humiliation experienced in the eyes of others. This could be due to repeated sexual rejection, blaming females for their arousal or failure to perform adequately.

This can be seen in male machismo where some males equate distress and fear with weakness and convert this into excitement and anger to fuel aggressive sexuality as a mask for their shame. When accompanied by a sense of entitlement, this allows them to feel pride in their sexual prowess and success as they replace connection and mutuality with contempt and projected shame. To unleash eroticised rage requires the objectification and dehumanisation of the victim through counter-shame, humiliation and devaluation. While such humiliation is typically represented in sexual fantasies or pornographic imagery, in some cases this is enacted through sexual practices such as urinating or defecating on partners, or sexual violence and rape. Committing such shameless and degrading acts is a way to evacuate their shame and project it into the other. The relationship between eroticised rage and shame will be explored in more depth in Chapter 8 (Carnes 2008).

SEXUAL COMPULSIONS AND SEX ADDICTIONS

Shame is also the central component of sexual compulsions and sex addictions. To escape feelings of shame and humiliation the sex addict needs to seek to numb or soothe unbearable inner states through dissociation, alcohol or drugs to heighten excitation and arousal. Sex addicts typically present with a history of broken or impaired attachments in childhood which are characterised by humiliation, rejection, abandonment and shame (Carnes 2008). In addition, many have been exposed to negative sexual messages or seductive caregivers who eroticise the child and reward sexualised responses and arousal. Many sex addicts also have a history of childhood sexual abuse in which their only worth as a sexual object was conditioned, which they then replay through their sex addiction. Such experiences are drenched in crippling shame and lack of relational worth. As they fear connection to others, their only viable refuge is in sexual excitement through other means such as masturbation, pornography or sex addiction.

THE SEXUAL COMPULSION AND ADDICTION CYCLE

As in the addiction cycle (see Chapter 7) shame underpins the sexual addiction cycles in which sex and sexual arousal are used to numb shame-based thoughts and feelings. As shameful feelings, self-loathing and humiliation threaten to overwhelm, sexual thoughts and fantasies intrude as a way to soothe or block out unbearable painful feelings. In this the individual enters a dissociative state in which they become immersed and preoccupied with sexual arousal cues and feel compelled to pursue sexual stimuli to masturbate to, or engage in sexual activity. Once orgasm is achieved, rather than feeling pleasure and relief, the addict is suffused with self-loathing and shame which confirm their core beliefs that they are worthless, inadequate and loathsome. This activates associated feelings of shame and starts the cycle again (see Figure 6.1). As the desired relief is never really achieved the sexual cycle is repeated, leading to compulsive masturbation or compulsive pursuit of sexual encounters. You will need to ensure when working with clients with sex addictions that the underlying shame is explored and processed to break the sex addiction cycle.

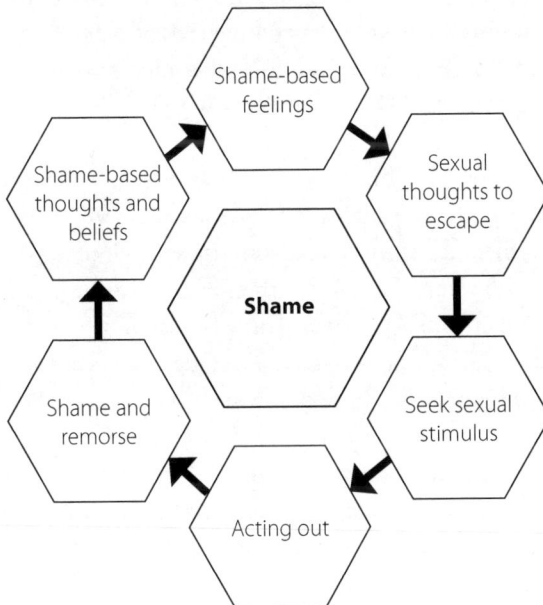

Figure 6.1 Shame and sexual addiction cycle

In clients who have been sexually abused in childhood or suffered sexual violence the sexual thoughts are often unbidden and unwanted and the opposite of what they really feel or want. Typically the content of these unwanted sexual thoughts represents a replaying of elements of the CSA. This is often seen in males who were sexually abused in childhood or raped by a male and are flooded by obsessive sexual thoughts about having sex with men. Although many of these sexually abused males present as heterosexual they feel compelled to masturbate to gay pornography, or seek gay sexual encounters of which they feel deeply ashamed. Similarly, female survivors of CSA may feel compelled to masturbate to images of their sexual abuse, only to be suffused with shame, self-loathing and disgust. Many survivors misinterpret this as evidence for being complicit in their sexual abuse and false belief that they orchestrated and wanted it.

Most clients who present with compulsive masturbation and sex addiction report that they enter a dissociative state in which they are compelled to act out the sexual thoughts and over which they have no control. This is often done in an automatic and ritualistic way until they reach release through orgasm. Given that they are largely disembodied they often feel no conscious pleasure during masturbation or sexual encounter but feel compelled to seek release through orgasm. There is rarely pleasure after orgasm as the individual comes out of the dissociative state and is suffused with shame and self-disgust. Given the automatic nature of compulsive masturbation and the lack of pleasure or satisfaction the cycle needs to be repeated. As a result compulsive masturbation can be repeated sometimes 10 to 20 times a day.

It is clear that sexual compulsions and sex addictions are a form of obsessive compulsive disorder (OCD) in which the individual feels compelled to engage in ritualistic behaviours over which they have no control and which are rarely comforting or satisfying. You will need to help clients with compulsive masturbation to become more embodied and aware of inner experiencing and how obsessive sexual thoughts are a way of avoiding sexual shame which is paradoxically intensified through the sexual addiction cycle. In addition you will need to help the client see that they are re-enacting the trauma or shame-based experiences to gain mastery, rather than confirmation, of their shame or responsibility for the abuse. Severely traumatised clients who are terrified of connecting to others find that their only relationship is to their wound(s). This is typically seen in traumatophilia in which the client is submersed and preoccupied by their trauma and the need to revisit traumatic experiences. The ensuing excitation and arousal compel the individual to pursue stimuli that represent trauma, sexual abuse or sexual violence through pornography, films or literature. This can be extremely distressing and confusing for clients, and it is essential that you do not judge or shame the client in this and help them understand how this was conditioned in early childhood and continues to exert control over their sexual arousal and behaviour.

Remember
Clients who can only have a relationship with their wound and are preoccupied with trauma-related stimuli are re-enacting aspects of their trauma and this is not evidence of their depravity.

WORKING WITH SEXUAL COMPULSIONS AND SEX ADDICTIONS

When working with clients with sexual compulsions and sex addictions it is critical to understand their behaviour within the context of shame and ensure that they are not judged. In addition you will need to work with the underlying shame rather than just focusing on managing the compulsion or addiction. It is also essential to distinguish between sexual obsession and compulsions that are enacted in fantasy and those that are enacted through sexual contact with others. If the sexual fantasies are dominated by sexual violence or rape you will need to do a safeguarding risk assessment with regard to posing a danger to vulnerable children or adults. This will need to be done sensitively as many people do not act on their sexual fantasies, while others do. You need to ensure that you are supported in this through supervision and peer consultation.

Warning
You will need to assess the likelihood that sexual fantasies dominated by sexual violence or rape will be enacted, and perform a safeguarding risk assessment to ensure that vulnerable children or adults are protected.

The highly intrusive thoughts characteristic of sexual compulsion and sex addictions usually manifest as sexual fantasies, obsessions and preoccupations which are heightened by masturbation or supercharged through sexualised encounters and environments (Carnes 2008). Typically sexual behaviour is primarily with the self rather than partners as this allows full control to escape into the ultimate fantasy without interference by others. This is usually achieved through masturbating to online or print pornography, or cybersex. Preoccupation with sex as a solitary process is usually underpinned by shame and despair associated with sexual contact which is often disappointing. A lot of time and energy is invested in searching for sources of stimulation or in the gathering, maintenance and utilisation of images and collections (Sanderson 2004), or finding the optimal online pornographic website or printed pornographic images. These are often categorised, with complex inventories, and guarded in case resources dry up. Due to the concomitant shame the addict may be caught in a binge/purge cycle which needs to be addressed in the therapeutic process.

Most fantasy sex is conducted anonymously online, although some may share their obsessions or fantasies with anonymous partners who have similar fantasies. Some addicts, however, habituate to these fantasies and need to heighten or modify the fantasies by escalating their content, or acting on the fantasy and engaging in risky behaviour (Sanderson 2004). This can lead to the pursuit of anonymous sex, voyeurism, exhibitionism, paying for sex, inflicting or receiving pain and humiliation or the exploitation of vulnerable others (see Chapter 8).

For some the preoccupation and obsession focuses on a specific person, in which they fantasise about having a relationship with that person without any basis for that in reality. This commonly leads to stalking to declare and prove their love. While the object of desire is typically a celebrity or public figure, it can also be someone known to the individual, or in their social world. This is a form of erotomania, or what is called de Clerambault's syndrome, in which unrequited love allows the individual to have all the feelings associated with being in love, being in a relationship and having sex. As the object of desire does not reciprocate these feelings it enables the individual to give free rein to their fantasy whilst avoiding relational or sexual shame.

Some addicts are preoccupied with fantasies of multiple sexual relations in which the primary motivation is conquest and novelty. The predominant feature is that once the object of desire has been captivated and sexual conquest has been achieved the addict moves on to seek a new partner with whom to repeat the pattern. Many addicts report that, once having had sex, the romance is over and they need to find someone else to heighten their arousal. This cycle is often accompanied and fuelled by alcohol, which allows them to behave in a shameless way, including coercing or drugging potential partners to ensure a constant supply of novel sexual encounters. Some addicts prefer to have sex with anonymous partners, usually in public or semi-public places in which they risk being seen. The emphasis is on avoiding relationships and frequent and novel sexual encounters that reinforce and intensify shame. This is also characteristic in many sadomasochistic encounters in which the preoccupation is with receiving or inflicting pain and humiliation. A commonality that links many of the sexual compulsions and addictions is secrecy and the use of money to gain access to sexual behaviour, which further fuels the sense of shame.

It is clear from the above that unbearable feelings of shame can be so overwhelming that sex addiction becomes only one of many soothing behaviours. A range of other substances such as alcohol, drugs and food or process addictions such as gambling and relationships can be used to numb shame-based thoughts or feelings. What they have in common is the need to regulate overwhelming feelings of shame and humiliation through substances or behaviours that calm, soothe or numb aversive internal states, even if these prove to be a further source of shame. The next chapter will look at the range of addictions and addictive behaviours in greater depth to uncover the relationship between shame and addiction.

SUGGESTED READING

Nathanson, D.L. (1992) *Shame and Pride: Affect, Sex, and the Birth of the Self.* New York: W.W. Norton.

Sanderson, C. (2006) *Counselling Adult Survivors of Child Sexual Abuse,* 3rd edn. London: Jessica Kingsley Publishers.

Sanderson, C. (2010) *The Warrior Within: A One in Four Handbook to Aid Recovery from Childhood Sexual Abuse and Violence.* London: One in Four.

Sanderson, C. (2013) *Counselling Skills for Working with Trauma: Healing from Child Sexual Abuse, Sexual Violence and Domestic Abuse.* London: Jessica Kingsley Publishers.

7

SHAME, ADDICTIONS AND COMPULSIONS

There is considerable scientific, clinical and anecdotal evidence that shame is inextricably linked to addiction and plays a central role in the development and maintenance of addictions and compulsions (Carnes 1983, 2001; Flores 2004; Khantzian 2014; Potter-Efron 2011). Early attachment experiences which are disorganised or where the primary caregiver is a source of shame are a fertile ground for developing chronic shame as the child is conflicted in its need for emotional attunement and fear of rejection or ridicule. As a result the child learns that basic needs for connection are shameful (Herman 2007) and the attachment system is de-activated to avoid the constant shame of rejection and abandonment. In this the opportunities for the regulation of unbearable emotions are reduced and the child is unable to learn how to comfort or soothe themselves. It is these impaired relational dynamics and lack of healthy affect regulation that provides a fertile ground for developing addictions and compulsions.

This chapter will look at how defences against shame can lead to addictions and compulsions as a form of escape and distraction from overwhelming thoughts and feelings. It will also highlight how addictions become a substitute for relationships and a way to avoid intimacy and closeness and lack of relational worth. Emphasis will also be placed on enhancing awareness of the role of shame in the addiction cycle and how the loss of control becomes yet another source of shame. The saturation of past and present shame leads to increased reliance on external sources of affect regulation, which makes it harder to relinquish the drug of choice. The role of shame, control and affect in compulsions is also explored, especially in obsessive compulsive disorders such as Pure O.

ADDICTION AS A DEFENCE AGAINST SHAME

One of the defences against shame proposed by Nathanson (1992) is avoidance, in which clients feel compelled to ward off the conscious experience of shame by avoiding it at all costs. This can be achieved either by by-passing shame through dissociation, or through numbing unbearable feelings of shame through a range of addictive behaviours. These commonly cluster around the use of substances such as alcohol, drugs or food, compulsive behaviours or process addictions, such as gambling, sex addiction, exercise, thrill seeking, compulsive spending or work. In substance dependency clients use external substances either to suppress or numb feelings or to induce a state of euphoria through neuro and bio-chemical changes. Process addictions have the same aim in regulating mood and inner experiencing, albeit through compulsive behaviours that produce internal neuro and bio-chemical changes stimulating endorphins and adrenaline, as seen in sex addiction, exercise and thrill-seeking behaviour.

Irrespective of the type of addiction the desire is to avoid overwhelming feelings of shame, inadequacy and abandonment. However, the relief of emotional pain is always temporary, which reinforces the need to self-medicate. This sets up a dependency cycle which in turn becomes a source of shame, especially if the client was shamed for their dependency needs in early childhood. In addition the loss of control over the compulsion or desire for the drug of choice can evoke shame as the client sets unrealistic expectations on themselves to be in control of their thoughts, feelings and actions. Failure to be in control activates past shame, which reinforces a sense of failure and inadequacy, and the client is catapulted into a cycle of shame where past shame is evoked and intensifies current shame. As the feelings of shame heighten, the need to avoid them escalates, the desire to submit to the addiction and compulsive behaviour increases, and the cycle of addiction is re-activated (see Figure 7.1).

Figure 7.1 The cycle of addiction

Paradoxically, the euphoria and intoxication leads to dis-inhibition and thus removes the need or impulse to hide shame (Tomkins 1963) which has the potential to unleash shameful thoughts or behaviour. This is most prominent when individuals under the influence of alcohol, drugs or compulsive sexual behaviour behave in a 'shameless' way, which they often regret when no longer intoxicated and their shame resurfaces. This coalesces into a never-ending cycle of shame in which shame is avoided, unleashed and then suppressed. This cycle is also commonly seen in thrill-seeking behaviour where the pursuit for the desired adrenaline rush to distract from inner emptiness, or lack of aliveness, leads to increasingly dangerous or shameful behaviours. This exacerbates the need to hide past and present shame, which can lead to isolation and avoidance of relationships in order to avoid exposure.

SHAME AND ADDICTION

As can be seen there are several intertwined dynamics in shame and addiction that serve a number of functions (see Figure 7.2). For many addicts, shame is the central organising principle of their identity and the primary cause of the addiction, which is then amplified by the addictive behaviour. The unbearable feelings that accompany shame are so incapacitating that they need to be avoided either through escape or distraction in the hope of suppressing them. One way to escape feelings is to suppress or numb them through alcohol, substances or compulsive behaviours (Potter-Efron 2001). In this addictions can be viewed as a form of self-medication, or 'sedative script' (Kaufman and Raphael 1996), which numbs and reduces the conscious experience of shame. Conversely, it can help the individual to transform feelings of inferiority, lack of potency or inadequacy into euphoria and a concomitant sense of superiority, power or dominance. As these altered states are only ever a temporary relief they need to be repeated, which can lead to dependency. As the dependency increases, the addict begins to fear the loss of the substance or compulsive behaviour more than exposure to shame. Over time the link between the original shame and the addiction may get severed as the addict justifies their behaviour. This makes it hard to explore the underlying shame as the addict is more preoccupied with getting access to their drug of choice.

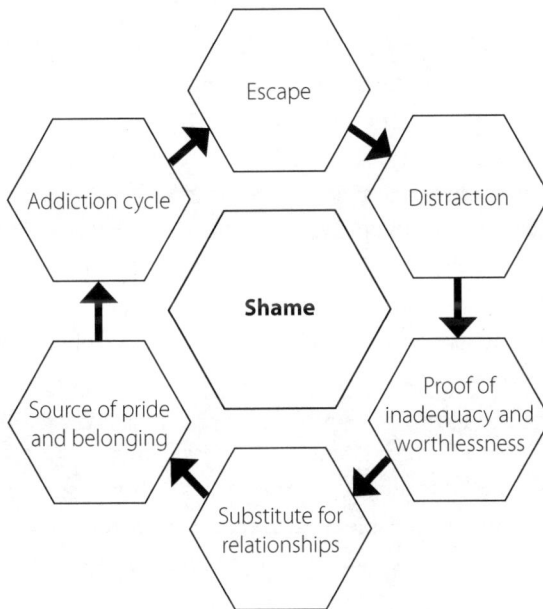

Figure 7.2 The relationship between shame and addiction

Much like escape, the function of distraction is to defend against the conscious awareness of shame and shame-based thoughts such as 'I am no good', 'I am less than' or 'I am defective'. These intrusive thoughts can become so intrusive that the person needs to distract from them. One way of doing this is to engage in the addictive behaviour or become preoccupied by the need to obtain the drug, or by planning compulsive behaviours (Potter-Efron 2011). Thus thinking about the drug of choice drowns out unbearable feelings and shame-based thoughts. One can see the link here between obsessive compulsive behaviour in which obsessive thoughts are cauterised, or avoided, through the enactment of a compulsive, ritualistic behaviour. This is commonly seen in rituals around alcohol and drugs, and in self-harming behaviour and in sex addiction (see Chapter 6).

ADDICTION AS A SUBSTITUTE FOR RELATIONSHIPS

Clinical research has shown that the origins of addiction lie in early developmental attachment failure with the primary caregiver and as such can be seen as an attachment disorder (Carnes 1983 1991; Flores 2004; Khantzian 2003, 2014). These early impaired attachment patterns are typically characterised by lack of empathic attunement and emotional regulation. This leads to an inability to self-regulate, and it is this dysregulation that creates a vulnerability to addiction as a way to soothe underlying emotional pain (Adams 2011; Schwartz and Brasted 1985). Baumeister (2003) argues that most addicts have not been able to internalise self-soothing strategies and have learned to escape or avoid strong feelings through the use of substances or process addictions.

When this is accompanied with shaming experiences in which the child is made to feel ashamed for basic human needs, or is made to feel defective or inadequate, the loss of the relationship is threatened and the child is cast into an abyss of loneliness and isolation (Trevarthen 2005). As a result the child associates closeness with shame and a source of terror rather than comfort. Such shaming and rejecting relationships cause deficits in the development of the individual's self-concept, which cannot be assuaged as they are unable to turn to others to get what they need.

The ridicule and deprivation of needs leads to object hunger (Flores 2004) and intolerable and unrealistic affects that are shameful to the addict, which impact on relational worth and ability to trust others. As relationships are perceived as further sources of shame, rejection and abandonment, comfort is sought in non-human sources such as substances or compulsive behaviour. Clients commonly report that their drug of choice is infinitely more dependable and predictable in providing relief from their pain than human relationships. In addition the shame that they feel for not being able to share their vulnerabilities, in not being able to control their addiction, and any concomitant shameful behaviour, forces them to hide away and suffer in isolation.

The avoidance of relationships is seen in a range of addictions. Katehakis (2009) found that an avoidant attachment pattern is linked to sexual addiction, while Carnes (1991) found that 78 per cent of the 204 sex addicts in his study came from disengaged or avoidant families. Furthermore, Karter (2014) found that 84 per cent of women with an addiction to slot machine gambling in her therapy group had a history of child sexual abuse and reported difficulties with relationships. These women reported that gambling provided the soothing that was often lacking in their relationships and that their addiction was a replacement partner who would never abandon her, let her down, betray her trust or judge or punish her. Thus the addiction serves not only to regulate emotions but also replaces unsatisfying and frightening relationships (Khantzian 2003; Kurtz 1981) and acts as proof and validation of intrinsic worthlessness.

As relationships are often difficult, painful, unpredictable and a potential source of shame they need to be avoided. Retreating into alcohol or drugs or compulsive behaviours serves to keep the addict safe from further hurt or shame. In this, the drug of choice becomes a steadfast friend which will not let the addict down or shame or reject them. As the addict becomes increasingly isolated, the drug becomes their only friend, which becomes a nominal price to pay to avoid shame through connection. In avoiding relationships addicts reduce opportunities to repair the underlying shame associated with early attachment experiences. It is not until they are in recovery that they will be able to repair these experiences through the therapeutic relationship. To repair the damage necessitates a healthy relationship which provides a consistent nurturing and mirroring environment to contain and manage destructive impulses in which shame is explored and authentic pride restored (Flores 2004; Khantzian 2013) (see Chapter 10).

In the absence of healthy relationships and limited sources of comfort, loving care or positive reinforcement addicts seek connection and pride through addiction (Potter-Efron 2002). A sense of belongingness is found in spending time with fellow addicts where the addiction is normalised and they feel accepted. For some this can also become a source of pride in terms of ability to consume prodigious amounts of alcohol or drugs, sculpting a perfect body through excessive exercise or body building, or success by working inordinate hours. Being able to hold their drink without getting a hangover, consume substantial amounts of drugs, take extreme risks or be the 'bad boy' can elevate the addict's status among their peers and become a potent source of pride. This creates a sense of accomplishment in which the addict, perhaps for the first time, feels a sense of achievement rather than failure, inadequacy or shame. The need for connection to other addicts and the sense of pride may be difficult for clients to relinquish and you will need to be sensitive to this rather than re-shaming them by guiding them gently towards more healthy sources of pride and belongingness such as group therapy, AA and the appropriate 12-Step Programme.

As the addiction takes hold, the addict becomes entrapped in the cycle of addiction, which reinforces their sense of inadequacy and shamefulness. The cycle of addiction becomes a self-fulfilling prophecy by proving on a regular basis how useless and fundamentally flawed and defective the addict really is and their addiction becomes an advertisement of their shame (Potter-Efron 2011). This is especially the case when through intoxication or euphoria the addict behaves in a shameful or shameless way. Conversely, some addicts use the addiction as a way to by-pass early or historical experiences of shame by becoming preoccupied by the shame that accompanies the addiction cycle and associated stigmatisation. You will need to ensure when working with clients who have an addiction or compulsive behaviours that they understand how their addiction serves to continuously re-contaminate them with shame.

OBSESSIONS AND COMPULSIONS

Shame is also highly correlated with a range of other compulsive behaviours such as self-harm, eating disorders and OCD, especially Pure O. 'Pure O' is a form of OCD in which unwanted obsessive thoughts intrude, causing considerable distress. Unlike OCD wherein obsessive thoughts and the concomitant anxiety are suppressed by engaging in compulsive ritual behaviours such as checking or hand washing, in Pure O the compulsion manifests as unseen mental rituals such as rumination and repetitive thoughts (see Figure 7.3).

As the content of the intrusive unwanted thoughts is typically pernicious the individual is too ashamed to share or reveal these to others and thus has no opportunity to gain reassurance from loved ones. Clients who suffer from Pure O may also be too ashamed to reveal these unwanted thoughts in the therapeutic process and you will have to be mindful of the role that shame plays in discussing these intrusive thoughts.

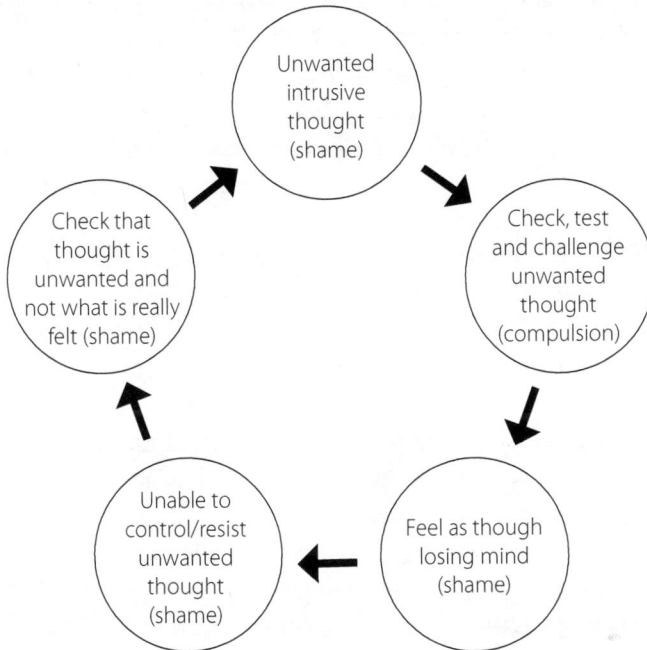

Figure 7.3 The Pure O cycle

THE ROLE OF SHAME IN PURE O

People with Pure O are typically plagued by unrelenting, intrusive and unwanted thoughts that they despise. These intrusive thoughts cluster around unjustified fears that they have, or will, cause harm such as through a car accident or murder, inflicting sexual abuse or rape – often on vulnerable others such as children or the elderly – turning against one's god or religion, switching sexual orientation, being unfaithful to a partner, or shouting something offensive or inappropriate. These fears are exacerbated as they often feature loved ones such as partners or ex-partners, parents, siblings or children. What is common in all these thoughts is an over-inflated sense of responsibility, shame and guilt for things they fear they have done, or might do. These thoughts are often so abhorrent that they create inordinate worry which cannot be allayed and as a result becomes amplified with the sufferer trapped in a cycle of torment.

These unwanted thoughts are fuelled by the deepest, innermost fears that exist within all of us but are magnified to the most extreme scenarios. Typically they represent what is considered to be most heinous in a particular society or historical time. Currently many people with Pure O fear that they are paedophiles or rapists as they are the most vilified and despised members of society. What is particularly distressing to those with Pure O is that the unwanted thoughts are the opposite of the sufferers' true feelings or actions. As they are unable to alleviate their fears they become convinced that they will lose control and act on their unwanted thoughts by harming someone, or that they lost control in the past and caused harm for which they need to be punished.

When working with clients with Pure O it is critical to remind them that these unwanted thoughts are just thoughts and not to give in to them but to let them pass. Rather than try to reassure the client, what is more helpful is just to accept the thoughts as thoughts rather than facts or predictions about what might happen in the future. You can help clients in this by encouraging them to practise the art of mindfulness to help them accept and let the thoughts go (see Chapter 10).

MINDFULNESS TO MANAGE DIFFICULT THOUGHTS

To help clients in the practice of mindfulness you may need to start with simple breathing exercises and 60-second mindfulness (see Chapter 10) until they feel comfortable in the practice of mindfulness and ready to tackle more difficult thoughts. It is important to emphasise throughout that thoughts are not facts; they are simply what the mind is saying or creating at any given moment, and learning to accept them without judgement is vital. The following exercise practises mindfulness with the client:

Exercise
Mindfulness of difficult thoughts
Encourage your client to sit comfortably while you say the following:

Start with a mindfulness of the breath. Sit with your breath for a few minutes. Now bring your awareness to something that is difficult for you in your life.

It may be thoughts of an event in the past that was painful or distressing, it may be something in your life in the present time that is causing you painful feelings, or it may be something you are worried about in the future. Allow yourself to bring your attention to focus on one of these worrying thoughts.

Notice what is happening in your body right now as you have these thoughts. Are there places of tension or tightness? What is happening to your breathing? Don't try to modify the sensations in your body, just allow yourself to notice them with curiosity. Notice now the thoughts that are going through your mind; just notice them as thoughts. Remember, thoughts are not facts, they are simply what your mind is saying or creating at any given moment. They may be based in factual events, but they are simply the mind thinking. Think about the thoughts you are having. Notice them as they change and notice each new thought as it replaces the previous one.

As you continue to notice the sensations in your body, see if you can put words to some of the feelings that come with these difficult and painful thoughts. They may be feelings like sadness, hurt, anger, loneliness, fear or pain. Feelings may be difficult, they may be deeply uncomfortable, but they are not right or wrong. They are simply part of your present moment experience.

Allow your awareness to move between the thoughts you are having as you notice them, the physical sensations you are having as you notice them, and the feelings and emotions you are having as you notice them. Finally, bring your awareness and attention back to your breathing for a while, noticing the physical sensation of taking breath into your body and releasing it.

SHAME, ADDICTIONS AND COMPULSIONS IN THERAPY

As shame pervades addictions and compulsions, both in terms of causality and the cycle of addiction, it is critical that you address both underlying, historical shame and shame that is due to the addiction (Flores 2004; Khantzian 2012 2013; Potter-Efron 2011). Most addicts in recovery tend to focus on the shame that is elicited in the cycle of addiction and believe falsely that once they give up their addiction their shame will evaporate and they will be shame free. You will need to disabuse them of this and help to make the link between the origins of their shame and how it is maintained and intensified through the cycle of addiction. If the underlying shame is not addressed the likelihood of relapse is increased as the client still feels inadequate and worthless.

Exploring and working through early shame experiences can be terrifying and needs to be appropriately paced until the client has mastered some of the necessary skills to manage shame more effectively (see Chapter 10). Throughout the process you will need to accept the client's shame rather than deny or avoid it so that the client can accept their shame rather than defend against it. Most importantly you need to provide a safe and secure therapeutic relationship in which the client doesn't feel judged or re-shamed. With this in place they can work through their shame and move towards self-acceptance, self-compassion and authentic pride.

SUGGESTED READING

Carnes, P. J. (1983) *Sexual Addiction*. Minneapolis, MN: Camp Care.

Carnes, P. J. (2001) *Out of the Shadows: Understanding Sexual Addiction*, 3rd edn. Center City, MN: Hazelden.

Carnes, P. J. (2008) 'The perfect storm: Assessing for sex addiction.' *Counsellor 9*, 3, 50–58.

Crossan, C. (2014) 'Technology, Attachment, and Sexual Addiction Risk.' In R. Gill (ed.) *Addictions from an Attachment Perspective: Do Broken Bonds and Early Trauma Lead to Addictive Behaviour?* London: Karnac Books.

Flores, P.J. (2004) *Addictions as an Attachment Disorder*. Lanham, ML: Jason Aronson.

Katehakis, A. (2009) 'Affective neuroscience and the treatment of sexual addiction.' *Sexual Addiction and Compulsivity 16* 1–31.

Khantzian, E.J. (2012) 'Reflections on treating addictive disorders: A psychodynamic perspective.' *The American Journal on Addictions 21* 274–279.

Khantzian, E.J. (2014) 'The Self-Medication Hypothesis and Attachment Theory: Pathways for Understanding and Ameliorating Addictive Suffering.' In R. Gill (ed.) *Addictions from an Attachment Perspective: Do Broken Bonds and Early Trauma Lead to Addictive Behaviour?* London: Karnac Books.

Potter-Efron, R. (2002) *Shame, Guilt and Alcoholism* 2nd edn. New York, Haworth Press.

Potter-Efron, R. (2011) 'Therapy with Shame-Prone Alcoholic and Drug Dependent Clients.' In R.L. Dearing and J.P. Tangney (eds) *Shame in the Therapy Hour*. Washington, DC: American Psychological Association.

8

SHAME, RAGE AND VIOLENCE

The defence against shame seen in addictions is avoidance, in which clients seek to numb their unbearable feelings through alcohol, drugs or food, or distract themselves by engaging in risky behaviour. Alternatively, some clients will try to compensate for feelings of shame and humiliation through attacking the self or attacking others (Nathanson 1992). In this they will either take the shame on themselves by becoming invisible so they cannot be shamed, or they will seek to displace their shame onto others through anger and rage. The defences in attacking the self range from modesty, self-effacement, self-deprecating humour, shyness, deference and self-neglect through to more active self-attacks such as self-sabotage, self-debasement, self-humiliation, masochism, self-injury and suicidal ideation and behaviour to annihilate the self. In attacking others the focus is on turning rage or humiliated fury onto others through either covert anger, as seen in banter, teasing and put-downs, or overt expressions of hostility, aggression, violence, sexual violence and murder.

This chapter will look at the relationship between shame and rage and how this is enacted. The focus will be on how shame is converted into anger and rage and then directed at others. This can lead to shameless acts of rage and violence to disavow shame through shaming and humiliating others. Attention will be focused on the shame and rage cycle and how this manifests in abusive relationships such as domestic violence. It will also explore how shame-related rage can become eroticised, leading to the sexual abuse and sexual exploitation of children, sexual violence, rape and sexually motivated murder.

THE ROLE OF SHAME IN RAGE AND VIOLENCE

The unbearable nature of shame makes it difficult to acknowledge and express. This is in part due to the need to conceal it not just from others but also the self. Many clients are aware of their shame but are too ashamed to reflect on it as they fear re-activating old shame wounds. As a result it lurks outside of conscious awareness yet is easily inflamed when threatened with rejection or abandonment. As there is little or no conscious recognition of shame, when shame-based rage is detonated it is typically experienced as being outside of the self, and caused by others rather than emanating from within. You will need to help clients to recognise that explosive rage is primarily elicited by an internal active shame wound which needs to be expunged. The release of tension experienced through the discharge of rage onto others is a powerful way to purge the self from the toxicity of chronic shame. In believing that the rage has been elicited by others, clients often rationalise their rage and violence as a legitimate response, which can lead to a sense of entitlement in expressing rage as it releases the pressure of shame. Such shame-based entitlement rage is commonly seen in domestic abuse, racism, personality disorders and sexual violence.

ATTACK SELF AS A DEFENCE AGAINST SHAME

The attack self defence against shame allows the shamed person to control the amount of external shame by inflicting it on the self. In this, self-shame signals an acceptance of shame through self-effacement or using humour to deflect the shame. In acknowledging and overtly expressing shame it allows the shame-prone person to remain affiliated and connected to others, and minimises the risk of rejection or abandonment. To achieve this, individuals have to render themselves invisible so as to reduce the likelihood of becoming the source for shame, although invariably attacking the self confirms their sense of worthlessness and that they deserve to be shamed.

The conflict between being invisible and the biological imperative of needing to be visible can result in anger and rage. As expressing anger risks more shame, it is safer to direct this anger at the self for having to submit to shame from others. This can lead to more active forms of self-attack such as self-injury, self-mortification, suicidal ideation and suicidal behaviour to destroy and annihilate the shamed self. Rage turned against the self is most commonly seen in eating disorders such as bulimia, where shame-based hunger is linked to food, which after being ingested has to be violently evacuated through vomiting, and anorexia, in which embodied shame can only be eliminated through starvation and wasting away. Shame rage is also prevalent in self-injury where the shame can only be released through cutting, carving or lacerating the body. In all of these the exposure or masking of shame is controlled by the individual rather than others.

In turning anger inward the individual is able to stay connected to others at considerable cost to the physical and psychological integrity of the self. The attack self defence against shame is also typically seen in abusive relationships and domestic violence where the victim is entrapped in a cycle of shame and humiliation that they cannot challenge for fear of more violence or abuse and in which they have no choice but to submit (see Figure 8.1).

ATTACK OTHER AS A DEFENCE AGAINST SHAME

The attack other defence is often the most primitive of the defences against shame and is typically triggered by shame around dependency, powerlessness, weakness, vulnerability, competency, physical size or strength. When shame is re-invoked in adulthood through real or imagined insults, disapproval, criticism or being rebuffed it can trigger silent rage or humiliated fury which compels individuals to annihilate those who have exposed them in their shame. This activates early shame wounds in which the child fears rejection and abandonment which could only be defended through rage. As these primitive wounds are not always in conscious awareness the individual is unable to link their rage to shame and early impaired bonds and recognise that by unleashing their rage they keep people at bay and thereby reinforce their isolation and desolation. The corrosive effect of rage, which blocks empathy and compassion while boosting contempt, ultimately prevents respectful and trusting relationships and the individual is trapped in an endless shame-rage cycle in which shame is intensified (see Figure 8.1).

In essence, anger and rage represent emotional substitutes for shame, allowing the individual to disown or by-pass shame (Lewis 1992) through humiliated fury which is expunged by projecting it into others. By shaming others through humiliation, or verbal or physical threats or assaults, the other is devalued, objectified and dehumanised. In this the other becomes the shamed one, while the attacker is flooded with a sense of power and control, hubristic pride and feels entitled to feel rage. In addition, it ensures that, rather than being invisible when saturated in shame, the attacker feels all powerful and highly visible when overpowering the victim. If left unchecked the rage can be eroticised and enacted through sexual violence, sado-masochism and sex addiction.

THE ROLE OF RAGE AS A RELEASE FROM SHAME

Anger is a natural response to pain, fear, sadness and frustration which is usually conscious and relatively easily dissipated. In contrast rage is a more overwhelming threat to the perceived annihilation of self from symbolic sources such as rejection or abandonment. As such, fears of annihilation are often fused with early experiences of shame, becoming highly combustible when reignited and bursting forth as rage and humiliated fury and potentiated violence. In response to the perceived threat to the physical or psychological self the biologically mediated alarm system of fight, flight or freeze response is activated. Freezing entails being drowned and overwhelmed by shame with no means of escape, while running away is an overt demonstration of weakness and vulnerability, both of which are sources for more shame. In contrast the fight response elicits anger, rage or violence which transforms the feeling of shame into a semblance of self-confidence (Asser 2014). This is a more active and potent way of managing rejection, ridicule or loss of respect by replacing shame with hubristic pride.

To avoid being overwhelmed by crippling feelings of shame and to restore respect, rage is elicited to defend against wounded pride and expunge feelings of shame and humiliation, or being seen as a victim. However, this is only ever fleeting, as the loss of control and shameless acts of violence that usually accompany shame-based rage intensify the shame, leading to more acts of violence (see Figure 8.1). It is also a potent way of masking shame by deflecting shame from the self to the other (Gilligan 2001). In addition the adrenaline, cortisol and physiological arousal in anger and rage can become addictive in making the person feel more alive and energised, which is the antithesis to the enervating effects associated with shame. This is most pronounced in sexual violence and sex addictions.

As rage is primarily driven by a cascade of neuro and bio-chemical hormones it is rarely under voluntary control. Potter-Efron (2007) argues that there four types of rage that come from different sources. These consist of survival rage that occurs in response to physical threat, impotent rage as a result of feeling threatened and utterly helpless, attachment rage in response to being abandoned or rejected by an attachment figure, and shame rage that is elicited as a result of feeling ridiculed, humiliated or shamed. Shame rage can also be elicited in other situations that might evoke shame such as loss of prestige or status, loss of potency and function or a deeply embedded sense of inadequacy, all of which have the potential to threaten self-esteem and sense of control.

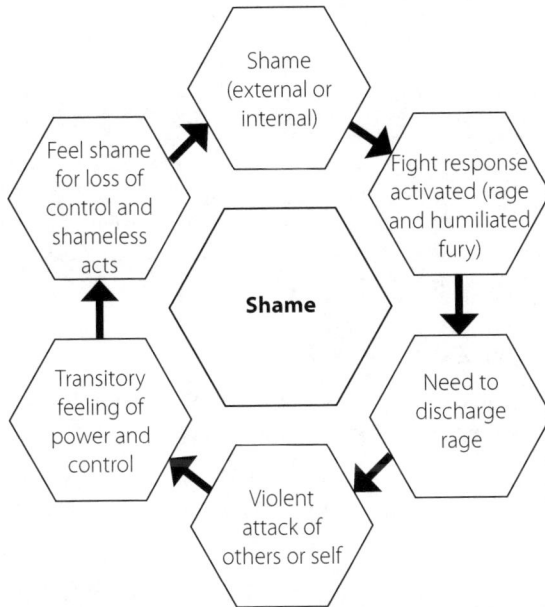

Figure 8.1 Shame-rage cycle

Shame rage has a number of other psychologically driven functions beyond threat management, in particular to induce shame in the other, to assert power by penetrating the other through overt or covert invasion of physical or psychological boundaries or to gain revenge through retaliation. Moreover, rage and violence are potent ways of disguising the truth by doing the opposite of what is actually felt or needed. They are ways of proclaiming invulnerability, independence and autonomy to cover up and suppress the shameful need for love, closeness, intimacy and care. This is most apparent in domestic abuse (DA) where the primary indicator for shame is the presence of explosive rage, humiliated fury and verbal and physical violence (see p.156).

Rage elicited by rejection and abandonment is also seen more subtly in clients who are self-sacrificing in taking care of others while masking a secret hope or expectation that this will be repaid with love and affection. When this is not forthcoming rage is detonated accompanied by a sense of entitlement in response to the lack of appreciation and care of others. Once the rage is dissipated the reality becomes clear again and the recognition of what has happened becomes intolerable, stimulating more shame which is either directed at the self or others, and the shame-rage cycle is repeated again. You need to be aware that as a practitioner you may also be vulnerable to this, especially when clients do not voice or show their appreciation of you. To avoid escalation of a shame-rage cycle you need to be aware of your own shame triggers (see Chapter 11).

! Warning

You need to be aware of your own potential for shame-based rage to ensure that this is not enacted when clients fail to show appreciation or are hostile and rejecting.

RELATIONAL SHAME AND RAGE

Shame is often activated in early relational experiences in which the child had to conceal infantile dependency needs for loving care or when threatened with rejection through withdrawal of love or support. To a young child the threat of abandonment is boundless and is the equivalent of annihilation or death. The ensuing terror increases dependency needs which are seen as shameful and must be concealed from self and others (Gilligan 2001). The shame associated with dependency and vulnerability fuse into a sense of being inadequate and unlovable, which when intensified is transformed into rage and hate and the impulse for violence.

This is compounded by the lack of attunement and mirroring characteristics of such early shame-based experiences which hijack the development of self-esteem (Dutton, van Ginkel and Starzomski 1995). As the child and later adult cannot derive self-esteem from within they become dependent on external sources. This leads to 'mirror hunger' (Sanderson 2013) in which the individual constantly seeks acknowledgement of their existence and worth through what is mirrored to them by others. In the absence of not being able to feel good about the self there is an increased dependency on others to provide the necessary self-esteem and release from shame. This places monumental pressure on partners to constantly mirror and reflect back positive esteem, which is hard to maintain or sustain consistently. Whenever there is a rupture in the reflection the shameful dependency and threat of abandonment returns to fuel the shame-based rage. In addition, giving the power to provide self-esteem and self-approval to an external source reinforces the individual's dependency, that produces more shame which is then converted into rage and violence to mask the shame. This is classically seen in DA where shameful dependency needs are hidden yet manifest in the dependency on the partner to be mirrored, loved and taken care of (see Figure 8.2).

DOMESTIC ABUSE

As the dependency needs are so great any sign of independent thought or life has to be obliterated, which results in the control and violence associated with DA. The need to conceal the shame and dependency needs means that they are converted into violence and repeated assaults to prevent the partner from having a separate, independent existence, as this is seen as evidence of abandonment and rejection. Many domestic abusers initially 'love bomb' their prospective partner in order to make the partner dependent on them and to ensure that they will never be abandoned (Sanderson 2008). This deflects the dependency needs away from the abuser and onto the partner who is expected to be totally devoted to the abuser. When there is any perceived change in the degree of devotion the abuser sees this as a threat of abandonment or rejection which needs to be punished so that the dependency needs are not exposed.

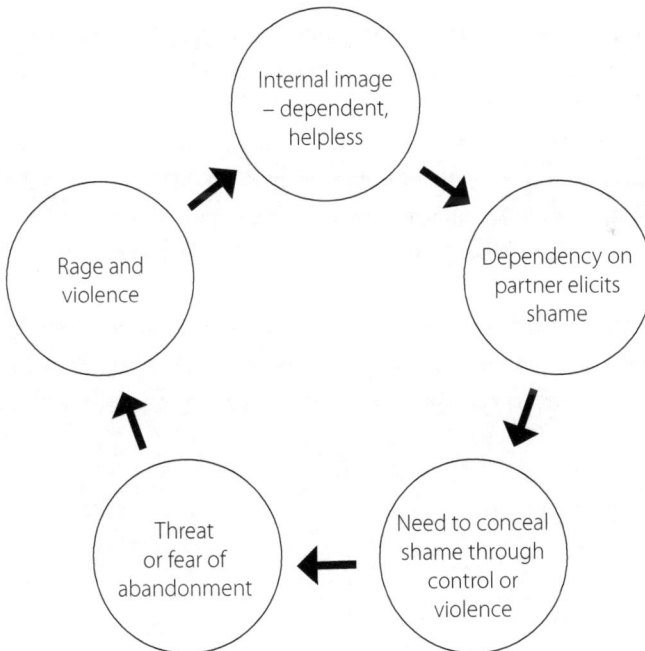

Figure 8.2 Shame-rage cycle in DA

As the perpetrator has disavowed the sense of inadequacy, self-contempt and shame, the partner absorbs these feelings, making the abuse more acceptable and less frightening (Motz 2014). This projected shame plus the partner's own shame renders them helpless, which generates even more shame as they submit to the abuser. As it is too dangerous to release their shame through rage, the partner turns this onto themselves. In attacking the self they begin to feel that they deserve the abuse and violence as punishment for their inadequacy, dependency and shame. In addition, the partner can deny and suppress their own feelings of rage and humiliated fury as the abuser has enacted the feelings for them (Motz 2008, 2014). In order to experience any sense of potency they focus on the importance they have in the abuser's life, even if only as a vessel for their rage and violence. This traumatic bonding in which the abuser and partner are fused together accounts for why many partners find it hard to leave, for fear that the abuser would not be able to live without them (Sanderson 2008, 2010).

When working with perpetrators or survivors of DA you will need to be aware that DA is not an event but a complex process (Motz 2014) in which both partners fear abandonment and project their unacceptable parts into the other, leading to polarisation of either complete dependency and vulnerability or murderous rage. In projecting their disavowed shame, dependency and vulnerability into the partner the abuser finds satisfaction in attacking this disavowed part of themselves. As their fear and helplessness are embodied in their partner it enables them to find a rationale for brutalising the partner in the way they were brutalised. The violence is also a way of marking the partner's body, which leaves a visible stain of shame on them and which helps the abuser to triumph over their own shame wounds. This complex process of traumatic bonding and projection of disavowed shame is also seen commonly in physical abuse, CSA and sexual violence.

SHAME, TRAUMA AND RAGE

These dynamics are also seen in physical abuse, CSA and sexual violence where unacceptable shame and vulnerability are projected into the child or victim and the abuser gains gratification in attacking these disavowed parts of themselves. As the victim has no choice but to absorb the disavowed shame their own shame is intensified (Sanderson 2014). This leads to distorted beliefs that they are complicit in the abuse and that they were to blame, and that this is evidence of their intrinsic badness. Often this is compounded by messages from the abuser that the victim seduced them, that they are bad, dirty and should be ashamed of themselves (Sanderson 2006). As in DA, it is too dangerous for the victim to allow the shame to be converted into rage which means their only option is to submit, which is a further source of shame. The overwhelming feeling of shame leads many survivors of physical or sexual violence to attack the self rather than externalise their rage. It is crucial when working with this client group to differentiate between legitimate rage as a response to their abuse and shame-based rage, and find healthy and constructive ways of releasing appropriate rage.

Remember

To facilitate the release of shame you need to help clients to differentiate between legitimate rage and shame-based anger.

Unleashing rage, including legitimate rage, needs to be carefully managed as shame inhibits empathy through excessive negative focus on self which precludes focus on others. If the rage is not regulated and discharged in a constructive way it can lead to hostility towards others which only serves to replicate the abuse, which in turn can be a further source of shame. In addition you will need to guard against being drawn into a 'blame boomerang' (Dalenberg 2000) in which survivors externalise their shame by consistently blaming others, including you (see Chapter 11). This can lead to undifferentiated and global hostility which only serves to amplify their isolation and alienation. You will also need to moderate your responses to such rage so that the shame-rage cycle can be interrupted.

As shame is inextricably linked to trauma it is highly likely that current shame will trigger reminders of the abuse and trauma, and concomitant submissive defence responses. These are then typically replayed in the therapeutic process. You will need to be mindful of how these might be triggered in the counselling setting. In the presence of such triggers many survivors tend to dissociate from both reminders of the abuse and the accompanying shame. You will need to help them to stay grounded and work through whatever is being triggered. It is also critical to help them to regulate their dissociation to reduce the risk of revictimisation while in a hypo-aroused or dissociative state in their environment. In addition helping survivors to break the silence and secrecy of shame in a safe and secure setting allows them to share this with others and build a good support network outside the counselling relationships. This will help them to build more healthy relationships and empower them to resist potentially abusive relationships or degrading sexual encounters.

EROTICISED RAGE

Rage and anger have long been recognised as a central component in sexual violence (Carnes 2008) especially in response to humiliation and shame which needs to be avenged in an attempt to restore the self. Eroticised rage is characterised by preoccupation with sexual fantasies and obsessions which in some can evolve into acting out sexual violence in an opportunistic or predatory way. While some rage-fuelled fantasies are never enacted due to social inhibitions or lack of opportunity, others may manifest in more subtle ways through serial affairs, angry sex after fighting, public humiliation or through put-downs. Alternatively they can develop into sexual compulsions, sex addictions or a range of paraphilias which involve the humiliation and degradation of others, as seen in CSA, incest, sado-masochism and rape of the most vulnerable (Carnes 2008).

The focus in eroticised rage is to diminish sexual partners and to feel superior, which in turn is highly sexually arousing. Stoller (1975) argues that eroticised rage is an 'erotic form of hatred' in which anger is channelled through sexual behaviour that is socially unacceptable. This is rarely erotically pleasurable as anger and sex can be fused without pleasure, as seen in sexual compulsions and sex addictions. Sources of sexualised rage are usually a result of grievance, insufficiency of the self or vulnerability. Eroticised rage in response to a grievance has its origin in a real or imagined sense of betrayal which fuels the need for revenge. This can lead to sexual, emotional or physical abuse in which the perpetrator feels entitled to avenge their shame and humiliation.

Remember
Anger does not have to be pleasurable to be erotic.

The eroticised rage underpinning insufficiency of self is driven by a deeply felt sense of inadequacy and intrinsic worthlessness accompanied by a belief that no one will ever be able to meet their needs. As this is usually pushed out of conscious awareness the individual is not aware of the inner source of shame and believes that their rage is in response to external factors or people. Such eroticised rage is commonly accompanied by dissociation and the compartmentalisation of self which make it easier to degrade and violate others, especially those who are most vulnerable. Eroticised rage in response to vulnerability is often the most powerful as the disavowed vulnerability of the perpetrator is fused with the vulnerability of the victim, which can lead to out-of-control heightened sexual arousal which is then directed at the victim.

The desire in eroticised rage is primarily directed at the invasion of boundaries, either overtly or covertly. Covert invasion can occur without the victim's awareness such as voyeurism, stealing underwear or masturbating to photographs and print or online pornography. In this the perpetrator remains a detached observer who is empowered to invade, direct or control others who are not available, while preserving a sense of safety. Covert invasion can also be enacted through the abuse of trust. This facilitates sexual access to others through the abuse of power or positions of trust in which deeply rooted feelings of anger are used to justify breaches of trust. Such abusers use their charisma or kindness to make the victim feel special and seduce them into a dynamic in which abuse and sexual violence masquerade as affection and care, making it very difficult to unmask the seduction.

In overt invasion force or trickery is used to violate others, especially children and those who are not able to protect themselves. When directed against unwilling sexual partners who are able to protest, increased force or drugs such as Rohypnol are used. Such overt invasion commonly involves humiliation such as urinating or defecating on the victim or forcing them to perform degrading sexual acts. All of these are designed to expunge the perpetrator's shame by projecting it into, or inducing it in, the victim. Eroticised rage can also be directed at the self, as in eroticised self-hatred, in which the invasion or degradation is directed at the self through engaging in meaningless or degrading and humiliating sexual activities, staying in sexually abusive relationships, sado-masochism, promiscuity or sex work. The shame inherent in these serves to intensify the already existing shame and amplifies the need for more self-humiliation.

In order to stop the shame-rage cycle it is critical that underlying feelings of shame are explored along with any other addictive behaviours. It helps to understand the concept of eroticised rage as restoring personal parity and revenge and how this can underpin a range of client presentations such as couples caught in endless cycles of fighting followed by make-up or angry sex, or how the disinhibiting qualities of drugs and alcohol release sexualised anger. Most importantly you will need to challenge any gender stereotypes that you may have and acknowledge that, as shame is, gender neutral, rage and eroticised rage can manifest in both males and females. This suggests that shame-based rage is not gender dependent but an abuse of power and intimacy that can be enacted by either gender, especially in relationships where shame and vulnerability are most likely to be exposed. It is critical that the underlying shame is explored and processed in order to let go of rage.

Remember

Shame-based rage is a response to the abuse of power which can be experienced by either gender in intimate relationships.

In order to break the shame-rage cycle it is essential to identify and understand early shame experiences and what escalates the feelings in shame-based rage. Alongside this, shame-based messages, thoughts and beliefs that fuel rage need to be challenged and reconstructed. In addition it is crucial to learn to stay with the feeling of shame and regulate it rather than allowing it to escalate into rage. To facilitate this use the following exercise with your clients, which might also be useful for you to reflect on your own propensity for shame rage.

Exercise

Awareness of shame-based rage

Encourage your client to reflect on what triggers their impotent, helpless feelings and what sets these off. They should write these down and try to link them to early shame experiences. Take one and suggest they allow shame to arise, becoming aware of where it arises in the body, how it builds and escalates and when it threatens to detonate. They can then write down the physiological responses and draw these using different colours on a body outline. Help your client to use self-regulation skills to try to amplify and de-amplify the feeling of shame and rage so as to gain some control over them. Suggest they use mindfulness skills to try to let the feelings ebb and flow until they dissipate. Finally, ask the client to write down what they can do when the rage threatens to break through to circumvent a complete loss of control.

Use of this exercise over a period of time will help your client to monitor and track their shame-rage feelings until they diminish. Remind the client that rage, like any other feeling, is just a feeling and does not have to be acted upon. This work can be supported with grounding exercises that help to contain the feelings appropriately (for further exercises see Chapters 10 and 12). This will help clients to take responsibility for their actions and gain mastery and control over their feelings, which can become a powerful way to gain self-approval and self-esteem. It also helps to identify a pattern of violence that they may have learned in childhood or through other experiences, and to remind them that exposure to aggression and violence can shape how frustration and shame are managed. This allows the client to redefine themselves through self-compassion and self-acceptance and recognise that real strength is learning to allow feelings of hurt, disappointment and vulnerability.

This will help clients to find strength in being the one who chooses not to escalate the fight by removing themselves from the situation to calm down and reduce the risk of harming self or others. In this they will need to learn not to have the last word or make the final point and take pride in being the bigger person by managing their rage. Alongside this you will need to challenge the need to control and exert power over others and the sense of entitlement by challenging the client's belief that they have the right to act out when frustrated. This allows the client to replace grandiosity and hubristic pride with humility and compassion for self and others.

Remember
Chipping away at the shame-rage cycle takes time and patience to learn new skills and break old patterns of behaviour.

You will need to adopt a similar approach when working with eroticised rage and link this to early childhood experiences and how these have shaped clients' sexual script or sexual arousal template (see Chapter 6). In addition, it is essential to challenge any shame-based thoughts or distorted thinking and rationalisations that maintain eroticised rage and the sense of entitlement, which prevent the individual from taking responsibility. Whatever the source of rage, eroticised rage or humiliated fury, you will need to understand this within the context of a defence against shame. Rather than focusing on the acting out or behaviour you will need to address the underlying shame and work with it so that these destructive defences can be relinquished and the person can allow themselves to feel the shame, rather than escalating it. This will allow the client to experience their shame without judgement but through the prism of self-compassion and self-acceptance. Ways of working with shame in the safety of the therapeutic process are the focus of the next chapters, which introduce a range of skills and exercises to release shame and build shame resilience.

SUGGESTED READING

Dutton, D.G., van Ginkel, C. and Starzomski, A. (1995) 'The role of shame and guilt in the intergenerational transmission of abusiveness.' *Violence and Victims 10* 121–131.

Gilligan, J. (2001) *Violence: A Reflection on the National Epidemic.* New York: Pantheon Books.

Herman, J.L. (2007) 'Shattered shame states and their repair.' From the John Bowlby Memorial Lecture 10 March, Department of Psychiatry, Harvard University School.

Motz, A. (2001) *The Psychology of Female Violence.* London: Routledge.

Motz, A. (2014) *Toxic Couples: The Psychology of Domestic Violence.* London: Routledge.

Sanderson, C. (2008) *Counselling Survivors of Domestic Abuse.* London: Jessica Kingsley Publishers.

9

SHAME IN THERAPY

Shame is ubiquitous in therapy due to the inherent unequal power dynamics in the therapeutic relationship. Clients typically come to therapy because they are in need of help and in the process are asked to reveal themselves fully, and yet this is not reciprocated by the therapist whose narrative remains hidden. The very process of the 'client in need' seeking help from the 'expert' therapist sets up an unequal power dynamic in which both parties may experience shame. In revealing themselves clients are encouraged to talk about intimate thoughts, feelings, fears, needs and feelings of dependency under the scrutiny of the therapist's gaze. In turn, bearing witness to the client's exposure of self may invoke or re-evoke shame in the counsellor, especially when clients have experienced repeated shame, humiliation or abuse.

This chapter will look at a range of factors that elicit shame in the therapeutic process such as the nature of the therapeutic setting, client and counsellor experiences of shame and counsellor responses that can evoke shame in clients, and how these become entwined in the therapeutic process. To manage these most effectively, client and counsellor need to be aware and share responsibility for the creation and maintenance of shame in therapy. In acknowledging the role of shame in counselling, practitioners will enhance awareness of how shame manifests in the therapeutic process, how to work through the layers of shame, and how to regulate exposure to shaming experiences to minimise therapeutic ruptures. Equipped with this you will be able to help your clients to give shame a voice by breaking the silence and secrecy that fuels it, and thereby provide a powerful antidote to shame. Crucially, you need to balance acceptance of the client's shame with apposite reminders of the client's sources of healthy pride. A creative way to balance shame and healthy pride is to encourage clients to identify positive aspects of the self and record these either in their journal or on the 'tree of growth' in the following exercise.

⚙ Exercise
Balancing shame with healthy pride
Invite your client to record positive aspects of the self, strengths, achievements and sources of healthy pride in their journal or on the blank leaves on the tree template (see Figure 9.1), drawing in more leaves where relevant. They should record negative elements that they would like to let go of on the leaves on the ground – to be blown away by the wind. This is a working document which can be added to as they begin to recover and heal from shame, and move towards self-acceptance.

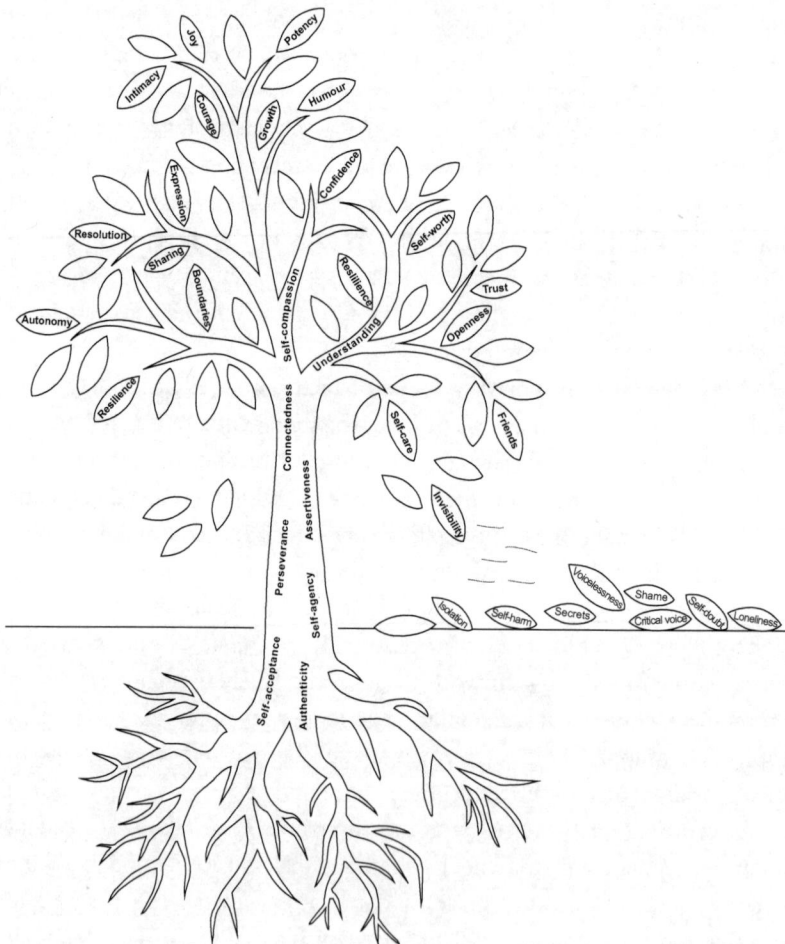

★ Figure 9.1 The tree of growth template
Copyright © Sanderson and Shalev 2015

Top tip

Emphasise that good aspects of the self can co-exist with the shamed parts in order to counterbalance and reduce the dominance of shame.

EFFECT OF THE COUNSELLING SETTING

The centrality of shame in the therapeutic process has been largely ignored in the practice of counselling and psychotherapy and yet is often the elephant in the room. Many counselling and psychotherapy training courses allude to it but do not devote specific attention to how shame manifests in the therapy room, and how it can be managed effectively to reduce therapeutic ruptures and premature termination (Dalenberg 2000). This is further exacerbated by the absence of discourse on shame in many well-established counselling and psychotherapy textbooks and journal articles. Brené Brown's (2005) content analysis of shame involving 75 major texts used by mental health professionals found that only one addressed shame. Such limited discourse makes it very difficult for both qualified counsellors and counsellors in training to identify the presence of shame in therapy and how it impacts on the therapeutic relationship. You must address your own, and your clients', shame in order to practise ethically and effectively and to recover from shame and build shame resilience.

Reflection

Take a moment to reflect on your counselling or psychotherapy training and examine where you learned the language of shame. Does your theoretical orientation address shame, and acknowledge its role in the therapeutic process? Did you have any lectures on shame? Did any of your trainers conduct research in this area? Which books did you read in which shame was addressed? Did your supervisor ever discuss shame with you? In your own therapy did you work on shame? Or did you learn about shame from your client work or supervisor?

To fully explore the nature and dynamics of shame you will need to develop a language with which to explore the impact that shaming experiences have had on clients and how these have prevented growth. To do this you need to provide a safe, empathic and compassionate space in which clients can talk about shame without fear of judgement or being re-shamed. In many respects, the therapeutic setting is designed to facilitate this, and yet it can also be the arena in which shame is reproduced, albeit unwittingly. The nature of shame is that it can be contagious in that the presence of shame can trigger further shame (Lewis 1971), including in the therapeutic setting, and in both client and practitioner. As shame is a social and self-conscious emotion that occurs primarily in relation to others it is inevitable that it will arise in the therapeutic relationship, especially when there is an unequal power dynamic.

Remember

You must address your own, and your clients', shame in order to practise ethically and effectively and to recover from shame and build shame resilience.

GROUP THERAPY

To reduce the intensity of the one-to-one therapeutic setting it can be helpful to explore shame in group therapy. This is a valuable modality as it offers compassionate support from other group members in an atmosphere of acceptance and equality. This can be a powerful source in which to experience inclusion, cooperation, mutuality and a sense of belonging, all of which are a powerful antidote to long-held feelings of shame and stigma (Herman and Schatzow 1984). Group therapy, however, needs to be carefully regulated to ensure that individual members are able to remain present and do not use shame defences to shame others. To guard against this group therapy may be more appropriate to use with clients who already have some awareness of their shame or who are part of a particular client group that have been stigmatised, such as survivors of childhood sexual abuse or those who struggle with addictions (Herman and Schatzow 1984; Potter-Efron and Potter-Efron 1989).

POWER DYNAMICS IN THE COUNSELLING SETTING

The practice of counselling is intrinsically shaming due to the inherent power imbalance (Herman 2011b). Clients who are in need and seek help enter the strange world of the therapy room with little or no knowledge of the process of therapy, what to expect or how to behave. They enter the counsellor's domain, in which the practitioner is seen as an authority figure who is all knowing, all powerful and psychologically healthy. Clients will have arrived in a state of anxiety, fear, trepidation and often shame as their vulnerability and dependency needs are exposed by the very act of seeking help. This implies that they are not competent or lack the skills to manage their lives, which is typically a source of shame.

The power differential is further amplified by the fact that the client is entering the counsellor's consulting room typically in a respectable location, or institution, at a time that is primarily convenient to the counsellor's schedule, and which may require payment. Entering this unfamiliar space can be daunting as it will be full of expectancies for both client and practitioner. The expectancies associated with the practice of therapy such as the therapeutic contract, boundaries of time, frequency, duration, confidentiality, payment and disclosure will be familiar to the counsellor and not yet known to the client. This not knowing can elicit shame anxieties and defences, making the initial session extremely fraught. To fully understand such anxieties you might find it helpful to reflect on your own experience when entering personal therapy during your training to recapture the impact of being a 'naïve client' in the presence of the 'all-knowing' therapist.

Reflection

Try to remember your very first session in your personal therapy. What were your hopes and expectations? What were your fears and anxieties? Did you experience an unequal power dynamic? How did this feel? How did you react? Did you experience any shame? If so, were you able to talk about it then, or later on? Reflect on these to remind you how clients might feel on entering your consulting room and how you can equalise the power in the therapeutic relationship.

What is often not known to the client is that the counsellor will also have anxieties, doubts and expectations of themselves in the first meeting. These vulnerabilities usually cluster around 'Do I have the necessary qualities, skills or expertise to help this client?', 'Will I be able to respond to the client in a way that is beneficial to him or her?', 'Will I have enough respect and liking for the client to sustain the work?' or 'Will I be able to connect to the client?' In this counsellors may be wracked with their own insecurities. The fear of being exposed in their self-doubts and inadequacy becomes a powerful source of shame which must be hidden at all costs. Thus both client and counsellor are concerned about being stripped bare or having their defects exposed. Thus, 'from the first meeting, much of the trajectory of the patient–therapist relationship is shaped by the shadow of shame, whether as a potential or as an actuality' (Jacobs 1995, p.86).

Reflection

Take a moment to reflect on some of the anxieties or fears that you have when first meeting a new client. Are these similar to anxieties you experience in other relationships? How do you manage these doubts or fears? How do you hide them from your clients? What would you like to do differently?

As clients are invariably unaware of the restrictions and limitations of therapy, and what is expected of them, it is essential that you are explicit when establishing the therapeutic contract to articulate the rules of engagement including what is expected from the client and what the client can expect from you. This will not only help in de-mystifying the therapeutic process but also provide requisite information to equalise the balance of power. This restores some control to the client in being better informed of what to expect and thereby minimise feeling shamed in their lack of knowledge.

BOUNDARIES

While therapeutic boundaries ensure safety for both client and counsellors they can often be a source of frustration for both. Clients can find such boundaries limiting and restrictive in that they may desire a greater degree of reciprocity in wanting to know their counsellor. Such uneven exposure of client and therapist disrupts the social code of reciprocity and can feel like an unequal balance of power. In wanting to share more, clients might feel ashamed for being needy, and in giving more you may also feel ashamed for breaking therapeutic taboos. In a similar vein, clients may feel ashamed for desiring more overt signs of empathy and compassion such as being comforted through touch or physical holding.

In turn, you may feel frustrated at having to remain abstinent in terms of self-disclosure or needing to adopt a neutral, objective stance which can be interpreted by clients as cold, dispassionate or detached. Some counsellors may feel restricted in being too open or available to their clients for fear of violating traditional therapeutic boundaries. This can lead to a constant battle between remaining professional yet being emotionally available to the client. This is a delicate balance that needs to be constantly monitored and calibrated.

THE PROCESS OF THERAPY
The therapeutic relationship

The therapeutic relationship is often a source of relational shame for clients in which there is 'a felt sense of unworthiness to be in connection, a deep sense of unlovability, with the ongoing awareness of how very much one wants to connect with others' (Jordan 1997, p.2). It can equally elicit shame in clinicians and practitioners. While clients will fear exposure of dependency needs and be preoccupied by anxieties around being accepted, loved, held or touched, you may fear exposure of your own shame and have doubts about your ability to stay empathically connected to the client and be competent and professional in facilitating client growth and healing. In combination this can lead to anxieties for both you and the client in the quest for mutuality and authentic connection (DeYoung 2015; Hartling *et al.* 2000).

In clients relational shame tends to cluster around vulnerabilities such as feelings of helplessness, powerlessness, dependency needs and disclosure of intimate thoughts, feelings or past behaviours which may be a source of shame and humiliation. This is especially the case in clients who have experienced physical or sexual abuse or domestic violence or who have a history of self-destructive behaviours such as self-injury, addictions or compulsions. These become further sources of shame, adding layer upon layer of shame onto what is perceived as an intrinsically flawed self. These layers of shame will need to be explored in order for the client to accept the self (see Chapter 12).

Layers of shame

The nature of shame means that it is hidden and clients may have several layers of shame that are only gradually revealed over time. Potter-Efron and Potter-Efron (1989) argue that shame can manifest in several ways in what they call the 'spheres of self'. As can be seen from Figure 10.3 on p.201 these spheres of self consist of the presentation sphere, which is what is presented to the world; the defensive sphere, which consists of defences against shame; the flawed sphere, which is where shame is located; and lastly the core sphere, the very essence of the self, which in some clients has been contaminated by shame.

According to Potter-Efron and Potter-Efron (1989) the presentation sphere comprises aspects of the self that are presented to the world and are available for public scrutiny. It is this sphere that shame-prone individuals attend to the most to cover up a felt sense of shame. Tending to this façade can be exhausting and result in an ever-widening gulf between a cultivated image of the self and the authentic self. It is in the presentation sphere that the initial layer of shame is first encountered in the therapeutic process. In order to uncover deeper layers of shame, you will need to gently explore the gap between the presenting image and the authentic self.

This is likely to trigger the shame alarm (Potter-Efron 2007) and activate the defensive sphere which serves to preserve the presented image from scrutiny or exposure. It is at this point that a range of shame defences such as denial, withdrawal, attacking the self or attacking others is revealed. Some clients may become aggressive and attack the counsellor, while others may become grandiose and avoidant, or withdraw emotionally or psychologically. It is this layer of shame protection that is critical in identifying unconscious defences against shame which need to be explored. In helping clients to identify defensive patterns and understand how these perpetuate shame you can enable them to relinquish habitual defences and move towards greater acceptance of self.

In penetrating the defences the flawed self risks being exposed and clients become increasingly anxious that they will be judged. To expose the flawed self and its concomitant perceived weaknesses, deficiencies and shameful secrets also risks rejection by others, including the counsellor. When entering this layer of shame counsellors need to ensure that the therapeutic relationship and trust are well established so that clients feel safe enough to explore the flawed self in a secure and accepting environment. With this in place clients can come to see that their perceived flaws are what makes them human and that in accepting these they can begin to accept themselves.

The final layer of shame for some clients is in the core sphere of the self. The core sphere is the very essence of the person and usually represents the true, real self. While the core-self in most clients is untainted by shame, there are some clients, particularly those who have been traumatised, who are so 'shame bound' (Kaufman and Raphael 1996) that their very core has been stained by shame. It is these clients who feel intrinsically defective and so contaminated by shame that they feel they should not exist and do not deserve therapeutic support. These clients often feel that they are beyond help and will seek confirmation of their defectiveness and actively resist developing a more positive sense of self. Counsellors will need to be sensitive in exploring the client's shame and ensure that they are not shamed in the process so as to help them recognise their intrinsic worthiness.

The client's experience of shame in therapy

The most common form of shame reported by clients is exposure of dependency needs (Dalenberg 2000), especially in Western cultures where the emphasis is on independence and any sign of being dependent, 'needy' or 'clingy' is judged as shameful. This is exacerbated in male clients who believe vulnerability and dependency undermine their masculinity. This is due to invidious gender stereotypic traits in which vulnerability and dependency are seen as primarily passive feminine traits, while anger and rage are seen as active and empowering masculine traits. Thus the very act of entering therapy for some men can be a source of shame as it is evidence of their inability to be self-disciplined or self-controlled.

In addition clients may fear being judged or pathologised and that under the scrutiny of the therapist's gaze previously hidden character defects or flaws may be unearthed. This is reinforced when labelling clients in terms of diagnostic categories, rendering them invisible and further stigmatising them. Alongside this, the implicit demand that clients have to submit to the superior knowledge and interpretation of the therapist serves to reinforce a sense of shame as not having self-agency to define themselves. Due to the power and authority of the therapist many clients may fear challenging clinical interpretations in case they are seen as a difficult client and shamed for being assertive.

This fear of being shamed is more likely to be exacerbated with therapists who are model led rather than practice led and who rigidly adhere to theory rather than the uniqueness of each client. Such singular focus on trying to fit the client into the theory fails to recognise the client's phenomenological world, making them feel invisible, humiliated and ashamed. Furthermore models that are protocol driven can be dehumanising and objectifying and re-invoke shame-based experiences.

Clients may also feel judged and shamed in their positive or negative transference. Clients who want a more complete, reciprocal relationship or feel closer to their therapist may fear being seen as 'greedy'. In addition, clients who long for physical comfort or touch will feel ashamed of this need. This is amplified when clients feel that they like you more than you seem to like them, or if they are attracted to, or have, erotic fantasies, dreams or daydreams about you. Fear of being shamed will prevent them from talking openly about their feelings, rendering them voiceless and having to keep their needs secret, which creates even further shame. This is also the case in negative transference reactions in which feelings or disappointment, anger or rage arise without being able to express them for fear of being shamed or rejected. This makes it hard for the client to be authentic. As a result, feelings of shame become intensified, promoting retreat into silence and humiliated fury.

A further source of shame for some clients who see counsellors privately is the ability to pay. Money and financial status are often highly charged sources of shame as they are entwined with achievement, success and status. A powerful source of crippling shame is the sense that the client has to pay someone to feel connected (Dalenberg 2000) because they are unable to connect to others. This is associated with lack of relational worth, inability to form relationships and chronic loneliness.

Clients who have difficulty paying fees may feel too embarrassed to discuss this and end up going into debt, or may terminate therapy prematurely to avoid the shame of talking about financial difficulties. Similarly clients who are on a reduced fee may also feel ashamed as they see themselves as charity cases rather than valued clients who are able to pay the full rate. Some of the shame experienced by clients around the exchange of money may also be shared by practitioners who may feel embarrassed about being paid for their empathy and compassion, or seeming to profit from a client's unhappiness, distress or trauma (Dalenberg 2000).

Traumatised clients may well be more prone to shame than non-traumatised clients given that shame and humiliation are integral factors in abuse. Clients who have experienced physical or sexual abuse or domestic violence fear that professionals may think that they were complicit in their abuse and thereby believe that they were to blame, or that they deserved to be abused. This is especially the case in CSA if the client reveals that they were aroused, or enjoyed the attention or affection. Similarly in the case of domestic abuse there is intense fear of being seen as sharing the blame for the abuse, or being defined as masochistic, and that in revealing acts of humiliation and submission clients are exposing themselves to further shame.

Warning
Traumatised clients are commonly more prone to shame than non-traumatised clients given that shame and humiliation are integral factors in abuse.

Research has shown that almost 50 per cent of abused clients felt that their therapist was ashamed of them (Dalenberg 2000) or shocked and disgusted when disclosing CSA (Armsworth 1989). While this may be due to the felt sense of shame in the client that they project onto the counsellor, it may also reflect actual shame felt by the practitioner, or an interaction of the two. You need to be open and honest in acknowledging respective responsibility for shame experiences in the therapeutic process and explore these in a non-judgemental way.

It is highly likely that abused or shame-prone clients are more likely to react with shame to the therapy process. Traumatised clients are often hyper-vigilant and have a highly sensitised shame alarm that is easily tripped by the most subtle of non-verbal cues. While this is an important skill that has helped them to manage their abuse experiences this may be activated in the counselling process when the client is fearful of being judged or humiliated. This level of constant scrutiny means that they are actively searching for signs of disapproval, shame or humiliation and may infer this even when this is not the case. Equally such a highly active shame alarm and finely honed scrutiny means that they may pick up signs of shame responses which are outside the counsellor's conscious awareness. In this clients take the non-verbal signs of shame in the counsellor as confirmation of their own shame or self-degradation. You need to be aware of your own reactions when working with traumatised clients to minimise re-invoking shame in the therapeutic process.

Remember
You must be mindful of your own shame and how your reactions to this can impact the therapeutic process.

The counsellor's experience of shame in therapy

As shame is most likely to be evoked in the presence of others and in relationships, you need to be aware of your own shame in the therapeutic process (see Chapter 11). Given the lack of discourse on shame in counselling and psychotherapy training many practitioners have insufficient knowledge and awareness of shame, including their own.

Thus therapist shame is often denied (Dalenberg 2000) and rarely reported except in the case of sexual attraction to clients (Pope, Spiegel and Tabachnik 1986). You must remember that even if your own shame is unconscious, or invisible to you, it might be highly visible to the client, who will react to it with a range of defences (see Chapter 11).

Remember
Clients are likely to detect the presence of shame and shame reactions in counsellors even though it is outside of the practitioner's conscious awareness.

Emphasising the universality of shame

A powerful way of engaging with your client's and your own shame is to emphasise the universal nature of shame. While this can in part be accomplished through psycho-education, it is most effectively achieved by sharing the human experience of shame. You can facilitate this by providing a human relationship in which small universal experiences of shame are shared. To do this you will need to move out of a detached professional stance and be authentic in sharing examples of embarrassing or shaming experiences to highlight the universal nature of shame and that this is a normal part of being human.

Reflection
Reflect on some examples that would be easy to share with clients and write these down. These might include simple, universal examples such as being late for a crucial appointment, saying the wrong thing, falling over when trying to make a good impression or forgetting something important. Practise reciting these in a succinct way that makes the point that we all make mistakes which can be a source of shame and embarrassment. Remember to choose innocuous, everyday examples and be concise when sharing these so as not to shift the focus from the client.

This can help the client move through shame defences, accepting and tolerating their shame and feel accepted and understood. While sharing appropriate and illustrative examples of shaming experiences you have encountered can be extremely effective you must remain mindful of not elaborating too much and thereby shifting the focus away from the client.

COUNSELLOR SHAME

While shame in therapy has generated some research (Lewis 1971; Tracy and Robbins 2004) the focus has been more on client shame rather than shame in therapists. In order to increase awareness of therapist shame, Kulp, Klinger and Ladany (2007) conducted a number of studies on therapist and supervisor shame. Their findings identified a range of typical examples of shame-inducing behaviours such as falling asleep, poor time management, referring to a client by another client's name, forgetting significant client information, difficulties in bodily functions, recognition of poor interventions doomed to failure, and the sexual behaviour of clients, all of which impacted on the therapeutic relationship and the counsellor's sense of self (Kulp *et al.* 2007). Such research confirms the need for greater awareness of counsellor shame in the therapeutic setting to minimise risk of harm to you and your clients.

Counsellor shame rarely exists in isolation and will invariably consist of a fusion of the counsellor's own past experiences of shame, plus shame that is evoked by the nature of the therapeutic encounter and the client's shame experiences and defences. The relative contribution of these elements will vary from client to client and session to session and will need to be addressed as they arise. In addition, counsellor shame may also be evoked during training and supervision, which can exert a powerful influence in the therapeutic process. Increased awareness of the origins of your shame will enable you to take ownership and responsibility for your contribution and better understand and manage shame dynamics in the therapeutic process (see Chapter 11).

SHAME DEFENCES IN THERAPY

Both client and therapist will have defences against shame. These will typically consist of the defensive shame scripts of withdrawal, attack self, avoidance or attack other (see Chapter 5) of which both parties may be unconscious. It is these defensive scripts that can become entwined, leading to an escalation of shame in the therapeutic process. As shame is triggered in the presence of others (Lewis 1971) it can become palpable with no real understanding of its origins or whose shame it is.

Client defences against shame

Shame in therapy can be masked in many ways and often manifest as silence, compliance, anger, rage or humour (Lewis 1971). These masks of shame are part of the shame scripts identified by Nathanson (1992) of withdrawal, attack self, avoidance or attack other (see Chapter 5). Clients may use any one of these at different points in the therapeutic process or tend to use one of the defence strategies. Thus clients who use withdrawal may become psychologically or emotionally absent by retreating into silence or become submissive and compliant. They are often seen as 'good clients' and yet feel a deep sense of shame and humiliation.

Clients who withdraw, or escape into themselves, are probably the easiest to treat in therapy as their primary need is to experience relational safety to allow shame to be disclosed. You will need to provide a genuine empathic stance in which you enter the client's phenomenological experience of shame and truly understand how it feels. This must be conveyed to the client within a non-judgemental atmosphere in which unconditional positive regard counters the felt sense of shame. This allows the client to move from withdrawal to feeling safe enough to reveal themselves. Most importantly, you need to stay connected and ensure that the interpersonal bridge between you remains intact to balance perceived inadequacies with positive aspects, not to cancel out the shame but to counterbalance it.

When working with clients who use the attack self strategy to defend against shame you will need to accentuate how attacking self, rather than the source of shame, is a highly creative strategy that aids survival by ensuring affiliation and connection to others (Nathanson 1998, p.335). While initially highly adaptive to ward off fear of further shame, rejection or abandonment, it can become maladaptive wherein attacking self comes to feel better than the experience of having somebody else do it. Clients who attack self require an enormous amount of patience and perseverance to help them understand how shame figures and shame-based relational experiences shaped their nascent sense of self and how feeling bad becomes conflated with feeling good. Attack self clients typically present as masochistic in their belief that they deserve their shame and do not deserve to feel better.

This needs to be understood as a way to retain the internalised shaming parent and ward off the fear of obliteration through abandonment, and the client should not be re-shamed for what on the surface appears to be masochistic. Similarly, clients who use the attack self strategy by engaging in self-destructive or self-sabotaging behaviour, such as self-harm, self-injury or repeated suicide attempts, need to be understood within the context of shame defences rather than being judged. This is also the case in milder forms of attack self such as self-deprecation and humour in which the client deflects from shame in order to ensure the connection in the therapeutic relationship remains intact.

Clients who use avoidance to defend against shame may present as narcissistic, grandiose and arrogant, making it difficult to connect to them. Alternatively they may enter therapy because of addictions to alcohol, drugs, food or sex as a way of numbing unbearable states of shame. Working with clients who defend against shame through avoidance is particularly challenging because, in dissociating from their shame, they are unable to link their current behaviour to shaming experiences in the past. This is exacerbated when their narcissism, grandiosity, arrogance and sense of entitlement act as impenetrable barricades to establishing an authentic therapeutic relationship. You will need to be mindful that such clients will find it extremely hard to relinquish their narcissistic tendencies until there has been sufficient work to develop enough inner resources to build authentic pride and shame resilience. This can only be achieved through empathic understanding, working through the shame and replacing self-aggrandisement and narcissistic boasts with self-acceptance and humility. To do this you will need to remember that narcissism and its concomitant behaviours are protective defences against shame and resist the urge to react defensively or re-shame the client. Similarly, those clients who use addictions as a way to avoid or numb the pain of shame will need to explore the role of shame in their addictive behaviour rather than be shamed for their addiction.

Finally clients who use the attack other strategy may direct their humiliated fury and rage at the counsellor for witnessing the client's shame. You must be mindful of not personalising this as it is often safer to shame the witness, in this case you, the counsellor, than shaming the one who humiliated them – the abuser. In this the client, rather than experience shame and despair, furiously attacks the practitioner for exposing their shame, weakness or dependency needs (Livingston and Farber 1996). This is often a cover-up for a real need for connection and mutual respect which the client is too ashamed to acknowledge.

In their rage and fury the client will overtly attack the counsellor by being highly critical of their skills, competency and ability to provide the care and help needed by the client. This represents an attempt to shame the counsellor through constant exposure of their failures and shortcomings and to highlight their inadequacy. This can elicit reciprocal anger to defend against rising shame in the counsellor, which if unleashed will further escalate the shame felt by both parties (see Figure 9.3).

Counsellor defences against shame

Counsellors will also use similar shame scripts in the therapeutic process. Counsellors who use withdrawal as a defensive strategy will withdraw psychologically from the client by becoming emotionally absent, and hide from any form of contact. In attack self they might blame themselves for any therapeutic impasse or failure in outcome. In avoidance the counsellor may become arrogant, grandiose and self-righteous. They may also disown their shame by interpreting any intense or uncomfortable feelings as counter-transference reactions to the client's transference. In addition, if the counsellor feels unfairly attacked or misjudged, they may criticise the client or resort to defensive interpretation. Counsellors may also retaliate by shaming the client or becoming hostile, which can culminate in an escalation of shame.

THE ESCALATION OF SHAME IN THERAPY

When client and counsellor defences against shame become entwined they can intensify and escalate the sense of shame in both client and counsellor (see Figure 9.3). To minimise such escalation you need to be open to examining yourself and take responsibility for your own shame and shame defences, including your own projections and how these contribute to the client's feelings of shame. Most importantly you need to be able to apologise honestly and openly to truly rebuild what Kaufman (1992) calls 'the interpersonal bridge' and heal any breach or ruptures in the therapeutic relationship.

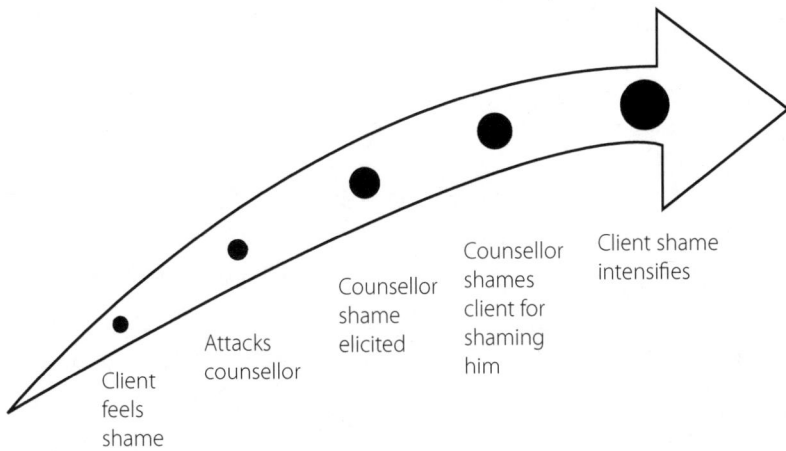

Figure 9.3 Escalation of shame in therapy

Blame boomerang and the Cycle of Shame

Another elicitor of shame which can result in shame escalation is what Dalenberg (2000) calls the 'Blame Boomerang' wherein the wish to protect the client and show compassion can lead to an over-reliance on 'other blame' (see Figure 9.4). This is most pronounced in clients who have experienced sexual or domestic violence where they present with severe self-blame which the counsellor recognises as disproportionate. In attempting to help the client realise that they were not to blame and acknowledge the harm done by others, the counsellor counters the self-blame by blaming others. While this permits clients to move towards a just re-allocation of blame, some clients may be enticed into adopting other blame as a default setting and indiscriminately project blame onto others, including the counsellor. As the client directs blame onto the counsellor, and the counsellor feels unjustifiably blamed or humiliated, there is an increased risk of activation of shame defences. This can lead to negative counter-transference reactions such as anger, rage and humiliation in the counsellor. If these are not contained, the counsellor risks blaming and shaming the client for not taking responsibility and thereby unwittingly escalates the client's shame. If left unchecked, this can lead to a pervasive and insidious cycle of shame.

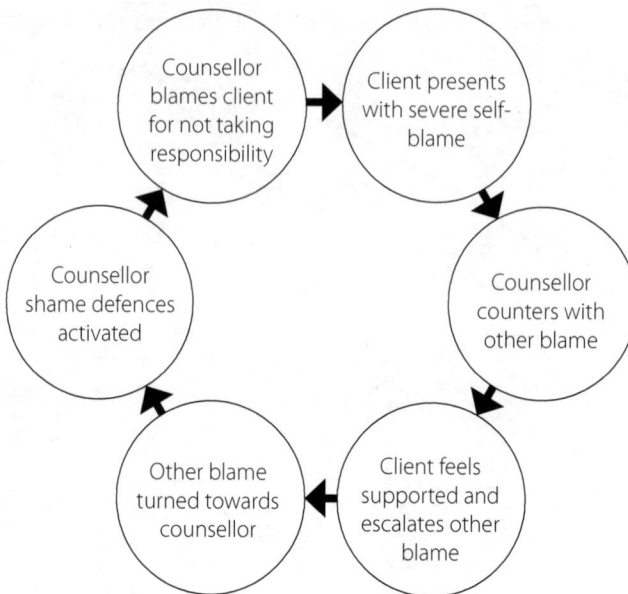

Figure 9.4 Blame Boomerang
(Adapted from Dalenberg 2000)

You will need to guard against this by understanding the protective function of self-blame and self-criticism in 'putting brakes on behaviour that will be punished by others' (Fisher 2013, p.10). In this, shame and self-blame are often the most effective ways to survive in dangerous and abusive families or relationships. To avoid becoming entrapped in yet another cycle of shame, which is all too familiar for the client, you need to listen to the client with what Joyce and Sills (2014, p.92) call 'creative indifference', in which you are open to hearing the extent and degree of negative self-attribution. In this the client feels accepted in their view of themselves and relieved to be understood, from which they can gradually start to challenge themselves. You need to reflect back to the client how they feel about themselves, rather than telling them how they should view themselves, as this is yet another source of shame. As you support the client in challenging themselves, they will be able to come to a more objective balance between self and other blame.

Remember
Shame and self-blame are often the most effective way to survive in dangerous and abusive families or relationships.

To help you identify some of your defences against shame in therapy you will need to reflect on how clients can elicit, or induce, shame in you. Such awareness will identify trigger points and areas of vulnerability. It will also help enhance awareness of your physical, emotional and cognitive responses which, although invisible to you, may be all too visible to clients.

Reflection
Remember a time when you felt shame when working with a client. Describe the circumstances and what preceded it. What were the triggers? When did you become aware of feeling shame? Try to identify your bodily responses and any areas of tension. How do these leave a mark on the body – blushing, feeling flushed, increased heart rate, rapid thoughts or speech or being rendered silent, or dissociating? Try to listen to any messages you are telling yourself such as 'I need to hide, disappear, vanish or get away', 'I am not good enough' or 'I don't deserve this', or do you feel anger and want to retaliate by lashing out? Try to get a sense of your projection of what you think other people may be thinking or feeling about you.

REGULATING SHAME IN THERAPY

In order to manage the escalation of shame and potential shame cycles in therapy, you need to be able to acknowledge your own shame as well as the client's and how these interact. In this you need to identify and take responsibility for your defensive reactions to shame and the impact these have on the therapeutic relationship and endeavour to remain connected (see Figure 9.5). If you can acknowledge and convey to the client your own shame, and how this can be co-created in the therapeutic relationship, you and your client can reconnect to explore and release the felt shame. If, however, you refuse to acknowledge your own shame or shame defences then you run the risk of therapeutic ruptures. If this is repeated in a cycle of shame then the client's shame becomes embedded, leading to a replay of abuse experiences or premature termination.

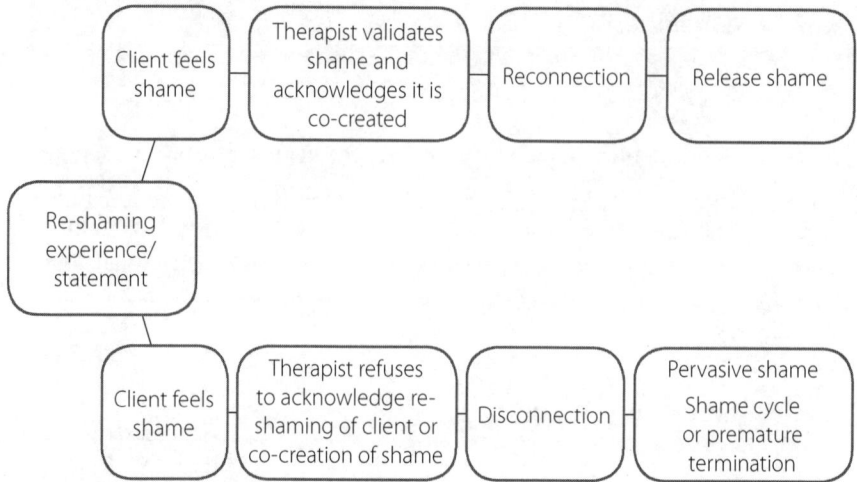

Figure 9.5 Regulating shame in therapy

Throughout you need to be mindful that hostility, grandiosity, flippancy, humour, aggression or criticism in either you or the client are often protective strategies against unbearable feelings of shame, or fear of humiliation. In understanding these defences, and by not reacting to provocation, you can minimise the potential for re-shaming the client. This will allow you to acknowledge the needs and vulnerability of your clients and offer empathy and compassion as the much-needed antidote to shame (Brown 2007a). How this can be achieved is the focus of the next chapter, which looks at a range of skills that can help when working with shame.

SUGGESTED READING

Dalenberg, C.J. (2000) *Countertransference and the Treatment of Trauma*. Washington, DC: American Psychological Association.

Dearing, R.L. and Tangney, J.P. (eds) (2011) *Shame in the Therapy Hour*. Washington, DC: American Psychological Association.

DeYoung, P.A. (2015) *Understanding and Treating Chronic Shame: A Relational/Neurobiological Approach*. Hove: Routledge.

Hartling, L., Rosen, W., Walker, M. and Jordan, J. (2000) *Shame and Humiliation: From Isolation to Relational Transformation*. Work in Progress No.88. Wellesley, MA: Stone Center, Wellesley College.

Miller, S.B. (1985) *The Shame Experience*. Hillsdale, NJ: Erlbaum.

Miller, S.B. (1996) *Shame in Context*. London: Routledge.

Sanderson, C. (2013) *Counselling Skills for Working with Trauma: Healing from Child Sexual Abuse, Sexual Violence and Domestic Abuse*. London: Jessica Kingsley Publishers.

10

SKILLS FOR WORKING
WITH SHAME

Given the nature and impact of shame it is often the most difficult emotion to reveal as it re-invokes shame. This is particularly the case if shame is not acknowledged and out of conscious awareness. While the therapeutic space provides ideal opportunities to explore shame and how it has impacted on clients, it is frequently overlooked in therapy (Lewis 1971; Lewis 1992; Nathanson 1992). This chapter will look at how to work with shame in the counselling process by exploring the main aims of working with shame, and the role of psycho-education to enhance awareness, the origins of shame and its impact. It will focus on how to identify layers of shame and how to interrupt shame spirals and circumvent cycles of shame. Emphasis will be placed on the importance of accepting and tolerating client shame and balancing this with positive aspects of the self and healthy pride.

In order to achieve this it is critical to establish a safe and secure therapeutic relationship in which shame can be regulated in order to minimise re-shaming clients. To assist this, the chapter will provide a range of exercises to help uncover shame, enable clients to connect to unacknowledged shame and release this and build healthy pride and shame resilience. It will include exercises to help break the silence and secrecy of shame and encourage clients to critically evaluate their shame and look at ways of relinquishing it by reapportioning shame and reframing negative evaluations of the self. It will also explore how both client and counsellor can transform shame through acknowledging what it means to be human without fear of judgement, ridicule or humiliation.

THERAPEUTIC AIMS

When working with shame, counsellors will need to be mindful that there will be huge variation in client presentation of shame. Some clients will enter therapy with very little understanding or conscious awareness of shame, while others may recognise their shame and how it has affected them. Given that shame is ubiquitous in therapy irrespective of degree of client awareness, counsellors will need to ensure that shame, like any other emotion, is addressed, released and worked through. However, unlike other emotions, shame is often harder to explore because of its hidden nature and the masks that clients use to defend against it. In addition, the fear of being re-shamed can make clients very resistant to exposing their perceived flaws and vulnerabilities, which can make it difficult to talk about or to release shame. In order to minimise re-shaming clients and reinforcing their shame you will need to be sensitive when working with shame and implementing the range of therapeutic techniques (see Table 10.1).

Remember

Addressing and exploring shame can feel overwhelming and shaming for both client and counsellor.

As the expression of shame can amplify shame many clients disguise it by expressing a range of other emotions such as embarrassment, self-blame or guilt rather than give voice to shame. In addition they may cover up their shame through anger, hostility, grandiosity or dissociating. You will need to be aware of how these defences make it hard to identify and label shame and ensure that you attend to both non-verbal and verbal cues to shame through empathic and active listening. This is particularly critical when working with clients from cultural environments which do not permit talking about shame or demand shame-appropriate behaviour. This must be understood by practitioners and managed sensitively to avoid intensifying the client's shame.

As many clients have little understanding of shame it is helpful to enhance awareness through psycho-education of the nature and origins of shame and how this can impact on the self and self-identity. In becoming more aware of shame clients will be able to make implicit or unconscious shame more explicit or conscious. This will enable them to identify their shame and how it has shaped negative beliefs and thoughts about the self, absorbed unwanted identities and generated the negative self-talk that keeps them in thrall to their shame. In exploring these, clients can begin to release shame and begin to develop self-acceptance, empathy and compassion, and rebuild authentic pride.

Table 10.1 Summary of therapeutic aims of working with shame	
Aim	**Process**
Psycho-education	Function, origins and impact of shame. Break the secrecy and silence of shame by emphasising the universality of shame
Therapeutic relationship	Building a safe and secure therapeutic relationship in which it is safe to explore shame and build trust and relational worth, in which the client's shame is accepted and tolerated, and shame can be shared
Shame awareness	Begin to reveal layers of shame to make implicit shame explicit and identify shame triggers, shame screens and defences against shame
Identify impact of shame	Negative self-beliefs, unwanted identities, negative self-talk
Releasing shame	Break the secrecy and silence of shame and reapportion shame
Self-acceptance	Critical awareness of negative impact of shame, reframe expectations and develop self-definition
Empathy and compassion	Develop empathy and compassion for self and others in order to reconnect to others
Build authentic pride	Reclaim accomplishments and achievements and take pleasure in competency, and joy in self-efficacy

In working with shame, counsellors will need to prioritise building a secure therapeutic relationship in which it is safe to explore shame without judgement or being re-shamed. This is crucial in order to build trust and restore relational worth so that clients can value themselves as individuals and feel accepted. This will require you to be aware of your own vulnerability to shame, how this is elicited in the therapeutic relationship and how you defend against it. With such knowledge you can minimise the risk of contaminating the therapeutic process with unacknowledged shame and prevent enmeshment or client and counsellor shame.

PSYCHO-EDUCATION

The silence and secrecy surrounding shame means that most clients will try to avoid thinking or talking about it. In addition, as the sense of worthlessness and defectiveness gets embedded, shame-prone clients begin to surrender to their prison of shame and believe that they are beyond help. This can be challenging in the counselling process where any attempt to discharge the shame and reverse distorted beliefs is fiercely resisted by the client. In avoiding or denying shame clients are unable to develop an understanding of the function or origins of shame, or the distinction between healthy and toxic shame. Counsellors will need to emphasise the universal nature of shame and the role it plays in regulating behaviour and forming social bonds, but which under certain circumstances can become toxic. See Chapter 9 for more about the universality of shame. In normalising healthy shame and distinguishing this from toxic or destructive shame you can help clients to feel less ashamed and more open to exploring the role shame plays in their lives. Such understanding will make it easier to see how shame shapes the sense of self and influences behaviour, both positively and negatively.

Top tip

Emphasising that shame is normal and has a healthy function can help clients to feel less ashamed and more open to exploring how shame has impacted on them.

As clients begin to acknowledge that healthy shame is part of the human condition they can acquire a better understanding of shame and the range of factors that underpin shame such as early attachment experiences, family dynamics and cultural attitudes. Initially you will need to address these factors in general terms rather than the client's own experiences and may find the Circle of Shame (see Chapter 4) a helpful guide to common sources of shame. From this clients can begin to identify some of their own sources of shame which they can insert into the blank segments of the exercise on p.91. This circle is most effective when seen as a working document which can be revised and edited throughout the therapeutic process as clients begin to explore their shame.

Clients will also benefit from understanding how shame experiences and shaming messages in early childhood shape neural networks in the brain and how these direct and influence the formation of self-identity, feelings, cognitions and behaviour (Badenoch 2011; Gerhardt 2004).

This can be a relief to many clients who blame themselves for their shame and shame-based behaviour. In recognising that shame is often imposed by others and not a true measure of their value or worth they can lessen their sense of shame. In this they will need to be reminded that while they were not to blame for their shaming experiences in early childhood they do need to acknowledge that they are responsible for changing those patterns now (Potter-Efron and Potter-Efron 1989).

It is also helpful to explore common defences against shame and how these manifest and impact on current relationships. This normalises the need to cover up and defend against shame, which enables clients to feel less ashamed of their defensive strategies, especially when they manifest in the counselling process. Clients need to know that when defensive strategies are activated they will be understood rather than judged by the counsellor, and develop sufficient trust to allow themselves to be authentic in the therapeutic relationship.

Clients will also need to know that it is possible to recover from chronic shame rather than feel condemned to a lifelong prison of shame. To facilitate this, counsellors will need to discuss the process of working through shame and emphasise the antidotes to shame. This will help clients to embrace the possibility of letting go of shame and replacing it with self-acceptance, authentic pride, empathy and compassion for self and others. This can be supported by reminding clients that shame is only a part of them and not the whole of them, and by counterbalancing shame with recognition and acknowledgement of achievements and sources of healthy pride.

BALANCING SHAME WITH HEALTHY PRIDE

It is essential that you balance working with shame with acknowledging positive aspects of the self, achievements and sources of healthy pride. To facilitate this it is helpful to encourage clients to keep a record of their signature strengths, achievements and sources of pride. Clients can do this in their journal or may prefer to log these in a more creative way (see the exercise on p.165 using the 'tree of growth').

Other useful sources of psycho-education are Brené Brown's self-help books (see, for example, Brown 2010). These will reinforce the universality of shame and show how to recover and heal from crippling shame.

THE THERAPEUTIC RELATIONSHIP

Shaming experiences have taught clients that safety lies in disconnection and detachment and that to be connected is a source of further shame. This makes it difficult for them to trust others and have confidence in relationships. You will need to be mindful of this when building the therapeutic relationship as clients commonly test the practitioner in terms of their commitment and authenticity of connection. It is crucial to establish a reliable, safe and trustworthy therapeutic relationship in which to explore shame without fear of judgement or rejection. Moreover, in providing empathic connection and compassion, shame can be transformed and intrinsic worth restored. The therapeutic relationship is also an opportunity to provide a template to guide and restructure other relationships and build shame resilience.

Remember

The shaming gaze of the counsellor can be reduced through inclusion rather than being a detached observer – an ally and companion rather than judge and jury.

ACCEPTING THE CLIENT'S SHAME

In order to facilitate working with shame it is imperative that counsellors can accept the client's shame rather than try to argue it away. While it is tempting to avoid shame, or try to minimise or dispel it, this can be counterproductive as it prevents the client from working through it. To heal shame you must be able to bear witness to the excruciating agony of toxic shame rather than avoid talking about shame or deflecting attention away from it. The danger of ignoring shame is that the client will feel silenced and judged and come to believe that their shame is beyond repair. Equally it is important to avoid facile reassurances that the shame is not that bad, or that it will simply dissipate or heal over time. You need to be able to enter into the client's experience of shame – to be able to sit with it and be seen to tolerate it. This will help the client to tolerate their shame and to know that they no longer need to suffer shame alone. This can only be achieved if you have worked on your own shame (see Chapter 11) and are able to maintain appropriate boundaries to ensure you are not engulfed by the client's shame.

Top tip

It is important that you can accept the client's shame and avoid minimising it through facile assurances or deflection.

Modelling that shame is a feeling that can be tolerated, accepted and shared with another human being will enable the client to tolerate and accept their shame. This is most likely to occur when you are able to stand next to the client as a sensitive companion rather than a detached observer. Being present and able to attune and resonate with the client's shame will provide the basis of compassionate responses. Clients struggling with shame will be able to experience, perhaps for the first time, that another person can respond empathically to their experience, in an atmosphere of mutual respect, in which shame can serve as a signal to move toward deeper connection rather than disconnection.

As a practitioner you have a responsibility to know your vulnerabilities and fears, especially around shame, so that your own shame does not re-shame the client. This is most effectively achieved through genuine engagement and mutuality in which you are able to move with the client, and allow the client to move with you. To do this requires an openness to our own vulnerabilities, or need for certainty, predictability or being the perfect therapist. Such a stance can be supported through the use of inclusive language such as 'What can we do together?', 'How can we stay connected in the therapeutic relationship?' and 'How can we bear shame, uncertainty or vulnerability together?' (Hartling *et al.* 2000). Working through shame collaboratively not only equalises the relationship between client and practitioner, it also conveys to the client that they are someone 'who is worthy of being met instead of someone worthy of derision, dismissal and rejection' (Jacobs 1995, p.90).

REGULATING SHAME

The complex nature of shame requires a sensitive and nuanced approach in which the exploration of shame is carefully regulated to ensure that it is within tolerable limits for the client. This involves sensitive pacing in managing the expression of shame. As the intensity of shame can fluctuate quite dramatically counsellors will need to assess the client's window of tolerance and regulate the exposure to shame.

In order to tolerate shame whether in the client or you, it is important to feel it. This can be difficult, as the feelings of shame can be distressing and overwhelming, prompting a habitual defence mechanism. Shame can result in a desensitisation to body awareness or flooding of sensation wherein the body shuts down or collapses and somatic self-support is lost. It is important for both counsellor and client to stay present and embodied in order to feel the shame and work through it.

You can help the client and yourself in remaining embodied in the presence of shame by using grounding techniques such as breathing (see the following exercise). Through steady breathing clients will be able to tolerate shame rather than defend against it. This will enable clients to work through shame and transform it into an empowering emotion to be used as a source of internal strength and resilience rather than crippling fear and isolation (Feiring and Taska 2005).

Exercise
Feeling shame

You can help ground yourself, and the client, when feeling shame by being aware of how both of you are breathing. To regulate breathing it is essential to breathe through the nose to a slow count of three, hold to the count of three, and then breathe out through the mouth to a slow count of three. This can be repeated several times until you or the client are able to stay with the feeling of shame rather than activate habitual defensive patterns. Regular practice will help you and the client to tolerate feeling shame.

If habitual shame defences are activated it is important to ensure that you and the client remain in psychological contact. This can be achieved by checking with the client how present they are and how connected they feel to you. In addition, it is essential to check with the client how they are experiencing you by encouraging them to talk about how present they feel you are, and the strength of the connection between you. This has to be sensitively balanced to ensure that clients are offered an optimum level of support, as too little or too much support can be equally damaging. It is important to remember that being overprotective and seeing the client as too fragile can be re-shaming as it implies that they are too vulnerable to face their shame.

Top tip
Normalise shame as just another feeling that can be faced and worked through.

If clients become overly preoccupied with shame or overwhelmed, especially outside of the therapeutic sessions, it can be really useful to make a shame box in which they place the shame until they feel more able to explore it or they bring it to a session (see Chapter 2).

AWARENESS OF SHAME

Once the therapeutic relationship has been established and the client feels ready to explore shame you can invite them to engage in a number of exercises to identify their subjective experience of shame. This can be done in a number of ways and you will need to assess which particular approach is best suited to each individual client. You may initially wish to assess the degree of shame by using a range of clinical assessment measures such as the Internalized Shame Scale (ISS) (Cook 1994), the Other as Shamer Scale (OAS) (Allan, Gilbert and Goss 1994) or the Guilt and Shame-Proneness Scale (GASP)(Cohen, Wolf, Panter, and Insko 2011). While these measures will give some indication of shame you may find these somewhat clinical and wish to support these with other methods such as the projective shame exercise on p.193 or through exercises that encourage clients to begin to explore their subjective experience of shame.

Alternatively you could encourage the client to make a shame inventory to help them to identify their experiences of shame and how that felt at the time of the experience and how it feels now. This will enable them to recognise the impact shame has had on them in the past and how it continues to reverberate in the present.

Exercise

Shame inventory

Ask your client to list ten examples of shame, starting with their earliest experience and continuing to the most recent experiences. Encourage them to look at these and reflect on them while being mindful of any sensations, actions, thoughts or feelings.

Next they should identify their worst experience of shame and list their feelings, then and now.

1. Worst experience of shame _____

2. Feeling then _____

3. Feeling now _____

Ask your client to next list three current problems with shame and how it impacts on them and their relationships.

1. Shame still affects me _____

2. Shame still affects me _____

3. Shame still affects me _____

Remind clients to pace this. They do not have to do this in one go but can add to it over time.

As human contact is one of the best antidotes to shame, sharing shame with trusted others will reduce the sense of exclusion and isolation in which shame grows. It is helpful to remind clients that being accepted, understood and valued by someone in a non-judgemental way will enable them to release their shame and come out of hiding and become more visible. Before starting to talk about shame it is useful to explore any fears or fantasies the client might have around the exposure of shame and how these can be managed. This needs to be accompanied with grounding skills to help the client stay present and regulate concomitant emotions.

MAKING SHAME CONSCIOUS

As early experiences of shame are implicit and right brain dominated and thus not easily accessible to left brain cognitive processing and language, many clients will have little or no conscious awareness of shame. This will hamper the ability to talk about shame or know how to respond to shame-based questions. Such clients may find it easier to access their experience of shame through visual imagery such as the projective exercise below. You will need to be mindful that this can be a powerful exercise for some clients and can elicit unbearable shame, so you will need to ensure that there is enough time to explore overwhelming feelings and restore emotional regulation before the end of the session.

Exercise
Projective shame
Invite your client to look at the image (see Figure 10.1) and freely associate to what this person might be feeling or thinking. Next encourage the client to talk about what physical sensations, feelings, thoughts or memories are elicited, along with any responses and reactions.

Figure 10.1 Projective shame image
Copyright © Sanderson 2015

Warning

The projective shame exercise can elicit overwhelming feelings which need to be regulated before the end of the session.

Another exercise that can begin the process of getting into contact with the experience of shame is to encourage the client to talk about where and how they feel shame. This helps to identify the sensory experience of shame through the main sensory channels.

Identifying the sensory experience of shame is crucial in accessing the unique, subjective experience of the client. It also helps them to identify where shame might be located in the body. If clients respond well to the above exercises they might wish to elaborate a little further, locating where in the body they hold shame. This exercise needs to be carefully paced as some clients may have a strong reaction to being in contact with bodily shame.

Exercise

Embodiment of shame

Provide your client with body outline images (front and back) (see Figure 10.2) and ask them to colour in where they feel shame in their body. Different colours or shades can be used to represent the intensity of shame.

Encourage your client to reflect on the physical sensation of shame in the different parts of their body. They then choose one part of their body and place a hand over that area and direct comforting, affirming energy to that part to reduce their cortisol levels. Encourage them to reflect on any change in their sensations and how that feels.

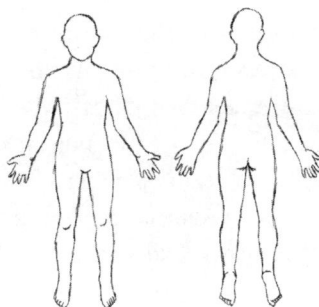

Figure 10.2 Body outline images
Copyright © Sanderson 2015

In beginning to identify the subjective experience of shame clients can begin the process of exploring and releasing shame.

RELEASING SHAME

To release shame clients will need to be able to explore the experience of shame by bringing it back into conscious awareness and break the silence and secrecy of shame by talking about it. While the above exercises are designed to facilitate the exploration of shame clients will need to gain confidence in talking about shame to fully release it. Initially clients will benefit from talking about shame in the therapeutic setting, but as they begin to release some of the shame it can help to share this with trusted others at a pace that is comfortable to them. Encourage your client to make a list in their journal of trusted people they could talk to about shame. To maximise the chance of being heard, remind them to check with the person whether they are happy to talk about shame to minimise the risk of rejection.

To make it easier to embark on talking about shame it is helpful for the client to make a list of what they feel ashamed of and to rank order these, with the most shameful at the top of the list and the least shameful at the bottom. You can then suggest to the client that when talking about their shame with trusted others they start with the least shameful experiences and gradually work up the list. Exploring shame in this order makes it less overwhelming and will build confidence.

LAYERS OF SHAME

As shame needs to be hidden from the gaze of others, it is often buried and contained in several layers which take time to uncover. As trust in the therapeutic relationship is established clients will begin to reveal these layers of shame, with each layer representing a test for the therapist. These tests are designed to ascertain whether you are robust enough to handle shameful revelations without judgement or disgust. You need to demonstrate that you can tolerate and accept the client's shame so that they can accept themselves and uncover and explore deeper layers of shame.

Remember

Shame comes in layers and clients will reveal them over time as trust builds, and these represent a test for the counsellor.

There are several techniques that can help to uncover layers of shame. One is to invite the client to identify the layers of shame and record these on concentric circles which represent the spheres of the self as introduced in Chapter 9.

⚙ Exercise
Identifying layers of shame
Enlarge the concentric circles of the spheres of the self (Figure 10.3). Invite your client to record the layers of shame in each of the spheres of self. This will help them to track how shame manifests in the four aspects of the self and guide what needs to be worked through to recover and heal from shame.

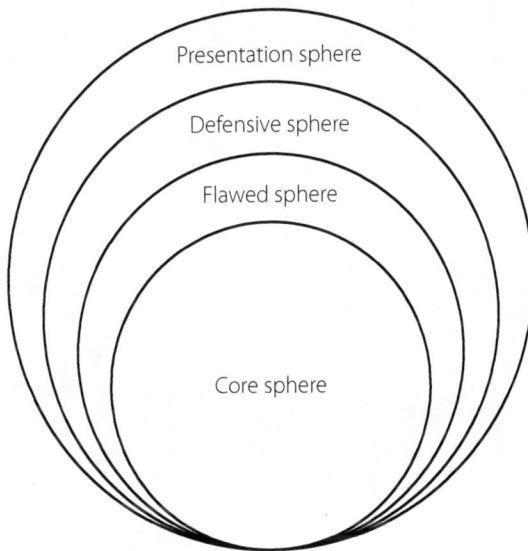

Presentation sphere

Defensive sphere

Flawed sphere

Core sphere

Figure 10.3 Spheres of self template
(Adapted from Potter-Efron and Potter-Efron 1989)

Alternatively some clients may find it easier to engage in uncovering layers of shame in a more creative way. A powerful way of working is through the use of nesting dolls, commonly referred to as Russian dolls (see Figure 10.4). These usually consist of five or seven dolls nesting inside each other which can be used to represent aspects of the self. Nesting dolls can be used in a variety of ways in the therapeutic setting to explore a range of the aspects of the self including those that are visible to others and those that are hidden or disavowed. In addition, they can be used to access different developmental stages throughout the life span from infancy to adulthood. In exploring hidden or split-off parts of the self the client can begin to uncover shame in a more concrete way. Clients often report that they are able to identify more easily with these hidden parts through the use of nesting dolls, with some purchasing their own for use at home.

Exercise

Nesting dolls

Invite your client to start with the outer doll and talk about the self that everyone can see, including ways in which shame is covered up. The next doll can be used to represent the self that only family and friends see, including any defences against shame. The third doll may be used to signify the hidden shameful parts of the self of which the client is aware but keeps hidden from others. The fourth doll can be seen as the perceived flawed self, some of which is hidden even from the client, while the last doll represents the core-self. As each doll is uncovered encourage the client to talk about what is being revealed and how they feel about those aspects of the self.

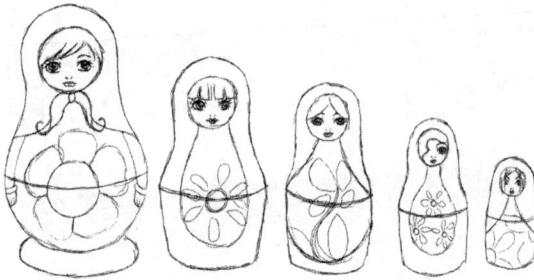

Figure 10.4 Nesting dolls illustration

Another creative technique to uncover hidden shameful parts of the self is to invite clients to draw this part as a character. This will appeal to clients who find it hard to express their shame verbally and who find it easier to use non-verbal forms of communication such as drawing. To help clients in how they might draw the shameful part of the self it can be useful to use Roger Hargreaves' Mr Men and Little Misses characters for inspiration. This exercise can help clients to name the shameful part and accept this as a part of the self. This exercise can be expanded to counterbalance shame by drawing characters that represent the positive aspects of the self.

⚙ Exercise

Mr Men and Little Misses

Using the Mr Men and Little Misses characters for inspiration invite your client to draw a shameful part of the self and talk about this part through the character they have drawn. This can be followed by drawing a character that represents a positive aspect of the self.

IDENTIFYING DEFENCES AGAINST SHAME

As you and the client explore the client's shame it is likely that a range of defences will emerge. A recurring conflict in shame is the need to be visible and the need to be invisible. This paradox of needing to be seen and needing to withdraw from others is paralysing, as seen in Chapter 5, and clients will activate a range of protective strategies to hide their shame. These usually cluster around moving away, moving towards and moving against (Horney 1945).

Clients who use the moving away strategy detach from relationships by withdrawing, silencing themselves or making themselves invisible. In contrast, clients who move towards tend to appease or please others to ensure that they stay connected. To do this they often have to keep important parts of their experience out of the relationship in order to secure and keep the connection. This usually necessitates a high tolerance level for abuse as they are terrified of losing the relationship. Clients who move against risk losing connection by directing anger, resentment and rage against those whom they believe to be the source of their shame. In therapy this is invariably the counsellor.

► Remember

A recurring conflict in shame is the need to be visible and the need to be invisible. This paradox of needing to be seen and needing to withdraw from others is paralysing.

Variations of these protective strategies are commonly seen in therapy both in the client and counsellor, which can diminish the capacity for mutual empathy and authentic connection. It is crucial that you recognise these as shame-induced protective strategies rather than personal attacks or attempts to deskill you. It is only through staying connected to the client through good relational practice that it is possible to transform shame and humiliation into opportunities for growth and deeper connection.

You will need to recognise the shame behind other emotions and be able to link these to the client's shame. Thus the client may express anger, rage or fury at you if an intervention or comment made by you has evoked shame in the client. This is exacerbated by envy toward you for the perceived power or competence in your role as counsellor. The client will focus on you in order to deflect from their perceived shameful weakness and attempt to reallocate shame by denigrating and undermining your power, or by deskilling. The danger of being the recipient of the client's contempt, criticism or anger is that it can trigger your own shame and any concomitant shame defences. It is essential that you are able to contain yourself during any onslaughts and keep your interventions short and empathic to show that you can survive such assaults without retaliating or escalating either your or the client's shame.

✓ Top tip

Don't personalise defensive shame attacks. You need to keep your interventions short and empathic and remain calm and contained to avoid escalating shame.

Counsellors need to view shame defences as a protective strategy against psychic devastation and understand aggression or avoidance as a form of assertion for fear of being put down or rejected. You will also need to recognise the full range of defensive strategies including silence, hostility, grandiosity, flippancy and humour to avoid re-shaming the client despite provocation and ensure that you do not disconnect and continue to provide a secure therapeutic relationship.

▼ Remember

Client hostility indicates that something has spooked them. You need to explore what has been triggered and work with it.

This means being mindful of managing any potential ruptures due to shame defences by maintaining an empathic and compassionate stance wherein you are able to mirror the client's shame in a non-shaming way. This can be conveyed through responses such as 'I can see how upset or angry you are and wonder what more can be done right now' or 'What would you like from me right now?' If the attack is particularly venomous or pernicious then an appropriate boundary needs to be drawn such as 'It is really hard to hear when you are shouting like that', 'It is difficult to connect when you are so hostile' or 'If you keep threatening me then we will have to suspend the session and take time out'.

Conversely some clients find shame to be so overpowering that they cannot bear to hear empathic responses and frequently interpret these as patronising or false. This is commonly seen in clients who have never received empathic responses or compassion and therefore misperceive it as pity, which evokes further shame. With such clients it is more useful to employ such responses as 'It looks as if you are feeling terrible right now. Shame has been a powerful presence in your life and it is hard to be reminded of that.'

Warning
Some clients find shame to be so overpowering that they cannot bear to hear empathic responses and frequently interpret these as patronising.

IDENTIFYING THE IMPACT OF SHAME
In working through and releasing shame clients can begin to make sense of how shame has impacted on their sense of self, self-esteem and self-identity. To concretise this, clients may find the following exercise useful.

Exercise
Identifying the impact of shame

1. Invite your client to make a list in their journal of how they feel shame has affected their self-esteem.

2. They should list some of the feelings, thoughts and beliefs they have about themselves (common examples are 'I have no right to exist'; 'I am inadequate'; 'I am defective'; 'I am not worth loving'; 'I am a mistake'; 'I don't belong'; 'I deserve to be abandoned'; 'I am a burden to others'; 'I don't count'; 'I am nothing'; 'I deserve criticism'; 'I am worthless'; 'I am not good enough'; 'I should not be').

3. Rank order these in order of severity.

4. To counterbalance these, ask your client to write down three things that are good about them, or what others tell them objectively is good about them.

Once clients have started to work through their shame experiences and gained increased awareness of the origins of shame and how it is maintained, they can begin to develop a more critical view of the origins of shame and how shaming messages from others have been internalised. This can help them to begin to challenge some of these internalised messages and reapportion shame.

CRITICAL AWARENESS OF SHAME-BASED MESSAGES

As clients become more conscious and aware of the origins of their shame they can begin to challenge internalised shame messages, negative thoughts and negative self-talk. Counsellors will need to support this by encouraging clients to challenge and re-evaluate shame-inducing cognitions and replace these with more affirming thoughts and beliefs about the self.

Exercise
Identifying and challenging shame-based thoughts and beliefs

1. Invite the client to write down their shame-based messages, thoughts and core beliefs and link these to the source of critical messages that have become internalised.

2. Look at these and encourage them to challenge and evaluate any cognitive distortions and reframe these with more affirming and self-accepting thoughts and beliefs.

3. Encourage the client to make a list of these in their journal to remind them of their value and self-worth whenever they feel that shame-based thoughts threaten to overwhelm them.

To prevent the constant replaying of shame-based beliefs clients will also need to challenge any internal dialogue and negative self-talk that serves to perpetuate shame. Clients will need first to identify the negative self-talk and then challenge and re-evaluate it in the same way as they challenged distorted beliefs. In doing so they will be able to replace it with a more affirming inner dialogue and self-talk reflective of the authentic self.

Exercise
Identifying and challenging shame-based inner dialogue and self-talk

1. Invite the client to write down the most frequently recurring shame-based internal dialogue and messages that have become incorporated into their self-definition and critical self-talk such as 'I am flawed'; 'I am not good enough, pretty enough, thin enough, strong enough, caring enough, independent or popular enough...'

2. Next take a piece of paper and make two columns and encourage the client to write down the adjectives they use to sustain their negative sense of self such as calling themselves stupid, pathetic, needy, unlovable or useless and place these in the first column.

3. In the second column they then list positive adjectives and statements about themselves.

4. Encourage the client to reflect on these and practise replacing the negative self-talk with more self-accepting adjectives and statements.

REAPPORTIONING SHAME

To release shame that has been imposed by others through criticism, invalidation, humiliation or ridicule clients may find it helpful to reapportion the responsibility of shame. This is particularly crucial for those clients who have been physically or sexually abused and blame themselves for this. Commonly clients who have been sexually abused or exploited in childhood, or who have experienced domestic abuse, not only take on the responsibility for the abuse, but also the disavowed shame of the abuser (see Chapter 8).

Exercise

Reapportioning shame

1. Invite the client to make a list of all those who contributed to their sense of shame.

2. Ask your client to draw two columns – one for those who imposed shame and one for their own shame.

3. Your client should reflect on these and evaluate the degree of shamelessness of others and their relative contribution and responsibility in inducing shame.

4. Next ask them to put this into a pie chart to show how others have contributed to their sense of shame, including those who did not protect them.

5. Encourage them to use this to begin to release themselves from the responsibility of carrying the shame that belongs to others.

6. If appropriate, your client should write a therapeutic letter or poem to the person(s) who caused them shame (without sending it to them).

SELF-COMPASSION, SELF-ACCEPTANCE AND AUTHENTIC PRIDE

As clients begin to reapportion shame and begin to accept themselves they are able to become more visible, and begin to connect to others. This is usually accompanied by a more empathic and compassionate view of the self. Self-compassion is a powerful tool to reduce self-blame and to relinquish distorted core beliefs and impossible expectations. When clients can accept themselves as they are rather than trying to be what others want them to be they can begin to let go of perfectionism and the need to compare themselves to others. In this, clients can allow themselves to make mistakes or show their vulnerabilities without the fear of being judged or shamed and truly come to know what it is to be human. As the preoccupation with the shamed self lessens they will be able to reach out and connect to others with greater empathy and compassion (see Chapter 12).

This will allow them to replace the crippling nature of shame with more self-affirming beliefs and replace their previous self-image 'laced with shame' (Jacobs 1995, p.87) with authentic pride. In reclaiming sources of healthy pride clients will be able to adopt a less shameful identity. One way to encourage clients to accept themselves is to remind them that it is human to err and make mistakes. This will enable them to see themselves as human and learn to replace self-judgement with humility and laughter rather than being crippled by shame. When clients are able to laugh rather than become embarrassed by awkward situations they are able to redefine their experience and maintain social bonds. In this way good-natured humour and laughter has a positive effect in disrupting the cycle of shame (Scheff 1990). Moreover, shared laughter is quintessentially human and a powerful tool for connecting to others.

SUGGESTED READING

Dearing, R.L. and Tangney, J.P. (eds) (2011) *Shame in the Therapy Hour*. Washington, DC: American Psychological Association.

DeYoung, P.A. (2015) *Understanding and Treating Chronic Shame: A Relational/Neurobiological Approach*. Hove: Routledge.

Hartling, L., Rosen, W., Walker, M. and Jordan, J. (2000) *Shame and Humiliation: From Isolation to Relational Transformation*. Work in Progress Npo.88. Wellesley, MA: Stone Center, Wellesley College.

Miller, S.B. (1985) *The Shame Experience*. Hillsdale, NJ: Erlbaum.

Miller, S.B. (1996) *Shame in Context*. London: Routledge.

Sanderson, C. (2010) *The Warrior Within: A One in Four Handbook to Aid Recovery from Childhood Sexual Abuse and Violence*. London: One in Four.

Sanderson, C. (2013) *Counselling Skills for Working with Trauma: Healing from Child Sexual Abuse, Sexual Violence and Domestic Abuse*. London: Jessica Kingsley Publishers.

11

COUNSELLOR SHAME

As shame is primarily a relational emotion it is not surprising that it is ubiquitous in therapy. Being in a relationship, whether personal or professional, can evoke relational shame, especially when it involves the search for authentic engagement and connection (Jordan *et al.* 2000). This is most likely to occur in therapeutic modalities that adopt a relational approach or when working with traumatised clients who need to transform the shame and dehumanisation that underpins all interpersonal abuse. It is essential that practitioners acknowledge that shame is a bi-directional process (Herman 2011b) in which past shame can be evoked in both client and counsellor, and in which both parties can shame and re-shame each other, no matter how unintentionally.

The very nature of being in relationship causes us to reflect upon ourselves in both past and present relationships, which can be a powerful elicitor of shame. It can remind us of early attachment experiences and relationships in our family of origin. As early attachment experiences are a powerful source of shame (see Chapter 2) which have often been implicitly stored, these can be re-invoked in both client and counsellor with little or no conscious awareness. As research has consistently shown that counsellor shame can significantly influence the process and outcome of psychotherapy (Covert *et al.* 2003; Leith and Baumeister 1998; Pope, Sonne and Greene 2006), it is critical to increase your awareness of your own shame to minimise potential aversive effects.

This chapter will look at counsellor shame and how this manifests in the therapeutic process. The focus is on enhancing awareness of the counsellor's experiences of shame and how these have impacted on them. This will enable them to name their shame and identify embedded defences against shame and how these manifest particularly in the therapeutic relationship. The chapter will also explore shame that is activated due to the nature of the therapeutic setting, how client shame can elicit counsellor shame, responses to clients' defences, and how these intermingle and are enacted in the therapeutic process. Consideration will also be given to the impact of shaming experiences whilst in training, in particular in supervision and in training institutes and clinical placements.

DEFINITION OF THERAPIST SHAME

Ladany, Klinger and Kulp (2011, p.308) define therapist shame as 'an intense and enduring reaction to a threat to the therapist's sense of identity that consists of an exposure of the therapist's physical, emotional, or intellectual defects that occurs in the context of psychotherapy'. This is commonly a conflation of the client's own historical shame experiences and the effects of the therapeutic setting as well as an intermingling of the client's and counsellor's shame and shame defences. Practitioners need to be aware of how these shame dynamics manifest in the therapeutic process in order to minimise misinterpretation of the source of shame. You will need to be mindful of whose shame is being elicited and how the interaction of your and the client's shame can escalate shame and lead to a range of iatrogenic effects that endanger the therapeutic encounter.

It is essential that you become familiar with the language of your own shame so that you can distinguish between your shame and that of the client and that which exists in the space between you. To facilitate this you will need to know your own sources of shame, and your vulnerabilities, anxieties and fears around these being exposed. With such awareness you will be able to regulate shame in the therapeutic process to ensure mutuality and authentic connection in which to explore shame without judgement or humiliation.

THE COUNSELLOR'S OWN SHAME

The degree to which individual practitioners have processed their own historical shame will vary enormously depending on how much this was addressed in their personal therapy and training. Nathanson (1992) argues that therapists tend to practise the same way as their own therapy and training. Thus, if shame was addressed during your own personal therapy and training, then it is likely that you will have considerable awareness of your own shame. If, however, shame did not feature during your training then it is likely that there may be some old unprocessed shame of which you are unaware. It might be helpful to reflect on this before proceeding.

Reflection

Take some time to reflect on how shame was addressed in your personal therapy and training. Did you work on your own experiences of shame in your personal therapy or did you learn about shame through what you were taught in your training, or from reading about it, or from your clients once you were qualified?

If you feel that you have had little or no opportunity to explore your own historical shame it might be helpful to devote some time to consider your experience of shame and how this has shaped you. You may wish to go back to some of the reflection points in earlier chapters to help you identify early shame experiences in the family and how these have shaped your sense of self (see Chapter 2) and link these to any shame-based traits such as a sense of inadequacy, perfectionism, negative self-thoughts or narcissistic tendencies.

Exercise

Counsellor awareness exercise: your own experience of shame

1. On a sheet of paper make a list of your experiences of shame in the past and present.

2. Reflect on how these experiences have affected how you view yourself and what beliefs you hold about yourself.

3. Next reflect on how your experiences of shame have impacted on your behaviour, how you relate to others, and your relational worth.

4. Make a list of what triggers your sense of shame in the present and how you manage this.

Given the centrality of the therapeutic relationship it is critical that you consider to what extent shame has impacted on your relational worth and how it feels to be connected to others. If early attachment experiences were shaming it can leave a nub of anxiety and doubt around our capacity to love and be loved, and a concomitant fear of intimacy and connection (Jordan 1991), which can be re-enacted in the therapeutic relationship. If you have shame-based fears about closeness you may avoid psychological contact or connection with clients through adopting an absent, detached professional stance, using prescriptive protocols or by retreating into intellectualisation, which can unwittingly shame the client by reinforcing their lack of relational worth. Similarly, shame-based narcissistic needs for power and control can manifest in power struggles in the therapeutic process in which any threat to your authority can elicit shame defences.

In exploring your experience of shame and shame-based tendencies you will be able to identify any habitual shame defences (see Chapter 5) and how these manifest in your personal and professional relationships, including when working with clients. Being equipped with an increased awareness of your own shame will make it easier to distinguish between shame that belongs to you, what is evoked in the client and how this is entwined in the space between you. This will help you to take responsibility for your contribution to, or co-creation of, shame, and manage shame dynamics in the therapeutic process more effectively.

Alongside shame, you may also experience embarrassment, humiliation or guilt, all of which are distinct from shame. Ladany *et al.* (2011; see Table 11.1) argue that embarrassment is less intense and extreme in that it is momentary and acute, and as such much milder than shame. In contrast humiliation does not stem from the self but is elicited by the actions of others and may be less disruptive to sense of self, while guilt results from a specific action which could harm someone else.

You may experience any one of these during a session with varying degree of impact on self or the client. For example, if you fail to turn up for a scheduled session, you might be suffused by a sense of shame which can haunt you as an example of your inadequacy and incompetence. If, however, you are late for a session you may feel deeply embarrassed but this will be fleeting and evaporate once settled into the session. You may feel humiliated if the client berates you for being tardy and recognise feelings of humiliation as a response to the client's rebuke. This will elicit guilt for harm done, which can be repaired through accepting responsibility for your lateness and a genuine apology.

Table 11.1 Examples of shame, embarrassment, humiliation and guilt in therapy (Adapted from Ladany *et al.* 2011)		
Construct	**Impact**	**Therapeutic example**
Shame	Intense and enduring reaction to a threat to the therapist's sense of identity	Missing a scheduled session, falling asleep
Embarrassment	Fleeting and acute, mild and less intense	Being late, being distracted
Humiliation	Response to action of client	Being reprimanded for lateness, challenged by client
Guilt	Specific action that can cause harm to client	Being late when client in crisis, falling asleep

COUNSELLOR SHAME DUE TO THE THERAPEUTIC PROCESS

The very nature of therapy can evoke shame, which can impact on how shame is managed in the therapeutic process. This tends to cluster around professionalism, the success or failure of therapy, and process dynamics such as sustaining empathy, compassion and acceptance. In addition shame can be evoked around competency and access to and mastery of requisite skills, as well as challenges arising from client shame and shame defences.

Most sentient clinicians will experience a degree of vulnerability around professionalism, especially in initial meetings with clients. This usually clusters around questions such as 'Can I really help this client?', 'Am I good enough, and do I have the right skills?' or 'Will I be able to like this client, and feel empathy and compassion for them?' Counsellors consistently face challenges in trying to solve unanswerable human questions, which can leave them bewildered, inadequate or confounded by client presentations and with doubts about their ability or fitness to practise. This is often the result of high levels of responsibility and expectation to engage in good ethical practice. When these expectations become unrealistic they can become powerful elicitors of shame.

COUNSELLING SKILLS FOR WORKING WITH SHAME

Remember

Both you and your client will have vulnerabilities around being inadequate, unseen, unmet and accepted, which can lead to fear of exposure, shame and humiliation.

This is typically due to what Maltsberger and Buie (1974) call the three narcissistic snares common to psychotherapists, which are to 'heal all, know all and love all' (p.138). These reflect counsellors' unrealistic expectations of themselves with regard to caregiving and an inflated sense of omnipotence. The pressure to live up to these unrealistic aspirations can be enormous, and when they are not attained can elicit a sense of failure and shame. It is helpful to remember that such expectations are not always possible and to focus on much more realistic aspirations. Other areas in which shame is elicited in the counsellor include competency and skills, the process of counselling, therapeutic stance, talking about difficult topics and the counsellor's own psychology.

Remember

Counsellor shame is often elicited due to what Maltsberger and Buie (1974) call the three narcissistic snares common to psychotherapists, which is to 'heal all, know all and love all' (p.138).

In order to heal, all counsellors need to feel confident in their knowledge and skills, and when this is undermined they may experience accompanying feelings of shame. Common sources of shame in this category are feeling deskilled, confused, overwhelmed or not knowing what to do, all of which contribute to a sense of incompetence and inadequacy. In addition, counsellors who feel that they are not all knowing can experience a real sense of failure, which can trigger feelings of shame.

The aspiration to love all is also a source of shame whereby counsellors believe that they should like all their clients equally and feel ashamed if they have unacceptable feelings towards them. Thus if practitioners find that they do not like their clients, or indeed dislike or hate them, they feel ashamed in not being able to 'love all' (Dalenberg 2000, p.190). This is amplified when counsellors who fear connection with their clients, or abhor dependency needs, recoil from their clients' neediness. As such unacceptable feelings escalate and the counsellor's congruence is compromised, they may feel increasingly ashamed and compelled to disown their negative feelings. This unbearable state of tension is all too frequently resolved by interpreting such feelings as negative counter-transference in response to the client's transference. While this is undoubtedly the case at times, it might equally be the counsellor's own shame around unacceptable feelings. Some counsellors may also feel envious of their clients for things they have that the counsellor feels they lack. This could be a more elevated status, career, wealth or family relationships and friends. Such envy can be corrosive in that it triggers feelings of shame or feeling 'less than'.

A further potent source of shame for some practitioners is if they develop romantic or sexual feelings towards their clients. The taboo and concomitant shame around erotic feelings towards clients can prevent practitioners from talking about this with colleagues or supervisors. As a result, many clinicians will want to deny or disown erotic feelings, or conceptualise these as a reaction to the client's erotic transference. It is essential that you explore any erotic feelings you may have about the client to ascertain what is due to the client's erotic transference and what emanates from your own desire and sexual interest irrespective of the client's transference (Sanderson 2013). Most importantly, in order to contain and manage erotic counter-transference, you will need to discuss this with a trusted colleague or supervisor to avoid the violation of sexual boundaries (Pope and Bouhoutsos 1986). To help you in this it is worth remembering that erotic feelings in both client and counsellor are not uncommon during the therapeutic process, and rather than being seen as a source of shame they need to be explored within the context of relational expectations and dynamics.

❗ Warning

Unrealistic expectations of self and the client can lead to feelings of inadequacy and shame defences.

Counsellors may also have unrealistic expectations of themselves with regards to physical and somatic reactions in the therapeutic process. You may feel embarrassed by the myriad sounds that accompany digestive processes, peristalsis or the inopportune need to relieve yourself. You may also feel ashamed of somatic responses to uncomfortable feelings such as blushing, hot flushes, uncontrollable laughter or tears, muscle spasm, sexual arousal or having an erection. All of these natural and normal responses may be suffused with shame as they do not fit the expectations you may have of yourself to be the perfect therapist. The desire to be the perfect therapist may also manifest in unattainable expectations such as being fully present at all times with no lapses in concentration or memory or never being distracted by your own concerns or worries. The pressure of such unrealistic expectations exerts a powerful influence on your felt sense of shame, which if left unchecked can impede the therapeutic process.

Remember

Physical reactions and bodily functions are normal even in the therapeutic setting and must be viewed as such rather than as a source of shame.

Some counsellors may also have unreasonable expectations of clients, which can be shame inducing. Practitioners may expect clients to be grateful for the time and effort invested by the counsellor, and desire overt demonstrations of appreciation for being there for them. Similarly, when clients challenge your interpretations or interventions, you may feel disrespected, inadequate or unappreciated and feel compelled to defend against these by becoming resentful or hostile. As it is hard to expose your own vulnerabilities or shame you may be reluctant to discuss this openly, which will make it hard to be congruent in relation to the client.

Not being able to speak openly about difficult topics is often hampered by feelings of shame. One topic that is typically hard for many counsellors is fees and non-payment. Many practitioners feel embarrassed about making money from a client's misery or distress and want to prove that their commitment and compassion is real, not just a paid-for service. This is poignantly reflected in Ablow's statement: 'I rent my soul... I still feel embarrassed when my patients mention clinic fees. No matter how much I care for a patient, the fact that dollars are the life blood of the relationships seems to colour my concern as impure – a hint of the prostitute feigning romance' (Ablow 1992, p.35). This is also a source of shame for clients who may feel humiliated by having to pay for the basic human need for connection.

Counsellors who offer low-cost counselling may oscillate between feeling exploited by the low-cost client and being the exploiter of full-fee-paying clients. A further source of shame is around non-payment, especially if the counsellor knows that the client is struggling financially and making considerable sacrifices to continue therapy. This is more prominent when there seems to be little or no movement in the therapeutic process and the desired change is proving elusive. Such slow therapeutic progress can become a further source of shame as practitioners may feel as though they are not helpful enough and not worth the client's expense (Dalenberg 2000). In addition you may feel frustrated with clients who leave all the responsibility for change and recovery to you and judge them for their passivity rather than understand their paralysis and work towards collaboration.

Another source of shame can arise when the practitioner becomes bored with the client's material or procrastination. Such boredom can result in becoming inattentive, yawning, feeling drowsy or falling asleep. Such signs of withdrawal can indicate a degree of dissociation in which the counsellor feels so overwhelmed by the client's trauma or distress that they disconnect from the client (Sanderson 2013). Either way, this is a source of shame for both counsellor and client and creates doubt about fitness to practise and competency. This is intensified if the counsellor's scheduled breaks or holidays occur at a critical point in the client's process. Practitioners might feel shame over a perceived contribution to the client's pain or being absent when they are most needed.

This is most commonly seen in practitioners who work with traumatised clients. In your endeavour to understand the impact of trauma and abuse and to avoid blaming the victim, you may need to ask detailed questions. In this you may fear re-traumatising the client, which results in either an avoidance of asking pertinent questions, or asking inappropriate re-shaming questions such as 'Why didn't you do something?' This can lead to misunderstanding, which is a source of shame for both you and the client. Practitioners may also feel shame over unacceptably strong feelings about the abuser as this is the antithesis of the neutral, objective and professional stance associated with good ethical practice. And yet strong feelings of outrage may be necessary to confirm harm done (Herman 2001) and show congruence in that 'One simply cannot face this degree of pain in someone with whom one is involved and not feel changed' (Dalenberg 2000, p.121).

In addition, you may have strong, negative feelings about the client for being a victim and allowing the abuse to continue. Alternatively you may envy clients who have had traumatic experiences and compare these with your less dramatic life experiences. This can lead to admiration of the courage and resilience of your clients, which can lead to a sense of shame, especially if you feel you are lacking in courage in your own life. You may also feel shame for being seen as voyeuristic in witnessing the client's pain, or as abusive in encouraging the client to talk about painful or traumatic material in detail. You may feel responsible for re-triggering painful experiences or re-traumatising the client. While this may be necessary therapeutically it can still become a source of shame for the therapist as being the cause of yet further pain. This is part of what is known as 'witness guilt' (Danieli 1994) in which shame is experienced when being a party to traumatic or evil actions, and in knowing how cruel humans can be (see Chapter 10). Such shame-related themes are commonly seen in trauma therapists (Danieli 1994) and warrant close monitoring and attention to avoid shame escalation.

While some of the shame experienced in the therapeutic process is in response to client material, the contribution of the counsellor's own psychology and past shame experiences cannot be ignored. Counsellors who have an avoidant attachment style or who fear closeness or intimacy may feel shame for avoiding psychological contact or connection with their clients. This shame may be disavowed by retreating into intellectual justifications for their behaviour and unwittingly shame the client in the process. Counsellors' need for power and control can manifest in power struggles in the therapeutic process. Any threat to the counsellor's power or authority can elicit shame or humiliation which needs to be defended at all costs. Such shame-based narcissistic tendencies must be monitored and acknowledged to prevent contamination of the therapeutic process. In addition you need to identify your own shame-based traits such as perfectionism and link these to your own shame scripts and defences. The following exercise will help with this.

Exercise
Tracking your shame triggers and defences in therapy
To track your shame triggers and defences in the therapeutic process use the format in Table 11.2 to make a list of things that trigger shame and the strategies you use to defend against shame. Reflect on these and consider more appropriate alternative strategies and make a commitment to introduce these into your client work.

Table 11.2 Tracking shame triggers and defences template		
Shame triggers	Shame defences	Alternative responses

SHAME-INDUCING THERAPIST RESPONSES

As counsellors have more power in the therapeutic setting you need to make sure that the disproportionate power dynamics are not exploited at the expense of your clients. In order to engender a more equal balance of power you need to acknowledge your own shame and shame defences. To this effect you need to be aware of how shame screens can manifest in the therapeutic setting and how these might induce shame in the client.

One way that counsellors can induce shame in their clients is through pathologising or labelling them. This has the effect of dehumanising or objectifying the client and rendering them invisible. This will re-trigger early shame experiences or humiliation. This can be reinforced by therapist interpretations, especially if they are primarily theory driven and fail to consider the client's perspective or subjective experience. When these are poorly conceptualised or insensitively articulated clients may feel re-shamed and withdraw. Any anger you feel at being misjudged may lead to defensive use of interpretation rather than examination of what emanates from you. You will need to be willing to examine yourself and your reactions and offer an authentic and heartfelt apology in order to rebuild the interpersonal bridge (Kaufman 1992).

There is a danger that when our own inadequacy and shame are triggered we resort to intellectualisation or protocol-driven techniques, which can feel shaming to the client as they feel they are not seen as individuals but rather as objects of scrutiny that must be fitted into the therapist's theoretical orientation. This is particularly the case when you interpret all your reactions to the client as a response to the client's transference. It is worth remembering that your counter-transferential reactions will always be a combination of the client's transference, your reactions to that, plus elements from your own personality and traits (Clarkson 2004). Being honest in your evaluation of these entwined elements ensures not only good ethical practice but also an opportunity for a more authentic therapeutic relationship.

Warning

Pathologising, dehumanising or objectifying your client will re-invoke shame and re-traumatise them.

Alongside this, counsellors who are too wedded to a specific range of techniques or interventions may unwittingly ignore the needs of the individual client. For example, if you believe that insight and awareness or cognitive re-structuring are sufficient to alleviate emotional pain, you may induce shame in the client who does not respond to these techniques in the expected, or anticipated, way. In this clients often feel that they are too difficult or damaged and this can re-trigger the shame of feeling inadequate and incompetent. This is often seen when a particular model is inappropriately applied to clients who have a range of experiences and difficulties that do not lend themselves to a single model or approach and who would benefit from a more integrative or pluralistic approach (Sanderson 2013).

Warning

Client shame may arise not out of a sense of inadequacy, but from what is done to them by others who try to control or disempower them. You must guard against eliciting such shame by your actions, interventions or interpretations.

This can be amplified when the counsellor takes too much control over the pacing of the therapeutic process. Rushing the client in order to progress therapeutic change can be shaming for the client as they feel they are letting the counsellor down or are beyond help. You must ensure that you find a healthy balance between when to accelerate and when to put your foot on the brake so that the client feels they have some control and autonomy in the counselling process. To facilitate this you must examine your own needs and expectations of clients and acknowledge when your frustration with lack of progress is due to your own needs or sense of shame. When you take a disproportionate amount of responsibility for the outcome or success of therapy you may end up feeling inadequate or deskilled, which can trigger shame.

Counsellors may also induce shame in clients by being disengaged or perfunctory in how they relate to the client. This may manifest in not really listening to the client, being insensitive to the client's needs, ending sessions coldly or abruptly, overly rigid boundaries and inflexibility in scheduling sessions, or preoccupation with your own needs. Conversely, counsellors who hide behind a professional mask of cognitive empathy rather than affective empathy will be experienced by clients as patronising and shaming (Sanderson 2013). Cognitive empathy is using the right language and phrases that are associated with empathy without necessarily feeling empathy. Associated with this is the adoption of a polite, professional tone of voice that clients often experience as being talked down to and thus shaming. To avoid being seen as patronising, begrudging or as just 'going through the motions' you must make sure that you are congruent in conveying genuine affective empathy and compassion.

Warning

A professional mask of cognitive rather than affective empathy will be experienced by clients as patronising and shaming.

Many clients are highly sensitive to nuances in non-verbal messages such as body language, facial expression and tone of voice. They use this to assess empathy, compassion, level of engagement and feeling understood. Thus it is essential that you are emotionally engaged and are able to convey this appropriately. Demonstrations of human warmth, reciprocal emotional engagement and genuine interest are seen by clients as indicators of relational worth and being accepted. In the absence of these, clients feel rejected, humiliated and shamed.

Top tip

Having the client in mind both in and outside of session, and conveying this, can enhance relational worth and minimise the experience of shame and humiliation in the client.

CLIENTS SHAMING THE COUNSELLOR

While it is difficult to bear witness to clients' shame on a daily basis it is exacerbated when clients mask and ward off their own shame by shaming the counsellor. This is most likely in those clients who use attack other as a defence against shame (see Chapter 5). To manage their shame they will attack others, in this case you, in order to evacuate their own shame and to make you feel shame. Typically these are automatic, unconscious defence reactions which the client has not linked to their own shame. The forms of attack can be both overt and covert and will need to be explored. Commonly these are interpreted as negative transference but may warrant more detailed examination. Overt examples of attack other include hostile criticisms of the counsellor and undermining the counsellor's capability and credibility with regard to credentials, knowledge, skills, competency and genuineness in their care, empathy or compassion. More subtle manifestations include passivity in engaging in the work, resistance to change, being stuck, non-payment of fees, missing or being late for session, premature termination or repeated threats of suicide. You will need to understand these as a protective strategy to ward off shame and not personalise such attacks.

Exercise

How clients elicit shame in you

Reflect on your clients and how they elicit shame in you. This may be due to witnessing their shame or through overt or covert defences against shame. You may wish to insert these on a pie chart to identify where you feel most vulnerable. Next consider what would help you to become more robust in the presence of client shame.

As these defence strategies can manifest in the therapeutic setting, counsellors need to ensure that they provide a safe environment to work through shame. It is critical that practitioners avoid re-shaming the survivor no matter how provocative they may be. This is part of testing the counsellor to ensure that they are truly safe to be authentic. Counsellors need to acknowledge the survivor's needs and vulnerability and understand the function of these defensive strategies. The expression of rage, grandiosity and arrogance is a cover for the deep hurt and narcissistic wounds and is designed to keep the practitioner at a distance. In addition, fierce self-sufficiency and the repudiation of needs and vulnerability are ways of avoiding dependency and intimacy and must not be personalised.

DANGER OF THERAPIST SHAME

As highlighted by research (Ladany *et al.* 2011), client and counsellor shame have significant impact on the outcome of therapy such as therapeutic impasses, ruptures in the therapeutic relationships, client and therapist outcomes, and premature termination. This is especially the case when practitioners are too wedded to their own perspective and out of touch with the client's, and therefore insensitive to the client's actual needs. Counsellors who are more preoccupied with satisfying their own needs for authority, being all knowing, right, self-righteous and emotionally absent, imply that they are more important than the client. In this they can appear to be indifferent to the client's experience and come across as dismissive, judgemental, patronising and shaming. This can lead to therapeutic passivity in which 'the decision to remain silent in the face of a humiliated, withdrawn patient…will always magnify shame because it confirms the patient's affect-driven belief that isolation is justified' (Nathanson 1992, p.325).

Top tip
Remember to acknowledge that shame can be co-created and take responsibility for your own shame and how this contributes to your client's shame.

The danger of therapeutic passivity or psychological withdrawal is that the counsellor will be perceived as cruel, punitive or uncaring, in which the client feels like an object of shame. As a result clients defend against rising shame by shaming the counsellor. The counsellor feels misunderstood and unappreciated as a result and feels shamed. If you have difficulty acknowledging or managing your own shame you are more likely to defend against this. This can manifest overtly by directly shaming the client through anger, humiliation and psychological withdrawal or in more subtle non-verbal ways such as tone of voice, body posture or adopting intellectual language designed to restore superiority over the client. All of these can lead to a spiral of reciprocal shaming which escalates shame and activates an insidious shame cycle in which both client and counsellor are re-shamed and humiliated. To avoid this you need to acknowledge your own shame, validate that shame can be co-created and take responsibility for your contribution to the client's shame. In conveying this to the client you will need to balance compassion for your own felt shame with compassion and empathy for your client's feeling

224 COUNSELLING SKILLS FOR WORKING WITH SHAME

of shame and humiliation. This will enable you to model how to accept and manage shame in a more authentic way. It is also an opportunity to explore human vulnerabilities and frailties, including how to repair ruptures in relationships and heal from the corrosive effects of shame.

COUNSELLOR SHAME IN SUPERVISION

Counsellor shame may also be elicited in a variety of other settings in the process of becoming a qualified counsellor and established practitioner. As a student you may have been exposed to shame in your training by your tutors, your training therapist or supervisor, or in your placements or internships. In addition, the danger of being shamed can continue post qualification by supervisors, clinical managers or work colleagues. While the potential for this occurs across all clinical settings, it is exacerbated in public or non-governmental organisations (NGOs) such as social work, emergency work such as the police, safeguarding and domestic abuse agencies, and charities who support survivors of complex trauma and abuse. These are often dangerously under-resourced with not enough staff managing extremely high case loads. This can lead to unrealistic expectations and concomitant shame when targets are not met, or the death of the vulnerable clients they are attempting to protect or support. The elevated risk of secondary traumatic stress in practitioners is often accompanied by a sense of shame for not being able to help clients as much as they would like to.

SHAME IN SUPERVISEES

As in therapy, shame is ubiquitous in supervision, especially when supervising counsellors in training. The power dynamic inherent in the training process is palpable and has to be managed appropriately to avoid shaming or re-shaming trainees. The very nature of trainee supervision is likely to promote feelings of shame as they are expected to reveal their nascent attempts at practice, which may expose anxieties, self-doubts, perceived inadequacies, unwitting errors or poorly managed interventions. The fear of such exposure and being judged as a poor candidate for clinical practice can lead to reduced self-disclosure (see Table 11.3). This is supported by research which indicates that counselling trainees often withhold information from supervisors for fear of being exposed or shamed (Alonso and Rutan 2012). In the need to hide and to avoid more shame, trainees tend to avoid disclosing material that might be viewed negatively. While many trainees withhold information around process-related material such as erotic transference and counter-transference, and their own shame when working with clients, Talbot (1995) found that trainees most commonly avoid disclosing their experience of the supervisory relationship, especially any felt sense of shame.

Reflection

Reflect on your experience as a counsellor in training and list examples of when and where you felt shame. Was shame elicited by tutors or trainers? Or was it elicited in supervision? Or in your clinical placements? Did this stop you from being authentic and avoiding disclosure? In considering these questions reflect on how shame was managed by yourself and the supervisor and what impact this had on your personal and professional development and on client outcomes.

This is interesting given the emphasis on the quality of the therapeutic relationship when working with clients in a relational way. There are a myriad of parallels between shame in therapy and supervision, not least the imbalance of power, authority and expertise. Supervisors have considerable power over trainees in terms of the future of their clinical career, making it even more important that they are able to make objective evaluations which are not predicated on shame-based judgements or supervisor defences against their own unprocessed shame (see Table 11.3). They need to apply here the same relational principles that underpin good therapeutic practice in their supervision of trainees. As trainees typically experience shame in supervision it is critical that supervisors are able to acknowledge not only the trainees' shame but also their own shame and how this manifests in the space between them. This is no different to the management of shame in the therapeutic process with clients, and supervisors will need to provide a safe and secure environment in which to explore and work through shame.

Table 11.3 Summary of supervisee and supervisor shame	
Supervisee shame	**Supervisor shame**
• Supervisee's own historical shame • Shame-based educational experiences • Focus on mistakes • Fear of not getting it right • Hypersensitivity to criticism • Lack of trust • Doubts about ability • Feeling overwhelmed • Being impacted by the work • Erotic transference or counter-transference • Fear of being judged • Fear of being seen as not fit to practise	• Supervisor's own historical shame • Unprocessed or unconscious shame • Unacknowledged shame defences • Feeling overwhelmed • Feeling deskilled • Having less knowledge about client, client group or presenting issue • Challenges to power or authority • Fear of authentic engagement in the supervisory relationship • Envy

To facilitate this, supervisors will need to distinguish the sources of shame in supervision and manage these appropriately. Talbot (1995) has highlighted three typical sources of shame in the supervisory relationship. These are shame that is evoked in the trainee in revealing their anxieties and fears, shame that emanates from the trainee around fear of not being approved of by an idealised supervisor, and the shame that arises from the intermingling of trainee and supervisor shame to minimise the risk of negative transference and counter-transference in the supervisory relationship.

Warning

If feelings of shame are not explored or processed the trainee's learning process will be impeded, which can inhibit personal and professional development and compromise the supervisee's well-being.

Shame is not just manifest when supervising trainees but also when supervising qualified counsellors (Ladany *et al.* 2011). To minimise the shame in supervisory relationships supervisors will need to be aware of supervisees' as well as their own shame and be willing to explore these and how they manifest in the supervisory relationship. Supervisors will need to adopt some of the necessary qualities to build a strong, collaborative supervisory alliance by creating a safe and secure environment where shame can be discussed in an open and candid way. In essence, if feelings of shame are not explored or processed, the supervisee's personal and professional development will be inhibited, which can lead to negative outcomes for both client and supervisee.

This is critical in order to repair ruptures and restore self-efficacy to the supervisee so that they are appropriately equipped to continue their work with their clients (Ladany *et al.* 2011). Most importantly supervisors need to ensure that they do not compromise the well-being of the supervisee or deliberately undermine their capacity to work with clients.

In acknowledging shame, supervisors may benefit from sharing common personal and professional vulnerabilities that are inherent in clinical practice through appropriate self-disclosure. This will facilitate a more optimal environment in which to explore shame and provide a good practice model of how to work through shame and shame defences with clients (Hahn 2001).

SHAME IN CLINICAL PLACEMENTS

Exposure to shame can also occur in clinical placements where there are unrealistically high expectations of trainees. This is especially the case in placements where clinical managers expect trainees to work with very vulnerable clients who have complex presentations that are often beyond qualified practitioners' capabilities, let alone trainees'. The stress and focus on not making mistakes because of the ramifications should this happen generate a fear of not getting it right. In addition, trainees who are dependent on good reports from clinical managers and supervisors may feel ashamed of wanting to not overload themselves and regulate the number of clients they take on, yet be too afraid to say 'no' in case they are perceived as lazy or incapable of managing a high case load, which undermines their belief in their ability.

The potential for shame in clinical settings is likely to increase, as access to clinical placements is highly competitive. This is because there are more trainees than there are clinical placements, which only reinforces the pressure of being judged and scrutinised. Clinical managers may overload trainees and expect them to manage case loads and client presentations that would stretch even highly experienced, qualified counsellors. There are many examples of clinical managers and supervisors shaming trainees and questioning their ability unfairly as they fail to acknowledge that they are still in training rather than fully qualified with years of experience behind them. Not only is this unethical but it serves to shame supervisees and trainees and undermines their ability to practise. Ultimately this does harm to the profession as well as clients who are trying to heal and recover from shame. Clinical managers, supervisors and trainers need to ensure that their trainees are fully equipped to enable clients to have a better understanding of shame, how to work through it and how to build shame resilience, which is the focus of the next chapter.

SUGGESTED READING

Dalenberg, C.J. (2000) *Countertransference and the Treatment of Trauma.* Washington, DC: American Psychological Association.

DeYoung, P.A. (2015) *Understanding and Treating Chronic Shame: A Relational/Neurobiological Approach.* Hove: Routledge.

Ladany, N., Friedlander, M.L. and Nelson, M.L. (2005) *Critical Events in Psychotherapy Supervision: An Interpersonal Approach.* Washington, DC: American Psychological Association.

Ladany, N., Klinger, R. and Kulp, L. (2011) 'Therapist Shame: Implications for Therapy and Supervision in Specific Action that Results in Harm to Others.' In R.L. Dearing and J.P. Tangney (eds) *Shame in the Therapy Hour.* Washington, DC: American Psychological Association.

Miller, S.B. (1985) *The Shame Experience.* Hillsdale, NJ: Erlbaum.

Miller, S.B. (1996) *Shame in Context.* London: Routledge.

Sanderson, C. (2013) *Counselling Skills for Working with Trauma: Healing from Child Sexual Abuse, Sexual Violence and Domestic Abuse.* London: Jessica Kingsley Publishers.

Tangney, J.P. and Dearing, R.L. (2011) 'Working with Shame in the Therapy Hour: Summary and Integration.' In R.L. Dearing and J.P. Tangney (eds) *Shame in the Therapy Hour.* Washington, DC: American Psychological Association.

12

SKILLS FOR BUILDING
SHAME RESILIENCE

Having explored, released and worked through shame, clients will have found ways to inoculate themselves against shame. This can be supported by building shame resilience through enhanced awareness, breaking the silence, becoming more visible and the consolidation of skills learnt so far. To ensure that the tyranny of shame no longer has the power it once did, clients will benefit from building resilience to manage future internal, or external, exposure to shame. Clients will need to be mindful that the most powerful antidote to shame is empathy and compassion, both for self and others, and it is this that leads to self-acceptance and authentic pride.

This chapter will look at how clients can consolidate the skills they have learnt in understanding shame and how these can be honed through daily practice to build resilience to shame. The emphasis will be on encouraging mindfulness, practising critical awareness, reaching out to others and developing self-acceptance through empathy and self-compassion. This will allow both clients and counsellors to embrace who they are rather than who they are supposed to be. In having the courage to accept the self and develop authentic pride both you and your clients will be able to cultivate self-acceptance in which imperfections and flaws are embraced and seen as marks of wisdom which increase our value rather than things that need to be hidden or disguised.

CONSOLIDATION OF SURVIVAL SKILLS
TO COUNTERACT SHAME

To master the range of skills that clients have acquired while working through shame it is helpful to identify the most useful survival skills and consolidate these to help build shame resilience. These survival skills will be essential for clients to refer to and implement throughout their journey in recovering from shame and will need to be practised regularly. As clients become more aware of what is most effective and gain self-confidence they can add to their repertoire by devising their own customised strategies. You may also begin to add to your toolkit with a range of techniques and exercises that are designed to build shame resilience.

Exercise
Top ten survival skills

Invite the client to reflect on what they have found most useful throughout the therapeutic process to recover and heal from shame. This could consist of metaphors, images, exercises or practical skills that have enhanced self-acceptance. Examples are images or grounding skills, strategies to interrupt shame spirals or cycles, critical evaluation of shame-based messages or giving voice to positive aspects of the self. Next encourage clients to list ten of the most effective strategies and remind them to implement these whenever they feel they are being overwhelmed by shame or shame-based defences.

Equipped with these strategies clients are able to move toward integrating shame-based experiences and rather than be crippled by them to become more connected to their inner experiencing and accepting of themselves.

MINDFULNESS

Mindfulness helps clients to become more alert and able to focus and is an invaluable technique for building self-acceptance. It also helps to calm the mind and access a more peaceful, relaxed state of awareness. Most importantly it enables clients to identify, tolerate and reduce difficult, painful or frightening thoughts, feelings and sensations. In practising mindfulness clients are able to gain a sense of mastery over thoughts and feelings, rather than being controlled by them. This gives them the sense of agency to feel more in control of intrusive negative thoughts and feelings of shame.

Remember

It is important that clients know they can explore different methods and techniques to practise mindfulness in order to find the ones that are most effective for them. Once clients have done this you will need to encourage them to practise these daily or when necessary.

Mindfulness is also a way of helping clients to be in the present moment, both internally and externally. Being present allows clients to manage overwhelming and painful past experiences of shame and fears about the future. There are a range of courses, downloads and apps available to help clients to practise mindfulness, in addition to your own techniques and the exercises below.

A good exercise to start with is mindfulness breathing. The aim is to move your client's attention from one sensory input to the next, taking 15 breaths during each part of the exercise. They can take more or fewer breaths. You will need to encourage your client to breathe from their abdomen and, on the out-breath, silently count the number of breaths they are on. Clients can try this anywhere because, to others, they are just sitting or standing in an ordinary way.

Exercise
Mindfulness breathing
Invite your client to relax while you say the following:

Sit quietly with both feet on the ground and your hands on your lap. Allow yourself to feel centred in the chair. Bring all of your attention to the physical act of breathing. Start to notice the breath as it enters your body through your nose and travels to your lungs. Notice with curiosity whether the inward and outward breaths are cool or warm, and notice where the breath travels as it enters and departs. Also notice the breath as your lungs relax and you inhale through your nose. Don't try to do anything with your breathing – simply notice it, pay attention to it and be aware of it. It doesn't matter if your breathing is slow or fast, deep or shallow; it just is what it is. Allow your body to do what it does naturally.

You will start to notice that each time you breathe in your diaphragm or stomach will expand, and each time you breathe out your diaphragm or stomach will relax. Again, don't try to do anything – just be aware of the physical sensations of breathing in and breathing out. If you find that thoughts intrude, this is okay. Don't worry, just notice the thoughts, allow them to be, and gently bring your awareness back to your breath. Start this exercise initially for five minutes, building up daily. You can also do this exercise lying down in bed if you have difficulty sleeping. It is simply a way of allowing you to have more mindful and conscious awareness of your body and its surroundings, its breathing and its capacity to relax. When our breathing relaxes our muscles relax.

Some clients may initially feel that mindfulness is not for them or that they are frightened to engage in it for a prolonged period of time.

These clients may benefit from very brief mindfulness exercises that they can do in 60 seconds (see Box 12.1). Once your client finds the one that works for them, they can be encouraged to build up to five minutes and longer.

Box 12.1 60-second mindfulness exercises

1. **Mindful breathing** Try to pay attention to what one breath feels like. Feel the sensations of one breath flowing into and out from your body. Notice the sensations in your nostrils, your shoulders, your rib cage, your belly, etc.

2. **Mindful brain break** Use mindfulness to give your brain a break rather than filling up every tiny space in your day by automatically reaching to check your email. Instead spend a few seconds looking outside the window, at things such as the leaves fluttering on the trees.

3. **Mindful eating** Try mindful eating for the first two bites of any meal or snack. For the first two bites, pay attention to the sensory experiences – the texture, taste, smell and appearance of the food, as well as the sounds when you bite into your food. Just pay attention to the sensory experience in an experiential rather than evaluative way.

4. **Mindful actions** Pick an action you do at the same time every day and plan to do that action mindfully, for example the moment you wake up or when you go to bed.

5. **Mindful sensation** Pay attention to the feeling of air on your skin for 10–60 seconds. This is best done when wearing short sleeves or with some skin exposed.

6. **Mindful body** Scan your body from top to toe for any sensations of discomfort or tension. Attempt to soften the sensations of discomfort. Next, scan your body for any sensations of comfort or ease.

As clients become more comfortable with the practice of mindfulness you can encourage them to focus their attention on their inner experiencing by focusing on each of the sensory channels.

Exercise
Mindfulness for each of the sensory channels
Ask your client to do each of the following (on different occasions).

1. **Visual**: Look around you and name five different objects, or five blue/black/green objects.

2. **Hearing**: Close your eyes and listen for five different sounds.

3. **Touch**: Look at, name and touch five different objects, noticing their texture, temperature, mass and weight.

4. **Smell**: Look in a garden or park and smell five different plants, shrubs or trees, noticing their colours, texture and aroma.

5. **Taste**: Look in the kitchen and name, taste and smell five different foods or ingredients, noticing their colours, texture, taste and aroma.

Mindfulness of shame-based thoughts

The practice of mindfulness can also be applied to shame-based thoughts. Clients often treat thoughts as if they are facts, especially their shame-based thoughts such as 'I am no good' and 'I am unlovable'. If clients are unable to evaluate these thoughts, or if they are consistently reinforced by others, they become internalised beliefs. Over time these beliefs become so embedded that clients construe them as facts and a true and accurate reflection of their core identity. It is essential when building shame resilience that clients challenge shame-based thoughts and beliefs about themselves, and find ways of becoming more aware of their present shame-based thoughts so that these do not become solidified as beliefs and facts. You can help your clients by encouraging them to pay attention to their thoughts through the use of the exercise below. You could encourage clients to find a personally meaningful metaphor for allowing thoughts to float in and out of awareness without judgement such as the ebb and flow of a wave or tide, leaves floating on a stream or clouds in the sky.

Exercise
Mindfulness of thoughts

Ask your client to sit comfortably while you read the following:

Start with mindfulness of the breath. Allow yourself to notice any thoughts that come into your head as you are aware of your breathing. Notice, pay attention to and accept these thoughts, without judgement. Thoughts are not bad or good, positive or negative, they just are what they are – the thought that you happen to be having at this particular moment.

You may become aware that you are having difficulty thinking about your thoughts, so think about that. You may be thinking: 'I can't do this very well.' This is a thought, and so allow yourself to think about that. Notice each passing thought and then the one that comes after it, and then the one that comes after that. You may notice that, just at the moment you become aware of a thought, it passes and is replaced by another thought. That's what happens – thoughts come, and they go. Finally, bring yourself back to awareness of the breath.

PRACTISING CRITICAL AWARENESS

Through challenging shame-based thoughts and beliefs clients will be able to develop greater capacity for critical awareness of the familial or sociocultural origins of these thoughts to assess their validity. Clients typically find when evaluating these that they begin to question their own and others' expectations and what purpose they serve. Invariably such expectations serve others more than the client and thus need to be explored so that the client can let go of false or toxic beliefs that prevent them from accepting themselves. Most importantly, it is through reality checking and practising critical awareness that clients can begin to identify who they want to be rather than trying to be who others want them to be (Brown 2007a). Through practising mindfulness and critical awareness you can help clients to build resilience to being defined and judged by others.

BUILDING RESILIENCE

There is considerable research that emphasises the role of resilience in helping individuals to adapt to stress and adversity, or recover from the aversive effects of trauma, abuse and shaming experiences (American Psychological Association 2014; Rutter 2008; Werner and Smith 2001). While resilience is in part linked to temperament it is not a personality trait and therefore can be learned. You need to help clients to see resilience as a process rather than a character trait so as not to shame them, and to emphasise that they too can build resilience.

The most fundamental factor in resilience is having positive relationships that offer mutual and reciprocal support and care. Many clients who have suffered shame often find it hard to be in a relationship and so typically lack the most essential ingredient in building resilience. Other factors that are crucial to building resilience include a positive self-concept and confidence in one's strengths and abilities, which are often eroded in shame-prone clients, along with the necessary communication skills to relate to others. In addition, the fear of being shamed prevents clients from reaching out to others for help, which reduces their ability to regulate or manage their emotions and which is also necessary for acquiring resilience. In combination these deficits impact on the ability to problem solve, making it harder to manage stress or adversity.

The American Psychological Association (2014) suggests that there are ten essential factors that allow individuals to build resilience which include maintaining good relationships, accepting circumstances that cannot be changed, developing self-awareness and self-confidence, developing realistic goals and moving towards them, taking care of both mind and body, paying attention to one's needs and feelings and maintaining a hopeful outlook. You will need to encourage clients to develop all of these throughout the therapeutic process in order to restore meaning and purpose in life (see Figure 12.1).

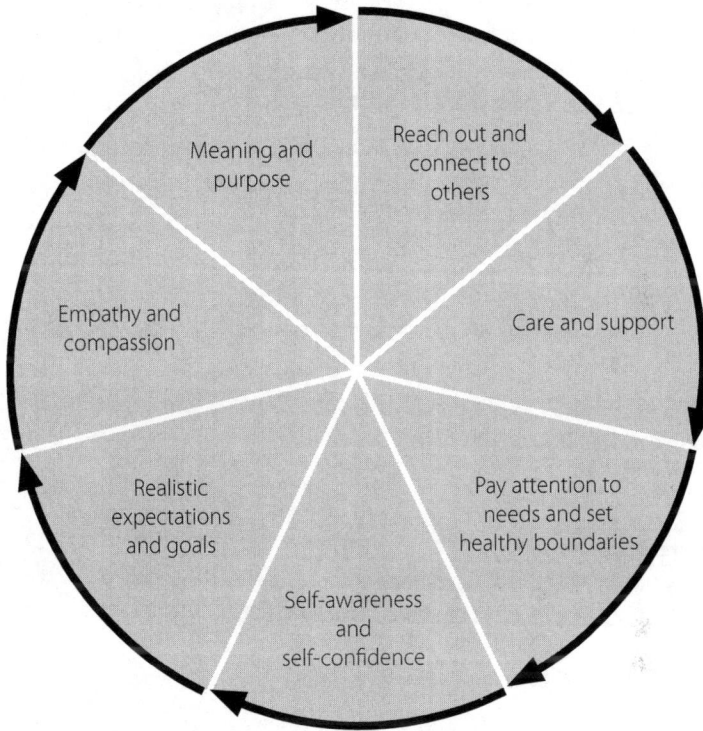

Figure 12.1 Wheel of resilience

BUILDING SHAME RESILIENCE

The fundamental factors that build resilience can equally be applied to the building of shame resilience. Brené Brown (2007a, p.5) defines shame resilience as the 'person's ability to recognise and understand shame, move through it constructively while maintaining a basic level of authenticity, and increase his or her level of courage, compassion, and connection as a result of experiencing shame'. This necessitates an awareness of the function of shame and the influence of sociocultural beliefs, and recognising early shame-based experiences, shame-based thoughts and beliefs and the loops and shame cycles that enforce and maintain shame. This is the focus of much of the therapeutic work when exploring shame in which you will have helped clients to identify shame triggers, shame cycles and the range of defences against shame. Once these have been identified the client can begin to move towards recovery from shame.

To facilitate this, clients will need to cultivate resilience by reaching out to, and connecting to, others and breaking the secrecy and silence that fuels shame. This can be done by talking to trusted others about shame, which gives a voice to shame and reduces its power. Many clients will initially fear reaching out to others in case they are judged and re-shamed, so you will need to help them pace this to make it more manageable. As one of the most common symptoms of shame is looking down and averting eye contact you could invite the client to become aware of eye gaze and to make eye contact with someone they perceive as compassionate. This will help them to make the initial contact to connect and build a relationship. As a trusting relationship develops the client will be able to share their shame and recognise that shame is universal and touches all. The relief in sharing shame is empowering and allows the relationship to blossom and become one of shared experience, laughter and joy rather than shame (Brown 2009).

Top tip
A powerful antidote to shame is making eye contact with compassionate people rather than hanging one's head in shame and averting one's eyes.

Authentic sharing requires taking risks and exposure to vulnerability which can be anxiety provoking and potentially re-invoke shame. It is for this reason that clients need to choose someone they can trust. To ensure that the client's shame is acknowledged it is helpful to ask the trusted friend to just listen rather than give advice, and ask them not to deflect or disqualify the felt sense of shame by telling the client that they are wonderful or that they shouldn't feel shame. It is critical that the client feels heard and is able to name their shame and not have it replaced with words that try to minimise or alter their experience. Some clients will find it hard to ask for what they need and will need to be reminded that giving shame a voice and sharing is the first step in reducing its toxic power.

Through reaching out, clients will increase their opportunities for care and support. In this they will need to pay attention to their needs and make sure they set healthy boundaries so that they do not get entrapped in a cycle of relational shame. When this is combined with enhanced self-awareness and self-confidence they can begin to adopt more realistic expectations of themselves and others, which allows them to set and attain more realistic goals.

EMPATHY AND COMPASSION

Along with connection, the most powerful antidotes to shame are empathy and compassion (Brown 2007a; Gilbert 2009) in which we see things from others' perspectives, withhold judgement and recognise and communicate our understanding of emotions to others as well as to ourselves. Empathy researchers continue this emphasis on general perspective-taking, defining empathy as 'an emotional response that stems from another's emotional state or condition and is congruent with the other's emotional state or condition' (Eisenberg *et al.* 1991, p.65). The need to hide and fear of judgement inherent in shame reduce the client's opportunities for empathic understanding or connection. You will need to ensure that you remain empathic to the client's experience of shame and how this has impacted on them. In conveying genuine affective, rather than cognitive, empathy to the client they can begin to develop empathy for themselves. You will need to be mindful that clients who have never experienced empathic responses and feel no empathy for themselves may experience your empathy as patronising by interpreting it as pity and yet another source of shame.

COMPASSION

To have compassion requires us to notice that someone is suffering and feel moved by this to the extent that we feel warmth, caring and a desire to help the person. It also means recognising that suffering, imperfections and failures are part of common humanity and require understanding and kindness to others when they make mistakes rather than judgement. Many shame-prone clients struggle with compassion as invariably they have little or no experience of this. This makes it difficult to receive compassion or have compassion for themselves as they feel that they are the architects of their shame. This is most prominent in those clients whose pain and suffering have been ignored and who have never received compassionate responses.

Many clients who have been shamed and felt rejected have little or no experience of compassion and it will seem alien to them. As a result they will regard compassion with suspicion and fear being humiliated and shamed in its presence. You will need to remain steadfast and remain empathic and compassionate despite the client's resistance so that they can accept compassionate responses and begin to feel compassion for themselves. This can be supported by a range of exercises which can help clients to develop self-compassion. A good starting point is mindfulness compassion (see p.234), especially with clients who have benefited from practising mindfulness techniques.

SELF-COMPASSION

Brené Brown (2007a) suggests that the way to restore intrinsic worth is through building self-compassion by 'treating ourselves the way we treat other people we love and respect' (p.5). Thus, self-compassion involves acting the same way towards yourself as you would for someone you care about. It is about noticing when you are experiencing pain, distress or shame and soothing this hurt, rather than ignoring or judging it. It is essential when building self-compassion that clients are able to be kind to themselves and move towards change because they care about themselves rather than needing to be perfect. Most importantly, clients need to know that having self-compassion is part of honouring and accepting one's humanness, in all its imperfections. In accepting rather than fighting the shared reality of what it means to be human they can begin to feel compassion for themselves and others.

THE THREE CORE ELEMENTS OF SELF-COMPASSION

There are three core elements of self-compassion: mindfulness, common humanity and self-kindness (see Figure 12.2). Self-compassion necessitates paying attention to all negative thoughts, feelings and experiences with openness to ensure that feelings are neither suppressed nor exaggerated and can enter mindful awareness. Mindfulness is a non-judgemental, receptive mind state in which clients can observe thoughts and feelings as they are, without trying to suppress or deny them. It also prevents becoming 'over-identified' with shame-based thoughts and feelings, and minimises the risk of becoming entrapped in the cycle of shame and negative reactivity.

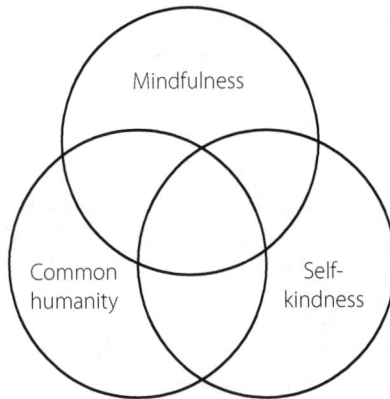

Figure 12.2 The three core elements of self-compassion

Common humanity is the recognition that being human means to be vulnerable and imperfect and that no one is alone in their suffering or sense of inadequacy. It is also about recognising that everyone is shaped by their environment, early experiences and expectations from others that they have little control over. In accepting this clients are able to see that everyone is interdependent and that any failings or inadequacies are not inherent character flaws but a record of the many experiences that shape all individuals. Thus, these are not personal defects but examples of being human and relating to others. With this recognition clients can begin to move towards self-kindness in which they are able to be kind and understanding toward the self when making mistakes, failing or feeling inadequate, rather than feeling shame. This will allow clients to accept reality rather than fighting it and through this gain greater self-acceptance.

In order to build self-compassion clients will need to incorporate all three core elements to transform shame. They will be aided in this by using their mindfulness skills and applying these to focusing on compassion and begin to develop self-kindness by paying attention to positive aspects of themselves rather than focusing on shame. This shift in attention will enable them to identify their inner qualities that have not been contaminated by shame and balance these with common human feelings of inadequacy and imperfection. The following exercises represent only a small proportion of the many available in books, podcasts, downloads or online (Brown 2009; Gilbert 2009). While these vary enormously they do share common themes. To help you have access to a wide range of exercises you may wish to build up your own toolbox for building self-compassion. Do, however, try to remember to give clients a choice to find which exercise appeals the most so that they can fully engage in it rather than feel shamed for not being able to do it. The use of these exercises will have to be sensitively paced as many clients will find it difficult to access self-compassion and will feel shamed if they are not able to do them perfectly, or the way they think you would like them to.

Remember

When using exercises give clients a choice so that they can fully engage in it rather than feel shamed for not being able to do it.

A good, generic exercise using mindfulness to focus on compassion follows.

Exercise
Mindfulness compassion

Invite your client to sit comfortably while you say the following:

1. Begin by breathing mindfully in order to notice your breath and become aware, curious and attentive to the physical sensations of breathing in and breathing out. Slowly allow your attention to focus on feelings of compassion and loving kindness.

2. Notice the physical and bodily sensations when you connect with feelings of compassion and loving kindness and what images and thoughts come to mind. Note these with gentle curiosity and without judgement.

3. Bring to mind someone in your life who is precious to you and imagine yourself enveloping him or her with these feelings and positive thoughts such as: may he or she find relief from his or her distress or suffering and may he or she experience peace, tranquillity, happiness and joy.

4. Next see whether you can direct some of that compassion and loving kindness towards yourself and envelop yourself in the same feelings and thoughts and notice how these feel in your body without judgement.

5. Now bring your attention, mindfulness and awareness back to your breath. Notice your inward and outward breath for a few moments.

Many clients who have experienced toxic shame find it difficult to apply compassion to themselves. You can help these clients to start the process of developing self-compassion through visualisations. This is often less threatening and easier to do as it is slightly removed from identifying positive aspects of themselves. As clients work through these visualisations and begin to feel more comfortable with the principle of self-compassion they can then start to embrace their positive qualities and allow themselves to build authentic pride.

A good starting point is to invite the client to generate a metaphor for their understanding of self-compassion which they can then use to build upon. It is better if the client generates this as they are more able to identify with it. You may need to start off by getting the client to freely associate to the words empathy, compassion and self-compassion. Typical words that are associated with self-compassion are non-judgemental, love, kindness, warmth, strength, courage and wisdom, although each client may have many others. From these words you could invite your client to develop a metaphor or build a compassionate image (Gilbert 2009) that represents their understanding of self-compassion.

Exercise
Creating a compassionate metaphor and image

1. Ask your client to freely associate to the words empathy, compassion and self-compassion and write these down. They should then rank order these in order of the most importance to them.

2. Encourage them to reflect on the most important words and try to find as many sensory images as they can that they associate with these (colour, sound, smell, taste, feel) and develop a metaphor for self-compassion that incorporates the spirit of these.

3. The client then reflects on what they have created so far and tries to capture this in writing or by drawing an image that represents compassion. If they prefer they can make a collage or use plasticine or playdoh to represent what self-compassion means to them.

4. When they have finished it encourage the client to reflect on how they feel when looking at this image and compare that to when they feel shame.

5. The client can keep this image somewhere easily accessible so that they can remind themselves of what self-compassion means to them.

Another useful exercise is to think of four compassionate people, either real or imaginary, and imagine asking them how they see you (Gilbert 2009).

Exercise
Visualisation of compassionate self

1. Ask your client to choose four compassionate and affirming people. These can be real or imaginary, living or dead and the client should imagine talking to them about themselves.

2. Encourage your client to ask them how they see the client, what qualities they notice and what strengths they see in them.

3. The client can list these in their journal where they will act as a visual reminder not to judge themselves and to counter-balance shame-based thoughts and beliefs. They can also be used to help the client identify sources of authentic pride by sight, so they will have a visual reminder to remember to not judge, but rather broaden their view and consider other perspectives.

This exercise can be expanded by inviting clients to visualise themselves as a compassionate person and asking themselves what they would be like.

Exercise
Imagine being a compassionate person

Ask your client to imagine being a compassionate person. Ask: what would you look like, how would you hold yourself, what would your voice sound like, what would your face look like? This can be visualised at any time when on the bus, walking, in between meetings or while doing tasks that do not require much thought. The visualisation can also be committed to paper through writing or drawing a character sketch.

When the client is ready you can encourage them to connect some of what they have discovered and apply this to their actual experiences. Clients often find this easier if they try to connect to the young child who was shamed. To help the client reconnect to the young child it helps to find visual records of themselves and significant others. Photographs are a powerful way to recover buried feelings and get into contact with childhood experiences and thoughts (Gilbert 2009).

Exercise
Using photographs to access self-compassion

1. Where possible, ask the client to collect a number of photographs of themselves, their family and significant others and make an album of these with notes about their feelings then and now. Seeing yourself next

to adults is a powerful way of recognising how small and vulnerable you were.

2. Invite your client to reflect and think about what they would like to say to the child, and consider writing a letter to him or her.

3. In this they can describe how they feel about the child's experience of shame and what they can do differently now to protect them from further shame.

4. Remind your client to end the letter by writing down three things that they feel genuinely proud of.

As clients begin to develop compassion for themselves, they can begin to shift their attention away from shame and attend to positive aspects of themselves. You can encourage them to focus on things that they like or appreciate in themselves, and identify qualities or achievements that they feel good about. Some clients will find this unfamiliar and may struggle to know what they like or dislike for fear of being shamed or seen negatively, so you will need to be gentle and allow them to build this gradually.

Exercise
Appreciation exercise

Encourage your client to make a note in their journal of all the things they like to see, touch, hear, smell, hold and taste such as the colour of the trees, sky and flowers, or the sound of birdsong or music, or the taste of food or beverages. Ask them to log things they have encountered during the day that they enjoyed or liked and then try to recapture that feeling. This can be expanded by listing their ten favourite things, films, books, poems, paintings or music.

As clients begin to identify what they like and dislike they can begin to turn their attention to themselves and identify what they appreciate about themselves. You will need to encourage them to look back in their journal at some of the exercises that they have completed throughout their journey and begin to collate what they have identified so far that they are able to approve of. You can guide your client to look back over previous exercises which logged positive aspects of the self (see Chapter 10). These can now be collected together and put into a jar which can be used as affirmations to remind clients of what they appreciate about themselves.

Exercise
Cookie jar

Ask your client to find a jar such as an old coffee or jam jar, and consider labelling or customising it. Ask them to take a piece of paper and write down their positive qualities and experiences in which they felt good about themselves, their achievements or authentic pride. Next they should cut each of these into separate strips of paper and then fold each strip and place them inside the box. Tell your client that each day, or when necessary, they should take one of these out and read it. They should allow themselves to recapture the feelings of pride and then put it back into the jar. As they feel and experience more positive things in their life, they can keep adding to the cookie jar.

It is important that clients generate their own positive self-evaluations, as many clients have difficulty accepting praise as they often feel that they cannot trust it, or experience it as patronising or humiliating. This is initially difficult for some clients as they may resist positive aspects of themselves or praise from others, especially as, in common with ridicule, praise uses exaggerated language. Some clients may have experienced praise as a precursor to shame through teasing. You can help clients to be more accepting of positive affirmations by reading out what they have written or said about themselves and ask them to monitor their reactions to hearing good things reflected back to them. It is worth exploring what sensations they experience, what they think and feel and to what extent they defend against them. As they become more familiar with hearing positive things about themselves they will be able to receive compassion from others.

SELF-ACCEPTANCE AND AUTHENTIC PRIDE

As the client begins to validate and integrate positive aspects of the self they become more accepting of themselves and start to restore authentic pride. To help clients identify a source of pride they can look at the Circle of Resilience (see Figure 12.3) and begin to fill in the blank segments. This is essentially a working document which can be filled in over time, as the client finds increasingly more sources of authentic pride and self-acceptance. It is also a powerful visual log of their achievements and positive aspects of themselves.

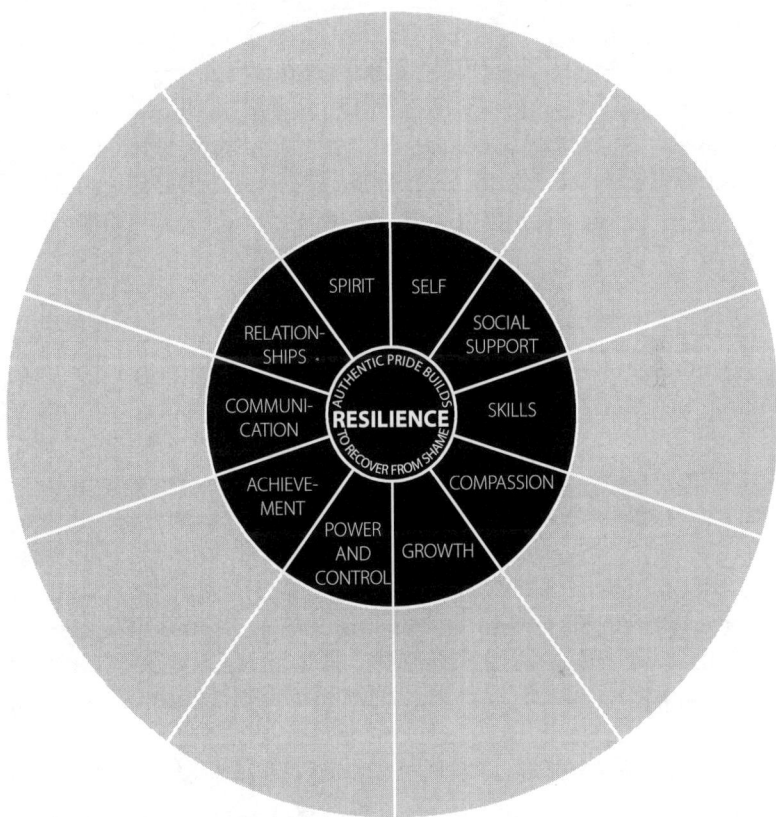

Figure 12.3 The Circle of Resilience

As part of self-acceptance clients may need to forgive themselves for any harm done to self or others. The powerful defences against shame can sometimes result in actions and behaviours which hurt others as well as the client. You will need to encourage clients to forgive themselves for doing things that they feel ashamed of or knew were wrong but had no control over. It is essential that clients remember that these defences are often activated outside of conscious awareness and are the only ones available to them at the time. Clients who have harboured rage or vengeful feelings towards those that have hurt, rejected or abandoned them will need to give themselves permission to forgive themselves for not being perfect.

Alongside this, clients will also need to take responsibility for actions and harm done to others. To help clients to take responsibility for their part you could encourage them to talk to any injured parties and apologise for any hurt they might have caused them. If this is not possible or too dangerous, it can help to write a therapeutic letter which they can choose to send or not. The main focus is on taking responsibility, maintaining integrity and behaving in a compassionate way towards self and others.

Cultivating self-acceptance reduces the need for perfectionism and enables the client to see that it takes courage to make mistakes and that these are an essential part of learning, creativity and curiosity. To facilitate true self-acceptance clients might find an apt metaphor in the Japanese art of Kintsugi (Japanese for 'golden journey') or Kintsukuroi (Japanese for 'golden repair'). This ancient art is used to repair damaged vessels by filling the cracks with gold and lacquer to create something new and even more valuable. This metaphor encourages acceptance of change through the compassionate embrace of breakages and damage that we all encounter in the course of our lives. In working through and repairing shame clients can learn that their imperfections and flaws are marks of wisdom which increase their value rather than something that needs to be hidden or disguised. Through self-acceptance both you and your clients can dissolve the stain of shame and begin to live more authentically.

SUGGESTED READING

Brown, B. (2005) 'Shame resilience theory: A grounded theory study on women and shame.' *Families in Society – The Journal of Contemporary Social Services 87*, 43–52.

Brown, B. (2007) *I Thought It Was Just Me: Women Reclaiming Power and Courage in a Culture of Shame.* New York: Penguin Group.

Brown, B. (2007) 'Shame Resilience Theory.' In S.P. Robbins, P. Chatterjee and E.R. Canda (eds) *Contemporary Human Behavior Theory: A Critical Perspective for Social Work* (rev. edn). Boston, MA: Allyn and Bacon.

Brown, B., Hernandez, R. and Villarreal, Y. (2011) 'Connections: A 12-Session Psychoeducational Shame Resilience Curriculum.' In R.L. Dearing and J.P. Tangney (eds) *Shame in the Therapy Hour*. Washington, DC: American Psychological Association.

DeYoung, P.A. (2015) *Understanding and Treating Chronic Shame: A Relational/Neurobiological Approach*. Hove: Routledge.

Gilbert, P. (2009) *The Compassionate Mind*. London: Constable.

Sanderson, C. (2013) *Counselling Skills for Working with Trauma: Healing from Child Sexual Abuse, Sexual Violence and Domestic Abuse*. London: Jessica Kingsley Publishers.

Tangney, J.P. and Dearing, R.L.(2011) 'Working with Shame in the Therapy Hour: Summary and Integration' in R.L. Dearing and J.P. Tangney *Shame in the Therapy Hour*. Washington, D.C: American Psychological Association.

REFERENCES

Ablow, K.R. (1992) *To Wrestle with Demons: A Psychiatrist Struggles to Understand His Patients and Himself.* New York: Carroll and Graf Publishers.

Adams, K.M. (2011) *Silently Seduced: When Parents Make their Children Partners: Understanding Covert Incest.* Deerfield Beach, FL: Health Communications.

Allan, S., Gilbert, P. and Goss, K. (1994) 'An exploration of shame measures II: Psychopathology.' *Personality and Individual Differences 17,* 719–722.

Alonso, A. and Rutan, J.S. (2012) 'Shame and guilt in psychotherapy supervision.' *Psychotherapy: Theory, Research and Practice 25,* 4, 576–581.

American Psychological Association (2014) *The Road to Resilience.* Washington, DC: American Psychological Association.

Andrews, B. (1995) 'Bodily shame as a mediator between abusive experiences and depression.' *Journal of Abnormal Psychology 104,* 277–285.

Armsworth, M. (1989) 'Therapy of incest survivors: Abuse or support?' *Child Abuse and Neglect 13,* 4, 549–562.

Asser, J. (2014) 'If I move he'll attack me: Mastering rage in prisoners.' *The Observer,* 9 March.

Badenoch, B. (2008) *Being a Brain-Wise Therapist: A Practical Guide to Interpersonal Neurobiology.* New York: W.W. Norton.

Badenoch, B. (2011) *The Brain Savvy Therapist's Workbook: A Companion to Being a Brain-Wise Therapist.* New York: W.W. Norton.

Barrett, K.C. (1995) 'A Functionalist Approach to Shame and Guilt.' In J.P. Tangney and K.W. Fischer (eds) *Self-Conscious Emotions: The Psychology of Shame, Guilt, Embarrassment and Pride.* New York: Guilford Press.

Baumeister, R.F. (2003) 'Ego depletion and self-regulation failure: A resource model of self-control.' *Alcoholism: Clinical and Experimental Research 27,* 2, 281–284.

Bowlby, J. (1969) *Attachment and Loss: Attachment.* London: Penguin.

Bradshaw, J. (2005) *Healing the Shame that Binds You.* Deerfield Beach, FL: Health Communications.

Broucek, F.J. (1991) *Shame and the Self.* New York: Guilford Press.

Brown, B. (2005) 'Shame resilience theory: A grounded theory study on women and shame.' *Families in Society – The Journal of Contemporary Social Services 87,* 43–52.

Brown, B. (2007a) *I Thought It Was Just Me: Women Reclaiming Power and Courage in a Culture of Shame.* New York: Penguin Group.

Brown, B. (2007b) 'Shame Resilience Theory.' In S.P. Robbins, P. Chatterjee and E.R. Canda (eds) *Contemporary Human Behavior Theory: A Critical Perspective for Social Work* (rev. edn). Boston, MA: Allyn and Bacon.

Brown, B. (2009) *Connections: A 12-Session Psychoeducational Shame Resilience Curriculum,* 2nd edn. Minneapolis, MN: Hazelden.

Brown, B. (2010) *The Gifts of Imperfection: Let Go of Who You Think You're Supposed to Be and Embrace Who You Are.* Center City, MN: Hazelden.

Budden, A. (2009) 'The role of shame in posttraumatic stress disorder: A proposal for a socio-economic model for DSM-V.' *Social Science and Medicine 69*, 1032–1039.

Carnes, P.J. (1983) *Sexual Addiction.* Minneapolis, MN: Camp Care.

Carnes, P.J. (1991) *Don't Call It Love: Recovery from Sexual Addiction.* New York: Bantam Books.

Carnes, P.J. (2001) *Out of the Shadows: Understanding Sexual Addiction,* 3rd edn. Center City, MN: Hazelden.

Carnes, P.J. (2008) 'The perfect storm: Assessing for sex addiction.' *Counsellor 9*, 3, 50–58.

CIVITAS (Institute for the Study of Civil Society) (2010) *Factsheet – Education in Prisons.* Available at www.civitas.org.uk, accessed on 9 April 2015.

Clance, P.R. and Imes, S.A. (1978) 'The impostor phenomenon in high achieving women: Dynamics and therapeutic interventions.' *Psychotherapy: Theory, Research and Practice 15*, 241–247.

Clarkson, P. (2004) *The Therapeutic Relationship,* 2nd edn. London: Whurr Publishers.

Cohen, T. R., Wolf, S. T., Panter, A. T., & Insko, C. A. (2011). Introducing the GASP scale: A new measure of guilt and shame proneness. *Journal of Personality and Social Psychology, 100*(5), 947-966.

Cook, D. R. (1994). *Internalized shame scale: Professional manual.* Menomonie, WI: Channel Press.

Covert, M.V., Tangney, J.P., Maddux, J.E. and Heleno, N.M. (2003) 'Shame proneness, guilt proneness and interpersonal problem solving: A social cognitive analysis.' *Journal of Social and Clinical Psychology 22*, 1–12.

Dalenberg, C.J. (2000) *Countertransference and the Treatment of Trauma.* Washington, DC: American Psychological Association.

Danieli, Y. (1994) 'Countertransference, Trauma and Training.' In J.P. Wilson and J. Lindy (eds) *Countertransference in the Treatment of Post-Traumatic Stress Disorder.* New York: Guilford Press.

de Hooge, I.E. (2014) 'The General Sociometer Shame: Positive Interpersonal Consequences of an Ugly Emotion.' In G. Lockhart (ed.) *Psychology of Shame: New Research,* 9th edn. Hauppauge, NY: New Science Publishers.

DeYoung, P.A. (2015) *Understanding and Treating Chronic Shame: A Relational/Neurobiological Approach.* Hove: Routledge.

Dorahy, M. (2010) 'The impact of dissociation, shame, and guilt on interpersonal relationships in chronically traumatized individuals: A pilot study.' *Journal of Traumatic Stress 23*, 653–656.

Duffell, N. (2000) *The Making of Them: The British Attitude to Children and the Boarding School System.* London: Lone Arrow Press.

Duffell, N. (2014) *Wounded Leaders: British Elitism and the Entitlement Illusion – A Psychohistory.* London: Lone Arrow Press.

Dutton, D.G., van Ginkel, C. and Starzomski, A. (1995) 'The role of shame and guilt in the intergenerational transmission of abusiveness.' *Violence and Victims 10*, 121–131.

Eisenberg, N., Shea, C., Carlo, G. and Knight, G. (1991) 'Empathy-Related Responding and Cognition: A "Chicken and the Egg" Dilemma. In W. Kurtines and J. Gewirtz (eds) *Handbook of Moral Behavior and Development. Vol. 2: Research.* Mahwah, NJ: Erlbaum.

Ekman, P. (2004) *Emotions Revealed: Understanding Faces and Feelings.* London: Weidenfeld and Nicolson.

Elison, J. and Harter, S. (2007) 'Humiliation: Causes, Correlates and Consequences.' In J.L. Tracy, R.W. Robbins and J.P. Tangney (eds) *The Self-Conscious Emotions: Theory and Research.* New York: Guilford Press.

Feiring, C. and Taska, L.S. (2005) 'The persistence of shame following sexual abuse: A longitudinal look at risk and recovery.' *Child Maltreatment 10,* 4, 337–349.

Ferguson, T.J., Eyre, H.L. and Ashbaker, M. (2000) 'Unwanted identities: A key variable in shame–anger links and gender differences in shame.' *Sex Roles 42,* 133–157.

Fessler, D.M.T. (2007) 'From Appeasement to Conformity: Evolutionary and Cultural Perspectives on Shame, Competition and Cooperation.' In J.L. Tracy, R.W. Robbins and J.P. Tangney (eds) *The Self-Conscious Emotions: Theory and Research.* New York: Guilford Press.

Fisher, H.L. (2013) 'Mind the gap – Pathways to psychosis.' *Psychologist 26,* 11, 798–801.

Fisher, H.L., Appiah-Kusi, E. and Grant, C. (2012) 'Anxiety and negative self-schemas mediate the association between childhood maltreatment and paranoia.' *Psychiatry Research 196,* 2–3, 323–324.

Flores, P.J. (2004) *Addictions as an Attachment Disorder.* Lanham, MD: Aronson.

Freyd, J.J. and Birrell, P.J. (2013) *Blind to Betrayal: Why We Fool Ourselves We Aren't Being Fooled.* Hoboken, NJ: Wiley.

Gagnon, J. and Simon, W. (1973) *Sexual Conduct: The Social Sources of Human Sexuality.* Hawthorne, NY: Aldine Publishing.

Gerhardt, S. (2004) *Why Love Matters: How Affection Shapes the Baby's Brain.* London: Brunner-Routledge.

Gilbert, P. (1997) 'The evolution of social attractiveness and its role in shame, humiliation, guilt, and therapy.' *British Journal of Medical Psychology 70,* 113–147.

Gilbert, P. (2009) *The Compassionate Mind.* London: Constable.

Gilbert, P. and McGuire, M.T. (1998) 'Shame, Status, and Social Roles: Psychobiology and Evolution.' In P. Gilbert and B. Andrews (eds) *Shame: Interpersonal Behavior, Psychopathology and Culture.* New York: Oxford University Press.

Gilbert, P. and Mills, J. (2002) *Body Shame: Conceptualisation, Research and Treatment.* Hove: Brunner-Routledge.

Gilligan, J. (2001) *Violence: A Reflection on the National Epidemic.* New York: Pantheon Books.

Goss, K., Gilbert, P. & Allan, S. (1994) 'An exploration of shame measures: I: The "other as shamer"scale.' *Personality and Individual Differences, 17,* 713-717.

Hahn, W.K. (2001) 'The experience of shame in psychotherapy supervision.' *Psychotherapy: Theory, Research, Practice, Training 38,* 3, 272–282.

Haidt, J. (2003) 'The Moral Emotions.' In R.J. Davidson, K.R. Scherer and H.H. Goldsmith (eds) *Handbook of Affective Sciences.* Oxford: Oxford University Press.

Hartling, L., Rosen, W., Walker, M. and Jordan, J. (2000) *Shame and Humiliation: From Isolation to Relational Transformation.* Work in Progress No. 88. Wellesley, MA: Stone Center, Wellesley College.

Herman, J.L. (2001) *Trauma and Recovery,* 2nd edn. London: Pandora.

Herman, J.L. (2007) 'Shattered shame states and their repair.' From the John Bowlby Memorial Lecture, 10 March, Department of Psychiatry, Harvard University School.

Herman, J.L. (2011a) 'Posttraumatic Stress Disorder as a Shame Disorder.' In R.L. Dearing and J.P. Tangney (eds) *Shame in the Therapy Hour.* Washington, DC: American PsychologicalAssociation.

Herman, J.L. (2011b) 'Shattered Shame States and their Repair.' In J. Yellin and K. White (eds) *Shattered States: Disorganised Attachment and its Repair.* London: Karnac Books.

Herman, J.L. and Schatzow, E. (1984) 'Time limited group therapy for women with a history of incest.' *International Journal of Group Psychotherapy 34,* 605–615.

Horney, K. (1945) *Our Inner Conflicts.* New York: W.W. Norton.

Jacobs, L. (1995) 'Shame in the therapeutic dialogue.' *British Gestalt Journal 4,* 2, 86–90.

Jordan, J.V. (1991) *The Movement of Mutuality and Power.* Work in Progress No. 53. Wellesley, MA: Stone Center, Wellesley College.

Jordan, J.V. (1997) 'Relational Development: Therapeutic Implications of Empathy and Shame.' In J.V. Jordan (ed.) *Women's Growth in Diversity: More Writings from the Stone Center.* New York: Guilford Press.

Jordan, J.V., Handel, M., Alvarez, M. and Cook-Nobles, R. (2000) *Applications of the Relational Model to Time-Limited Therapy.* Work in Progress No. 87. Wellesley, MA: Stone Center, Wellesley College.

Joyce, P. and Sills, C. (2014) *Skills in Gestalt Counselling and Psychotherapy,* 3rd edn. London: Sage.

Jung, C.G. (1957) *The Undiscovered Self.* New York: American Library.

Karter, L. (2014) 'Gambling Addiction: Seeking Certainty when Relationship is the Risk.' In R. Gill (ed.) *Addictions from an Attachment Perspective: Do Broken Bonds and Early Trauma Lead to Addictive Behaviour?* London: Karnac Books.

Katehakis, A. (2009) 'Affective neuroscience and the treatment of sexual addiction.' *Sexual Addiction and Compulsivity 16,* 1–31.

Kaufman, G. (1989) *The Psychology of Shame.* New York: Springer.

Kaufman, G. (1992) *Shame: The Power of Caring,* 3rd edn. Rochester, VT: Schenkman Books.

Kaufman, G. (2004) *The Psychology of Shame: Theory and Treatment of Shame Based Syndromes,* 2nd edn. New York: Springer.

Kaufman, G. and Raphael, L. (1996) *Coming Out of Shame: Transforming Gay and Lesbian Lives.* New York: Main Street Books.

Keltner, D. and Buswell, B.N. (1997) 'Embarrassment: Its distinct form and appeasement function.' *Psychological Bulletin 122,* 250–270.

Khantzian, E.J. (2003) 'Understanding addictive vulnerability: An evolving psychodynamic perspective.' *Neuro-Psychoanalysis 5,* 5–21.

Khantzian, E.J. (2012) 'Reflections on treating addictive disorders: A psychodynamic perspective.' *The American Journal on Addictions 21,* 274–279.

Khantzian, E.J. (2013) 'Psychodynamic Therapy for the Treatment of Substance Use Disorders.' In N. El-Guebaly, M. Galanter and G. Carra (eds) *The Textbook of Addiction Treatment.* New York: Springer.

Khantzian, E.J. (2014) 'The Self-Medication Hypothesis and Attachment Theory: Pathways for Understanding and Ameliorating Addictive Suffering.' In R. Gill (ed.) *Addictions from an Attachment Perspective: Do Broken Bonds and Early Trauma Lead to Addictive Behaviour?* London: Karnac Books.

Kinston, W. (1987) 'The Shame of Narcissism.' In D.L. Nathanson (ed.) *The Many Faces of Shame.* New York: Guilford Press.

Kluft, R.P. (1992) 'Dissociative disorders in childhood and adolescence: New frontiers.' *Dissociation 5,* 1, 2–3.

Kulp, L., Klinger, R. and Ladany, N. (2007) 'Embarrassment, humiliation and shame in therapy and supervision.' Poster presented at the Meeting of the Mid-Atlantic Society for Psychotherapy Research, New York, October.

Kurtz, E. (1981) *Shame and Guilt: Characteristics of the Dependency Cycle.* Center City, MN: Hazelden.

Ladany, N., Klinger, R. and Kulp, L. (2011) 'Therapist Shame: Implications for Therapy and Supervision in Specific Action that Results in Harm to Others.' In R.L. Dearing and J.P. Tangney (eds) *Shame in the Therapy Hour.* Washington, DC: American Psychological Association.

Leith, K.P. and Baumeister, R.F. (1998) 'Empathy, shame, guilt and narratives of personal conflicts: Guilt prone people are better at perspective taking.' *Journal of Personality and Social Psychology 66,* 1–37.

Leskala, J., Dieperink, M. and Thuras, P. (2002) 'Shame and posttraumatic stress disorder.' *Journal of Traumatic Stress 15,* 223–226.

Lewis, H.B. (1971) *Shame and Guilt in Neurosis.* New York: International Universities Press.

Lewis, H.B. (1987) 'Shame and the Narcissistic Personality.' In D.L. Nathanson (ed.) *The Many Faces of Shame.* New York: Guilford Press.

Lewis, M. (1992) *Shame: The Exposed Self.* New York: The Free Press.

Lewis, M. (2000) 'Self-Conscious Emotions: Embarrassment, Pride, Shame and Guilt.' In M. Lewis and J.M. Haviland-Jones (eds) *Handbook of Emotions,* 2nd edn. New York: Guilford Press.

Livingston, R.H. and Farber, B.A. (1996) 'Beginning therapists' responses to client shame.' *Psychotherapy 4,* 33, 601–610.

Maltsberger, J.T. and Buie, O.H. (1974) 'Countertransference: Hate in the treatment of suicidal patients.' *Archives of General Psychiatry 30,* 625–633.

Matos, M. and Pinto-Gouveia, J. (2010) 'Shame as a traumatic memory.' *Clinical Psychology and Psychotherapy 17,* 299–312.

Miller, R.S. (2007) 'Is Embarrassment a Blessing or a Curse in Self-Conscious Emotions?' In J.L.Tracy, R.W. Robbins and J.P. Tangney (eds) *The Self-Conscious Emotions: Theory and Research.* New York: Guilford Press.

Miller, S.B. (1985) *The Shame Experience.* Hillsdale, NJ: Erlbaum.

Mollon, P. (1993) *The Fragile Self: The Structure of Narcissistic Disturbance.* London: Whurr Publishers.

Mollon, P. (2002) *Shame and Jealousy: The Hidden Turmoils.* London: Karnac Books.

Montgomery, J.D. and Greif, A.C. (eds) (1989) *Masochism: The Treatment of Self-Inflicted Suffering.* Madison, CT: International Universities Press.

Morrison, A.P. (1987) 'The Eye Turned Inward.' In D.L. Nathanson (ed.) *The Many Faces of Shame.* New York: Guilford Press.

Motz, A. (2001) *The Psychology of Female Violence.* London: Routledge.

Motz, A. (2008) *The Psychology of Female Violence,* 2nd edn. London: Routledge.

Motz, A. (2014) *Toxic Couples: The Psychology of Domestic Violence.* London: Routledge.

Nathanson, D.L. (1992) *Shame and Pride: Affect, Sex, and the Birth of the Self.* New York: W.W. Norton.

Nathanson, D.L. (1998) 'From empathy to community.' Paper presented to the First North American Conference on Conferencing, Minneapolis, MN, August.

Orbach, S. (2009) *Bodies.* London: Profile Books.

Platt, M. and Freyd, J.J. (2012) 'Trauma and negative underlying assumptions in feelings of shame: An exploratory study.' *Psychological Trauma: Theory, Research, Practice, and Policy 4*, 370–378.

Pope, K.S. and Bouhoutsos, J.C. (1986) *Sexual Intimacy between Therapists and Patients*. Westport, CT: Praeger.

Pope, K.S., Sonne, J.L. and Greene, B. (2006) *What Therapists Don't Talk About and Why: Understanding Taboos that Hurt Us and Our Clients*, 2nd edn. Washington, DC: American Psychological Association.

Pope, K.S., Spiegel, P.K. and Tabachnik, B. (1986) 'Sexual attraction to clients: The human therapist and the (sometimes) inhuman training system.' *American Psychologist 41*, 147–158.

Potter-Efron, R. (2001) *Stop the Anger Now: A Workbook for the Prevention, Containment, and Resolution of Anger*. Oakland, CA: New Harbinger Publications.

Potter-Efron, R. (2002) *Shame, Guilt and Alcoholism*, 2nd edn. New York: Haworth Press.

Potter-Efron, R. (2007) *Rage*. Oakland, CA: New Harbinger.

Potter-Efron, R. (2011) 'Therapy with Shame-Prone Alcoholic and Drug Dependent Clients.' In R.L. Dearing and J.P. Tangney (eds) *Shame in the Therapy Hour*. Washington, DC: American Psychological Association.

Potter-Efron, R. and Potter-Efron, P. (1989) *Letting Go of Shame: Understanding How Shame Affects Your Life*. Center City, MN: Hazelden.

Ritzi, S.L., Brown, M.Z., Bohus, M. and Linehan, M.M. (2011) 'The Role of Shame in the Development and Treatment of Borderline Personality Disorder.' In R.L. Dearing and J.P. Tangney (eds) *Shame in the Therapy Hour*. Washington, DC: American Psychological Association.

Robinaugh, D.J. and McNally, R.J. (2010) 'Autobiographical memory for shame or guilt provoking events: Association with psychological symptoms.' *Behavior Research and Therapy 48*, 646–652.

Rutter, M. (2008) 'Developing Concepts in Developmental Psychopathology.' In J.J. Hudziak (ed.) *Developmental Psychopathology and Wellness: Genetic and Environmental Influences*. Washington, DC: American Psychiatric Publishing.

Sanderson, C. (2004) *The Seduction of Children: Empowering Parents and Teachers to Protect Children from Child Sexual Abuse*. London: Jessica Kingsley Publishers.

Sanderson, C. (2006) *Counselling Adult Survivors of Child Sexual Abuse*, 3rd edn. London: Jessica Kingsley Publishers.

Sanderson, C. (2008) *Counselling Survivors of Domestic Abuse*. London: Jessica Kingsley Publishers.

Sanderson, C. (2010) *The Warrior Within: A One in Four Handbook to Aid Recovery from Childhood Sexual Abuse and Violence*. London: One in Four.

Sanderson, C. (2011) *The Spirit Within: A One in Four Handbook to Aid Recovery from Religious Sexual Abuse Across all Faiths*. London: One in Four.

Sanderson, C. (2013) *Counselling Skills for Working with Trauma: Healing from Child Sexual Abuse, Sexual Violence and Domestic Abuse*. London: Jessica Kingsley Publishers.

Sanderson, C. (2014) 'The role of shame in child sexual abuse.' Optimus Education Safeguarding Hub, 20 March.

Sanftner, J.L. and Tantillo, M. (2011) 'Body Image and Eating Disorders: A Compelling Source of Shame for Women.' In R.L. Dearing and J.P. Tangney (eds) *Shame in the Therapy Hour*. Washington, DC: American Psychological Association.

Scheff, T.J. (1987) 'The Shame-Rage Spiral: A Case Study of an Interminable Quarrel.' In H.B. Lewis (ed.) *The Role of Shame in Symptom Formation.* Hillsdale, NJ: Erlbaum.

Scheff, T.J. (1988) 'Shame and conformity: The deference-emotion system.' *American Sociological Review 53*, 3, 395–406.

Scheff, T.J. (1990) *Microsociology: Emotion, Discourse, and Social Structure.* Chicago, IL: University of Chicago Press.

Scheff, T.J. (1997) *Emotions, the Social Bond, and Human Reality: Part/Whole Analysis.* Cambridge: Cambridge University Press.

Schimmel, S. (1997) 'The Seven Deadly Sins: Jewish, Christian and classical reflections on human psychology.' *Journal of Cross-Cultural Psychology 35*, 304–326.

Schore, A.N. (1994) *Affect Regulation and the Origin of the Self: The Neurobiology of Emotional Development.* Hillsdale, NJ: Erlbaum.

Schore, A.N. (1998) 'Early Shame Experiences and Infant Brain Development.' In P. Gilbert and B. Andrews (eds) *Shame: Interpersonal Behavior, Psychopathology and Culture.* New York: Oxford University Press.

Schwartz, M.F. and Brasted, W.S. (1985) 'Sexual addiction: Self hatred, guilt and passive rage contribute to this deviant behaviour.' *Medical Aspects of Human Sexuality 19*, 10, 103–107.

Stoller, R. (1975) *Perversion: The Erotic Form of Hatred.* New York: Pantheon.

Talbot, N.L. (1995) 'Unearthing shame in the supervisory experience.' *American Journal of Psychotherapy 49*, 3, 338–349.

Tangney, J.P. and Dearing, R.L. (2002) *Shame and Guilt.* New York: Guilford Press.

Tangney, J.P., Miller, R.S., Flicker, L. and Barlow, D.H. (1996) 'Are shame, guilt, and embarrassment distinct emotions?' *Journal of Personality and Social Psychology 70*, 1256–1264.

Tangney, J.P., Wagner, P.E. and Gramzow, R. (1992) 'Proneness of shame, proneness to guilt, and psychopathology.' *Journal of Abnormal Psychology 103*, 469–478.

Tomkins, S.S. (1963) *Affect Imagery Consciousness. Volume II: The Negative Affects.* London: Tavistock.

Tracy, J.L. and Robbins, R.W. (2004) 'Putting the self into self-conscious emotions: A theoretical model.' *Psychological Inquiry 15*, 103–125.

Tracy, J.L. and Robbins, R.W. (2007) 'The Nature of Pride.' In J.L. Tracy, R.W. Robbins and J.P. Tangney (eds) *The Self-Conscious Emotions: Theory and Research.* New York: Guilford Press.

Trevarthen, C. (2005) 'Stepping Away from the Mirror. Pride and Shame in Adventures of Companionship: Reflections on the Nature and Emotional Needs of Infant Intersubjectivity.' In C.S. Carter, L. Ahnert, K. E. Grossmann, S. B. Hrdy, M. E. Lamb, S. W. Porges, and N. Sachser. (eds) *The 92nd Dahlem Workshop Report. Attachment and Bonding: A New Synthesis.* Cambridge, MA: MIT Press.

Tronick, E.Z. (1989) 'Emotions and emotional communication in infants.' *American Psychologist 44*, 112–126.

Werner, E.E. and Smith, R.S. (2001) *Journeys from Childhood to Midlife: Risk, Resiliency, and Recovery.* Ithaca, NY: Cornell University Press.

Wurmser, L. (1989) 'Blinding the Eye of the Mind.' In E.L. Edelstein, D.L. Nathanson and A.M. Stone (eds) *Denial: A Clarification of Concepts and Research.* New York: Plenum Press.

Wurmser, L. (1995) *The Mask of Shame.* Northvale, NJ: Aronson.

Wurmser, L. (2013) 'Shame and its vicious cycles.' Paper presented at IPA meeting, Prague.

SUBJECT INDEX